Radical Sisters

WOMEN IN AMERICAN HISTORY

A list of books in the series appears at the end of this book.

Radical Sisters

Second-Wave Feminism and Black Liberation in Washington, D.C.

ANNE M. VALK

UNIVERSITY OF ILLINOIS PRESS
Urbana, Chicago, and Springfield

First Illinois paperback, 2010

Manufactured in the United States of America
1 2 3 4 5 C P 5 4 3 2 1
∞ This book is printed on acid-free paper.

The Library of Congress cataloged the cloth edition as follows:
Valk, Anne M.
Radical sisters : second-wave feminism and black
liberation in Washington, D.C. / Anne M. Valk.
p. cm. — (Women in American history)
Includes bibliographical references and index.
ISBN-13: 978–0–252–03298–1 (cloth : alk. paper)
ISBN-10: 0–252–03298–5 (cloth : alk. paper)
1. Feminism—United States. 2. African American
feminists—Washington (D.C.)
I. Title.
HQ1421.V37 2008
305.48'8960730753—dc22 2007035932

PAPERBACK ISBN 978-0-252-07754-8

Contents

Acknowledgments

The research and writing of this book extended over a long number of years during which I incurred numerous debts and relied on the goodwill of many people and institutions. As I took this project from a dissertation to a book, many friends and colleagues provided immeasurably important assistance, cooperation, and support. At the earliest stages of this project, my dissertation committee offered advice and direction that helped me produce an original piece of scholarship. Bill Chafe, Ray Gavins, and Bob Korstad introduced me to the study of social movements, especially the black freedom movement, and to the methodology of oral history. Jean O'Barr brought the interdisciplinary benefits of women's studies to the examination of second-wave feminism. In the past decade, they have continued to serve as vital mentors and supportive colleagues. Nancy Hewitt was, and has remained, a faithful advocate, a critical reader, and a brilliant scholar who consistently sets, and then surpasses, high standards for the profession. For whatever sparks of potential these scholars saw in me, I am grateful that they gave me an opportunity to learn from them.

More recently, other historians have given generously of their time and their feedback. Leslie Brown, Katharine Corbett, Andrea Friedman, Maggie Garb, Stephanie Gilmore, Nancy Hewitt, Ellen Nore, and Allison Thomason read and commented on parts of the book. From their very different areas of expertise, each raised important questions and extended encouragement that helped improve the manuscript. As I watched many of them bring their own books to fruition during the period that I worked on my own, I realized that it was possible to complete a manuscript while retaining one's grace, sanity, and good humor. Anne Enke, Stephanie Gilmore, and Nancy Hewitt helped connect me to the growing group of historians who are writing a second wave of scholarship on second-wave feminism by inviting me to participate in conferences, collaborative publications, and virtual communities. My work is better as a result. I also benefited enormously from former colleagues at Southern Illinois University Edwardsville (SIUE), especially those in history and women's studies, with whom I enjoyed exceptional camaraderie as we strove to balance steady scholarship, outstanding teaching, and fulfilling lives.

A number of institutions funded parts of the research and writing of this project. For support during the dissertation stage, I am grateful to Duke University and Mount Holyoke College. Summer research fellowships from the National Endowment for the Humanities and SIUE gave me time away from teaching to write, and travel grants from the Arthur and Elizabeth Schlesinger Library on the History of Women in America and the Sophia Smith Collection helped support the research. SIUE's Funded University Research and Faculty Development Fund programs extended monies to cover some of the costs of reprinting photographs and travel to archival collections. I also appreciate friends and family who opened their homes during my research trips, including Ken and Gretchen Davidian; Eli, Laura, Hayley, and Reggie Valk; and Heidi Valk and Conrad, Jackson, and Bennett Pitcher.

Because many of the materials that I used in researching this book are not available in archives, I had to rely on the address books, closets, and attics of people who participated in the activities about which I wrote. This book would not exist without the generous assistance that I received from many people, including Joan Biren, Sherry Brown, Charlotte Bunch, Dorothy Burlage, Sharon Deevey, Alexa Freeman, Valle Jones, and Loretta Ross, who not only recalled their own experiences but helped me locate people and holdings of written material. Mark Meinke and Billy X made available materials that filled crucial gaps in my research. Their projects, the Rainbow History Project and It's About Time, are playing a critical role in gathering and preserving first-person accounts and publications from the 1960s and 1970s that would otherwise be lost to history. I also appreciate those archives and libraries that have collected personal papers, organizational records, and other materials to document what is still a largely untold history. In particular, I am indebted to the staff at Duke University's Special Collections Library, the Sophia Smith Collection, the Schlesinger Library, the Moorland-Spingarn Library at Howard University, the State Historical Society of Wisconsin, the Henry Hampton Collection at the Film and Media Archive at Washington

University in St. Louis, the Gelman Library at George Washington University, and the Lesbian Herstory Archives. I found many treasures in the photograph collections, clipping files, and D.C. Community Archives at the Washingtoniana Division of the Martin Luther King Jr., Memorial Library. I also thank the staff of Lovejoy Library at SIUE for tracking down materials via interlibrary loan and for making it possible for me to bridge the many miles separating Edwardsville from the District of Columbia.

I would also like to thank the staff of the University of Illinois Press and the editors of the Women in American History series for remaining interested in this book despite my slow and unsteady progress. Susan Cahn and one anonymous reader offered generous and thoughtful comments that aided in revisions of the manuscript. Series editor Anne Firor Scott was a consistent source of encouragement and much-needed prodding. Laurie Matheson answered my many questions promptly and without any hint of impatience. I thank them for leading me through my first adventure in book publishing.

Finally, for general encouragement, I am beholden to my family and friends. Three of my grandparents, Marjorie Pickrell and Pauline and Melvin Valk, lived to see part of this project completed and I feel privileged to have enjoyed their companionship and benefited from their appreciation for history and good humor. My parents, Jim and Judy Valk, and my siblings, Jean, Heidi, and Eli and their families, entertained me during trips to Massachusetts and Florida, providing necessary breaks from the solitude of the archives and the loneliness of writing. Long-distance lunchtime conversations with Alex Byrd during our overlapping sabbatical year brought a sense of solidarity to the final push. Many friends in the St. Louis area helped me adapt to living in the Midwest, especially the Friedman-Sanguinettes, Laura Gates, Cathi O'Brien, Maggie Garb, Linda Markowitz, Laura Milsk Fowler and Scot Fowler, Michaela Hoenicke Moore and Michael Moore, Eric Ruckh, Nancy Lutz, Peg Simons, Shirley Portwood, Ellen Nore, and neighbors in Benton Park. Joy Allen's support and advice were critical as I neared the completion of this project. My greatest debt is to Leslie Brown. Through all stages of this project, Doc extended her unwavering interest in my research, unfailing belief in the worthiness of this project, steadfast confidence in my ability, and joyful companionship on countless nerd vacations. I thank her for her incredible love and commitment to me and to our partnership as historians.

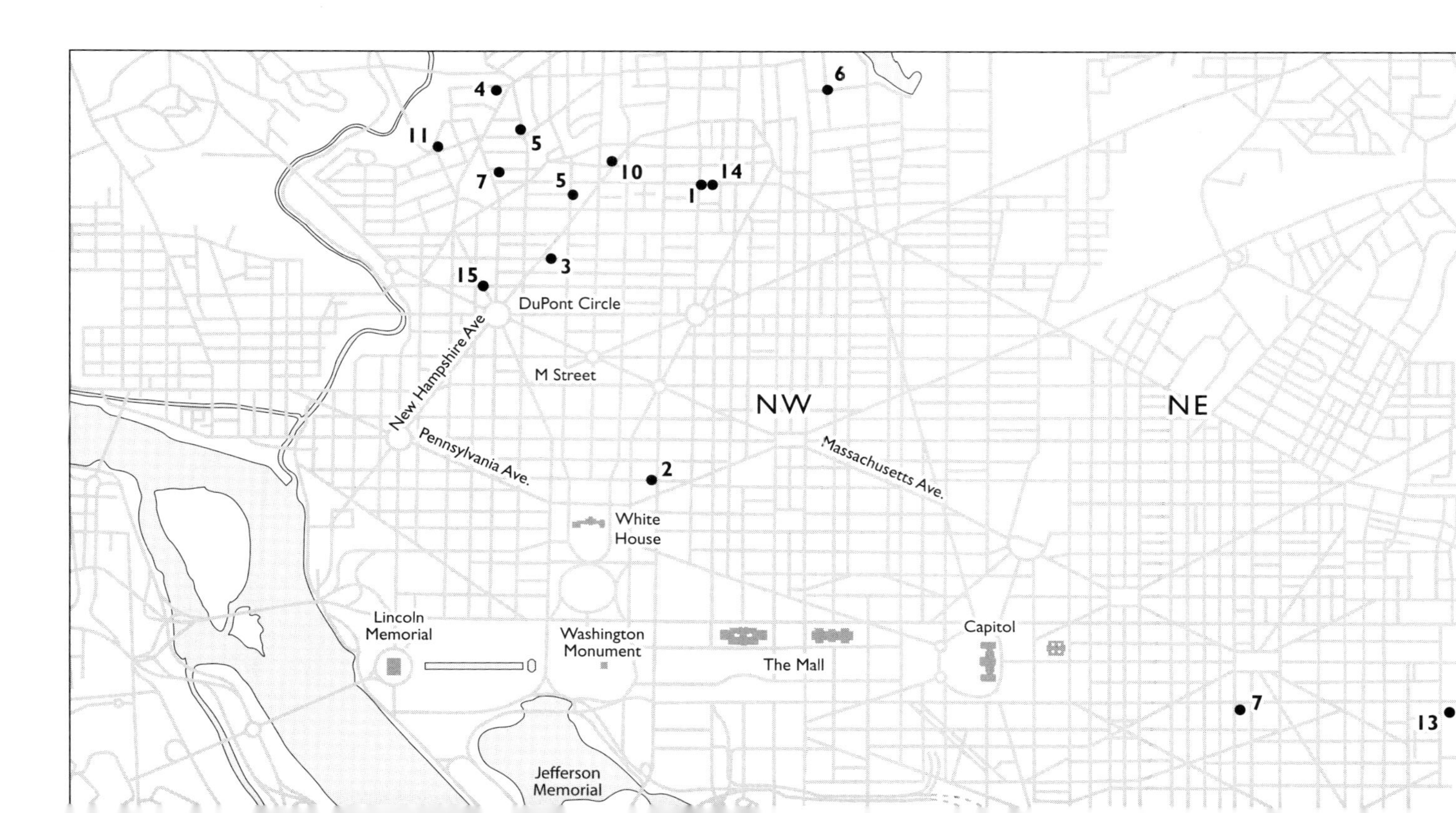

4
11
5
7
5
10
1
14
6
15
3
DuPont Circle
New Hampshire Ave
M Street
NW
NE
Pennsylvania Ave.
2
Massachusetts Ave.
White House
Lincoln Memorial
Washington Monument
The Mall
Capitol
7
13
Jefferson Memorial

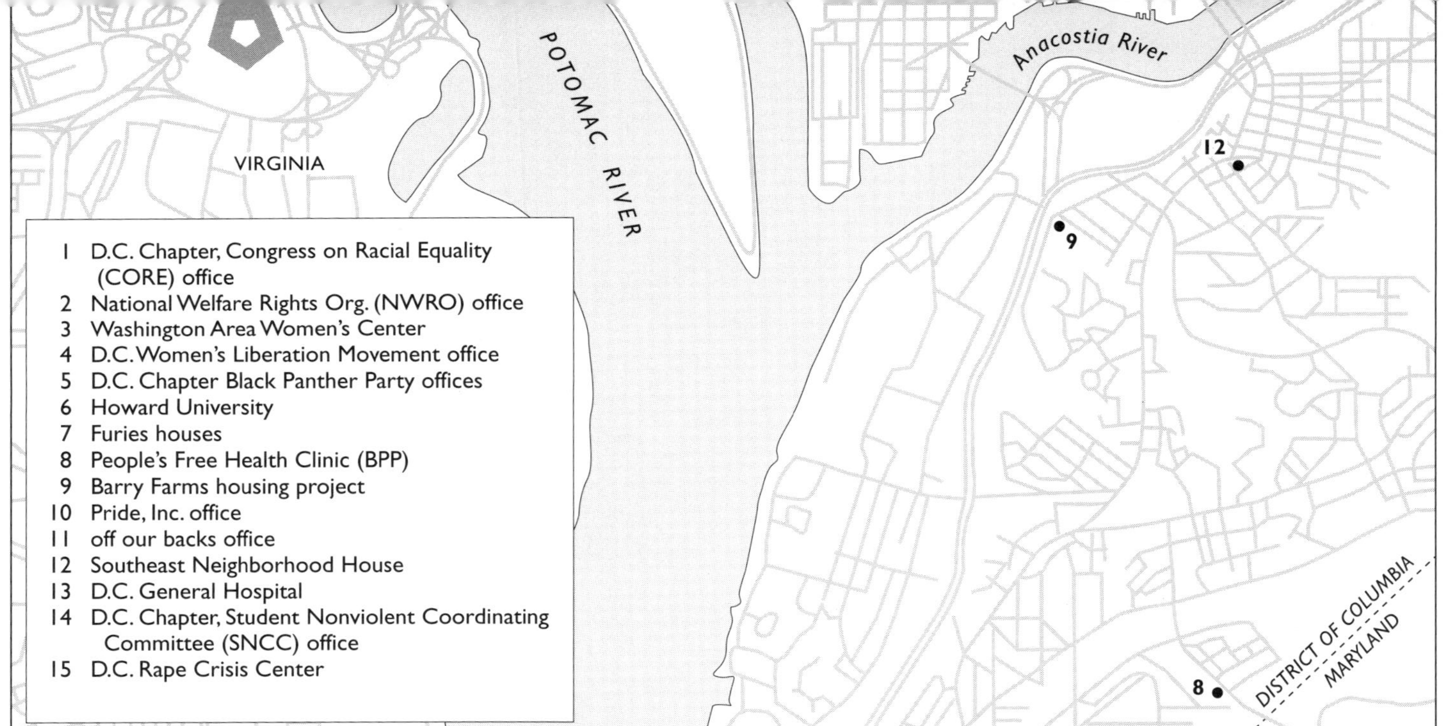

Map of Washington, D.C.

Abbreviations

BPP	Black Panther Party for Self Defense
CORE	Congress on Racial Equality
CWA	Citywide Welfare Alliance
DCAFA	D.C. Area Feminist Alliance
DCWLM	D.C. Women's Liberation Movement
FAAR	Feminist Alliance Against Rape
FEW	Federally Employed Women
GAA	Gay Activists Alliance
GLF	Gay Liberation Front
IPS	Institute for Policy Studies
LWV	League of Women Voters
MAA	Metropolitan Abortion Alliance
NAG	Nonviolent Action Group
NBFO	National Black Feminist Organization
NCHA	National Capital Housing Authority
NOW	National Organization for Women
NWRO	National Welfare Rights Organization
OEO	Office of Economic Opportunity
RCC	Rape Crisis Center
RPCC	Revolutionary People's Constitutional Convention
SDS	Students for a Democratic Society
SEH	Southeast Neighborhood House
SNCC	Student Nonviolent Coordinating Committee
SWP	Socialist Workers' Party
UPO	United Planning Organization

WAWC	Washington Area Women's Center
WITCH	Women's International Terrorist Conspiracy from Hell
WLDF	Women's Legal Defense Fund
WONAAC	Women's National Abortion Action Coalition
WPEC	Women's Political Education Coalition
WSP	Women Strike for Peace
YSA	Young Socialist Alliance

Radical Sisters

Introduction

On August 26, 1970, thousands of men and women gathered in the nation's capital for Women's Strike for Equality Day. Women's rights advocates marched through the Washington, D.C., streets and rallied in city parks, joining millions of individuals participating in similar activities across the country. A D.C. newspaper commented that the crowd included "Weatherwomen and League of Women Voters members: black women, suburban housewives, professionals, office workers, women of the peace movement, Black Panthers and religious orders." After parading through downtown's streets, women converged in two parks near the White House where they cheered speeches demanding equal opportunity in work and education and pledged to boycott corporations that sold products using advertising campaigns that belittled women. A group of federal employees publicized the results of a survey of congressional attitudes toward a proposed Equal Rights Amendment. Nearby, secretaries employed at the Pentagon, although forbidden from marching by federal law, nonetheless expressed support for the strike by filling a trash can with bras, girdles, and other accoutrements of women's oppression.[1]

The Women's Strike in Washington represented a historic moment, the largest women's rights demonstration held in the capital since suffragists had demanded the vote more than fifty years earlier. The highly visible activities, timed to coincide with others around the country, showed the rising strength of the national women's movement. Washington organizers' success in bringing together individuals from across the political spectrum—from the militant Weather Underground and the radical Black Panther Party, to the liberal ERA supporters and more conservative League of Women Voters—demonstrated an emerging consensus favoring the notion of women's equality. The Socialist Workers Party, one of the event's planners, applauded the strike for exemplifying "the real meaning of sisterhood—that is, the concept that women can unite as sisters on the basis of common struggle."[2]

But the apparent solidarity captured by the press masked the discord that also characterized the day. Protestors lined Washington's avenues, heckling the paraders. Men on lunchtime breaks leered and laughed at women passing by, giving evidence to support feminists' complaints about their second-class status. Some opponents avoided the event altogether, insisting that women's liberation would destroy society at large and damage the movement for black liberation. Finally, disagreement flared even among the organizers, who divided over issues related to political strategy and philosophy.[3]

The tension between unity and dissent present during the August 26 Women's Strike Day exemplified crosscurrents of second-wave feminism, the direct action women's movement that surged in the United States starting in the mid-1960s and crested in the 1970s. During the course of a decade, millions of Americans came to identify themselves as feminists, confident that women shared common struggles that could provide the basis for a liberation movement. Other Americans who never labeled themselves feminists nonetheless asserted that families, workplaces, government, and the media needed to change in order for an egalitarian society to emerge. But feminists' conviction of women's commonality obscured the realities of personal and political differences that separated women. These differences contradicted exclamations of sisterhood and complicated the attempt to sustain a movement for women's liberation.

Considering both paeans to sisterhood and challenges to gender solidarity, this book focuses on Washington, D.C., and examines how feminism evolved at the local level and within the context of concurrent grassroots initiatives for social, political, and economic change. In the 1960s and 1970s, a large and exceedingly energetic population of activists set up numerous local groups and branches of national organizations—including the Student Nonviolent Coordinating Committee, the National Welfare Rights Organization, and the Black Panther Party—that coalesced to identify and advocate for community concerns.[4] The campaigns these groups fought to win black liberation and defeat poverty were central to the developing discourse about women's roles in political movements and in society at large. Within the District of Columbia, mutual influence and interaction among overlapping movements became visible. African American residents made up more than 70 percent of Washington's population in 1970, and black women, many of them poor, contributed significantly to these movements, working as political actors as often as they were targeted as a constituency requiring attention by proponents of black liberation and economic justice. Although focused on defeating racial discrimination and expanding black power, participants in movements for African American liberation and economic justice also debated women's social and political roles, intending to improve women's lives as part of their fight against racism and poverty.

By the late 1960s a distinct movement to end women's gender-based oppression emerged that was philosophically and strategically tied to, but also separate from, contemporaneous struggles for black liberation and welfare rights. As this predominantly white women's movement evolved to fight for reproductive and sexual freedom, its participants drew on—and reacted to—the ideas and approaches generated within movements for welfare rights and African American liberation. At the same time, participants in campaigns for racial liberation and economic justice responded to arguments and priorities advanced within women's liberation organizations, adopting and adapting some while rejecting others. Many black women activists argued that racial unity should not come at the expense of women's liberation. But, keenly aware of the exclusive nature of the priorities and analyses advocated by many white activists who claimed to be addressing "women's issues," women of color and poor women resisted the notion of a universal sisterhood and contended that no single approach could guarantee the liberation of all women. By the early 1970s, many African American women had begun to publicly advocate gender equality as a central component of racial liberation, a notion that resulted in separate black feminist and Third World feminist movements that affirmed the common interests shared by African American, Latina, Native American, and other women of color. Black feminism also challenged white feminists and proponents of racial liberation to understand the intersectional nature of racism, sexism, and class oppression. Through this process of exchange and interchange, all of these movements transformed and further contributed to a widespread reconfiguration of societal expectations about gender roles.[5]

Feminism's dynamism resulted not just from the ideas presented by women of color and poor women. As the women's movement evolved over the 1960s and 1970s, participants recognized that feminism's broad umbrella could and should encompass diverse issues, people, and ideas. Frequent debates over tactics and philosophies took place even among self-defined feminists. White feminists often distinguished themselves politically on the basis of their views regarding the efficacy of reform versus the need for revolutionary transformations to forge an egalitarian society. Radical feminists, who identified as part of a larger left movement and took black liberation as their model, pushed to end male supremacy by overthrowing America's capitalist economy and creating a democracy that encouraged participation by all members of society. Radical feminists sought to liberate women within both personal and public realms, viewing individual transformation as a crucial first step for building a mass revolutionary movement committed to ending women's inferiority. In contrast, liberal feminists prioritized legal and statutory reform, pushing for sex equality and exhibiting a fundamental faith in the soundness of America's economic and political institutions. Although feminists used such categories to describe their approaches, their grassroots activities revealed frequent variations, compromises, and adaptations, suggesting that liberal and radical feminism often overlapped and transmuted to adapt to specific demands.[6]

This book shows how an array of activities, organizations, and people nurtured new models of womanhood and developed programs and projects to facilitate women's liberation. Indeed, the history of second-wave feminism should be understood within the context of the parallel, occasionally overlapping, and often contentious movements that arose at the same time. By analyzing the interactions between local social change efforts, this account of second-wave feminism differs from other histories that have attempted to understand the connections between the era's movements. Although acknowledging the important influence that the civil rights, student, and antiwar movements played on the emergence of second-wave feminism, previous studies typically have treated the histories of these movements separately. As a result, much of this scholarship has obscured the continuous and fruitful interactions that occurred even when each movement declared its independence from the others. In addition, such scholarship often perpetuates a declension narrative that correlates the birth of feminism with the dissolution of other left movements and stresses the decline of radical feminism in the mid-1970s, as the push for commonality gave way to cultural feminism.[7] Many recent studies, however, have focused on African American women's activism for racial and sexual liberation, thereby challenging the view that feminism was exclusively a white woman's movement; yet even this scholarship treats black and white women's activities as largely separate and generally antagonistic.[8]

By encompassing diverse campaigns that burst forth in Washington, D.C., over these two decades, this book acknowledges the divisions that occurred between various movements and groups of women, but still aims to understand the cross-fertilization of ideas that took place. Indeed, an examination of local movements demonstrates how political campaigns are not shaped solely by those people who declare their allegiance or who join affiliated organizations. Contemporaneous, converging campaigns to secure black liberation and end economic oppression inspired many individuals to support feminist demands, including those who did not belong to feminist organizations. Affinity for feminism could be expressed without identifying as feminist or joining feminist groups. Moreover, critics and outsiders, as well as occasional supporters and coalition participants, influenced each other's language, ideas, and agendas. Therefore, the book includes both women who explicitly defined themselves as feminists and activists for whom the elimination of sexual or gender oppression did not constitute a primary goal, but who fought to elevate women's status in their own communities and in the larger society through movements for economic justice and black liberation.[9] As they coordinated political campaigns within the same city at the same time, participants in movements for racial liberation, women's liberation, and welfare rights sometimes found little reason to ally across movement lines. But even when they conceived their movements as separate, activists borrowed, adapted, reconfigured, and disseminated ideas about political change and women's roles to suit the ideological and strategic needs of their organizations and movements. Through direct interaction and indirect exchange, these activists both created a distinct, multidimensional women's movement and advocated women's concerns within other social protest struggles.[10]

Internal dynamics also shaped the political campaigns in which women participated. Theory did not constitute the sole domain of educated women or scholars; instead, women in campaigns for sexual, economic, and racial liberation developed explanations for their conditions and analyses of oppression that they used to formulate short-term political strategies and long-term visions.[11] They discovered, however, that theory and action converged in complex and even contradictory ways. Sometimes theory and action inadvertently worked against each other, leading to strategic dead ends and the dissolution of alliances or individual groups. At other times, success required activists to compromise, bending their long-term goals for the sake of short-term benefits. Through attempts to align philosophical and practical approaches, activists struggled to maintain their ideals, negotiate alternative approaches, and incorporate change into extant organizations. These struggles generated criticism and conflict within the movement, yet they also accounted for feminism's evolution over time.

Perhaps most important, the conflicting forces of diversity and unity shaped the movement in Washington. Radical feminists' initial impulse was to build a mass liberation movement that would articulate women's common needs and establish a foundation for gender equality. They adopted the term *sisterhood* to stress the bonds they presumed women shared. Sisterhood also represented an ideal, a conviction that gender solidarity could be built through the process of collective struggles. But the realities of race, class, and political differences continually collided with calls for sisterhood. Many African American activists, discouraged by a history of interracial struggles and dismayed by the expressions of white privilege that suffused some feminist demands, questioned the efficacy of interracial alliances and contended that the language of sisterhood denied important interracial and intraracial differences. The very existence of these differences, and the reactionary anger sparked when white feminists denied such differences, prevented solidarity. Even white feminists often could not find unity, divided as they were by differing ideas about the nature of women's oppression and the need for either reform or revolution as the path to liberation. Moreover, the impulse to unify women frequently and inadvertently provoked activists to accentuate their dissimilarities. As women who embodied diverse organizational and theoretical approaches to social change came together for the purpose of meeting short-term goals—participation in a single march or repeated alliances to develop a project or series of activities—they articulated their differences in sharp and sometimes insistent ways.

Like any community study, aspects of the narrative uncovered here will illuminate activities in other places, but some elements will be unique. As previous histories of second-wave feminism have revealed, no single site can represent all aspects of the women's movement. The view from the local level reveals wide variations in the ideas and strategies taken up by radical feminists.[12] In this study, the predominance of African American residents within the city's population makes one striking feature. Other distinctions arise from Washington's function as the country's capital, a circumstance that both constrained and encouraged grassroots activism. Many national organizations based their headquarters in D.C., where large numbers of politically committed and astute people could potentially influence federal bureaucrats and the country's political leaders. Operating within this context, D.C. activists developed tactics that maximized the advantages of their location to generate visibility and provoke responses. But Washington's distinct political situation also stifled some forms of grassroots activism. National issues often eclipsed local concerns. Trying to protect the city's image and the security of the government, municipal and federal law enforcement kept a tight rein on radical activity. Furthermore, D.C. residents possessed limited political autonomy. Deprived of the right to vote in presidential elections until 1964, unable to elect any local officials until the late 1960s, and still without both voting representation in the Senate and fiscal control, residents faced restricted avenues for pursuing political change. Congressional committees controlled the city's governance and budget, creating a maze of bureaucracy that complicated municipal support for grassroots projects and limited residents' influence on politics and public policy.

Activists in the District of Columbia did, however, devise campaigns and institutions that reflected local demands and used available resources. Many of these pioneering projects inspired similar endeavors elsewhere and helped sustain the era's liberation movements. In 1968, men and women at Howard University took over an administration building and demanded changes that increased students' governance of campus affairs and led to the formation of an African American Studies program. The takeover came at the beginning of a wave of similar protests that swept United States campuses in the 1960s. In the fall of that same year, white feminists organized the first national women's liberation conference. In 1969, Washington feminists initiated and won the country's first successful suit against a public hospital when they sued to expand the D.C. General Hospital's abortion policies. In 1970, affiliates of the D.C. Women's Liberation Movement began publication of the *off our backs* newspaper. More than three decades later, the paper continues as perhaps the longest-running feminist publication to emerge from second-wave feminism. Other publishing endeavors, including *The Furies, Aegis,* and *Quest,* although not demonstrating the longevity of *off our backs,* provided women around the country with new analyses of women's oppression. In 1972, women from the Washington Area Women's Center established one of the country's first rape crisis centers. On the basis of their activism, women helped foment a shift in political power that granted more influence to local residents.

To examine the local women's movement, this book concentrates on the activities of so-called radicals, women whose activism connected to the broader demands articulated by the New Left, who generally prioritized grassroots issues and sought to transform, rather than reform, society. In the words of one observer, such women fomented a "revolution within the revolution," challenging mainstream society as well as left movements for racial and economic equality.[13] Pursuing broad goals, such as the elimination of patriarchy, capitalism, racism, and imperialism by dismantling social and political institutions including marriage and the nuclear family, such radical activists may seem like flukes and failures, dreamers or idealists to contemporary readers. Nonetheless, they transfigured women's lives in the District of Columbia and, like their counterparts elsewhere, helped shape ideas and priorities that spread throughout America. Other important activists and organizations, such as the local chapter of the National Organization for Women, also fought to secure women's equality and made vital contributions to the feminist movement. But they tended to use their D.C. location to mount national campaigns rather than address local concerns. In addition, the activities of politically conservative activists, those of the New Right, are excluded, as are many men who contributed time, energy, and resources toward the goal of women's liberation. Liberals and conservatives, and men of all political persuasions, certainly influenced the women's movement during these decades, shaping the arguments and strategies that radicals adopted and affecting the outcomes of women's campaigns. But radical women formed a cutting edge that helped introduce new styles of activism and ideas about women's oppression onto the local scene.

In fact, as this work shows, through the exchanges that occurred at the local level, the line separating liberals and radicals often blurred, particularly as the era progressed. Radical women in D.C. consistently compromised and moderated their demands, especially within the increasingly conservative political context of the 1970s.[14] This blurring also came when more mainstream activists adopted ideas and tactics that had been devised by radicals. Arvonne Fraser, who worked in a Congressional office and helped set up Washington chapters of numerous women's groups, acknowledged the singular role played by women who sought radical or revolutionary changes. Reflecting on the local movement, Fraser argued that "radical feminists identified and publicized 'the system's' oppression of women. They also made it respectable for women to work on women's issues." Fraser herself preferred working within established political channels and created ways to bring together women to influence federal laws and policies. She recognized, however, that "our group and others like it would never have been formed if the women's liberation groups had not staked out a more extreme position."[15] The movement's radical edge also helped liberal feminists appear more moderate, and hence made their demands seem more reasonable in the eyes of critics. Moreover, the contributions of radical activists are important to understand, for they created lasting and consequential initiatives, including rape crisis centers, battered women's shelters, children's programs, and feminist publications that altered women's lives and the broader society. These local initiatives provide an enduring legacy of the contributions made by activists of the era, signs of change in the face of more public setbacks like the failure to pass the Equal Rights Amendment or to equalize men's and women's salaries.

To explain how and why Washington women took part in such activities, this book traces women's participation in grassroots campaigns for political, social, and economic equality from the 1960s through the 1970s. The first chapter examines the direct action movements for civil rights and against poverty that pulled new groups of activists into the political arena. Urged on by organizers affiliated with the Student Nonviolent Coordinating Committee (SNCC), the Congress on Racial Equality (CORE), and publicly supported antipoverty agencies, the city's poor and black residents demanded improved conditions, developed confrontational approaches to pressure policy makers, and pushed the government not only to enforce existing constitutional rights but also to extend those rights to the dispossessed and thereby transform America's social fabric. With access to new monies to fight a federally funded "war on poverty" and inspiration from the Southern-based civil rights struggles, activists stimulated a full-scale mobilization of District residents. These new mass-based efforts addressed the economic and social needs of the poor and expanded resources and opportunities for African Americans. But although these campaigns spurred residents into action, participants recognized that the movements only went so far in addressing the specific needs of District women. Despite the limitations of these campaigns, civil rights and antipoverty movements played a critical role in moving poor and middle-class African American women into positions where they could influence public policy, shape agendas, and form the leadership for future movements.

Chapter 2 follows some of these women into the welfare rights movement, where public assistance recipients joined to reshape the welfare system. Stressing economic demands, welfare rights activists fought to increase public subsidies and to guarantee poor women a role in determining welfare policies. Although arguing in favor of welfare reform, activists in this movement sought broader goals related to altering society's understanding of the roles of mothers, especially African American mothers, and the resources they required to fulfill their maternal duties. Although they generally did not articulate welfare as a "woman's issue," welfare recipient-activists nonetheless raised issues that would become integral to feminism: the extent of state power over women's reproductive choices, the social value of motherhood, and the economic exploitation of women.

Taking up these issues, women's liberationists added a gender analysis to the welfare mothers' concerns. The radical feminists studied in chapter

3 intended to construct a movement on the basis of women's sex-based oppression and they emphasized conditions they believed united women as a sex. They advocated a revolution to overturn patriarchy and to bring about women's empowerment on both the individual and collective levels. Working as part of the D.C. Women's Liberation Movement, a citywide organization that coordinated numerous projects, radical feminists expanded their movement beyond its initial constituency of white, middle-class women who had previously participated in New Left and black liberation movements. But even as radical feminism expanded, it stressed women's shared experiences. In so doing, radical feminists diminished the importance of race and class as determinants of the conditions under which women lived.

Chapter 4 examines the diverse ideological and strategic approaches that women from welfare rights, black liberation, and women's liberation campaigns brought to a movement to secure women's rights to determine when and whether to bear children by gaining access to safe and affordable health care, contraception, and abortion. Using the tools of direct action perfected by civil rights and welfare rights organizers, the reproductive rights campaign became one of city's most vibrant and broad efforts to address a specific set of women's concerns. To an extent not seen in campaigns to address other issues, the movement for reproductive rights brought together diverse groups of activists who found points of strategic and philosophical compromise around the fight for abortion and birth control. Activists from women's liberation, black liberation, and welfare rights movements maintained distinct positions regarding the ways that race, class, and sex discrimination obstructed women's control of their bodies. But by collaboratively pushing for governmental and statutory change, activists created a movement, and a consensus, that asserted women's rights to control their fertility. After the 1973 *Roe v. Wade* decision upheld women's right to abortion, the reproductive rights movement lost the momentum required to fight off attacks on women's abortion access. Thus, organizing around reproductive rights represented a rare moment when women activists surmounted differences in race, class, and politics, but also demonstrated the movement's inability to secure reproductive rights for all women.

The next chapter follows women in the black liberation movement of the late 1960s and the 1970s, a period referred to as the Black Power era. The chapter examines how male and female activists on the campus of Howard University, in the local chapter of the Black Panther Party, and in other African American organizations conceived women's roles in politics and in liberated black communities. Most Black Power advocates reacted negatively to organized feminism and, unlike participants in most of the other movements included in this book, women in the Black Power movement worked closely with men. Yet within racial liberation groups, women organized on their own behalf to challenge the sexism of their black male allies. Even though Black Power women distanced themselves from many of the activities coordinated by Washington's white radical feminists and chose to work within mixed-sex groups, their organizational activities demonstrated how black women sought to advance gender equality through ending racial oppression.

Chapter 6 concentrates on lesbian feminism, a movement that emerged when former members of the D.C. Women's Liberation Movement joined with other leftist women to form a separatist collective. The Furies, as the collective was called, grew out of gay feminists' frustrations with the priorities of the movements described earlier in the book. Like Black Power advocates, lesbian feminists believed that feminists had failed to understand how women's oppression operated. Specifically, the Furies pushed other women's liberation advocates to consider the oppression that lesbians faced in the feminist movement and in the broader society. Identifying heterosexuality as an institution vital to patriarchy, members of the Furies collective sought to develop theories and practices that could ultimately direct a broad liberation movement. The Furies' ideas and programs, however, generated immense conflict inside and outside the collective, pushing feminists' analysis of the role of sexuality in shaping women's lives and helping to create a lesbian feminist identity, but also alienating many women.

The movement against sexual violence that emerged in Washington after 1972 attempted both to address local needs and draw African American women into feminist groups where white women dominated. The final chapter explores attempts to protect women from physical and sexual assaults and to address the causes of violence. While creating antiviolence campaigns in 1972, at a moment when separatism (racial and sexual) appeared to be a popular ideology among radical women, activists looked for ways to bring African American and white women together. They did so by developing a theoretical analysis of sexual violence that recognized the connections between racial, economic, and sexual oppression. In establishing services such as the D.C. Rape Crisis Center and battered women's shelters, lobbying for stronger laws, and educating the public, activists articulated sexual violence as an issue that crossed differences of race, class, and sexual orientation. They drew together the analytic frameworks that derived from welfare rights, women's liberation, black liberation, and lesbian separatism. In this way, the movement against sexual violence extended the activities and insights of women active in earlier campaigns. And to a degree not seen in the earlier campaigns, the movement against sexual violence broadened membership in explicitly feminist organizations and activities, thereby contributing to an important transformation in the voices and faces of feminism in Washington.

By detailing some of the activities undertaken by black and white women in Washington's grassroots movements, this book shows that feminism evolved at the local level through the connected and disconnected efforts of participants in the multiple campaigns of the time. It thereby yields a fresh picture of the myriad forces that shaped second-wave feminism and of the influence that feminism exerted on other movements.

Mary Treadwell (1971). Copyright *Washington Post;* reprinted by permission of the D.C. Public Library.

Washington, D.C., welfare rights activists submit applications for supplemental furniture grants (1970). Copyright *Washington Post;* reprinted by permission of the D.C. Public Library.

Washington, D.C., Women's Strike for Equality march (1970). Copyright *Washington Post;* reprinted by permission of the D.C. Public Library.

Rally for abortion law repeal, WONAAC (1971). Copyright *Washington Post;* reprinted by permission of the D.C. Public Library.

Abortion rights picket at HEW (1977). Copyright *Washington Post;* reprinted by permission of the D.C. Public Library.

People gathered outside administration building during student takeover, Howard University (1968). Courtesy of the Moorland-Spingarn Research Center, Howard University Archives.

Gathering on the steps of the Lincoln Memorial to announce the Revolutionary People's Constitutional Convention (1970). U.S. News and World Report Magazine Photograph Collection, Library of Congress Prints and Photographs Division LC-DIG-pppmsca-04303.

Members of the Furies, compiling the newspaper (1971). © 2006 JEB (Joan E. Biren)

The front of the Take Back the Night march, Stop Rape Week (1978). © 2006 JEB (Joan E. Biren)

1

Mobilizing for Political and Economic Rights

Mary Treadwell had lived in the District only a few months before she embarked on a path that would make her a significant figure in Washington's black freedom movement and earn her acclaim as a "soft-spoken, no-nonsense activist." Treadwell, from a middle-class African American family, had attended Fisk University in the early 1960s when hundreds of black Nashville students participated in desegregation sit-ins and other civil rights protests. After her graduation, she moved to D.C. intending to earn a law degree, a plan that was thrown awry one day in 1966 when she bumped into Marion Barry, an acquaintance from Fisk, who was marching in a picket line on the street near her workplace. As Barry and other black activists demanded that Congress "Free D.C." by expanding the voting rights of Washington residents, Treadwell overheard bystanders refer to the picketers as "monkeys." Incensed by these insults and radicalized by the disfranchisement of the city's residents, Treadwell joined Barry's efforts to increase local political power in the overwhelmingly black metropolis.[1]

Treadwell's accidental encounter with Barry irrevocably altered her professional and personal life. In contrast to Treadwell, who had little previous political experience, Barry was a seasoned activist, a member of the NAACP while in college, a veteran of Nashville's desegregation campaigns, and the first chairman of SNCC, the Student Nonviolent Coordinating Committee. Barry had come to the District in 1965 to take charge of SNCC's D.C. chapter, which concentrated on raising money and support for the Southern civil rights movement. Forging new directions for the chapter, he tackled the District's limited electoral power as a civil rights issue and fought to increase the economic resources of the city's black majority. Inspired by her encounter with Barry and the political demands SNCC raised, Treadwell joined the organization in the summer of 1966. The next year, Treadwell and Barry paired to start Pride, Inc., an agency dedicated to starting initiatives that would yield jobs for the city's young black men. In April 1968, when Martin Luther King Jr.'s assassination kindled violent unrest in Washington, Pride's staff protected the businesses owned by its supporters and distributed food donated by a local grocery chain. As Pride's executive director, Mary Treadwell oversaw its commercial activities and, moving far from her middle-class roots, she worked alongside young men from the city's poorest neighborhoods. Pride's codirector, Marion Barry, attested to Treadwell's conviction, telling a reporter, "She walks the streets every day. She goes some places in this city where even I'd rather not go."[2]

Over the next few years Treadwell volunteered time outside of Pride to numerous causes, including the antiwar movement, prison reform, and reproductive rights, through which she continued to prioritize racial liberation. In the spring of 1970, she mobilized African American activists to attend a massive protest against the Vietnam War, hoping to make the antiwar movement more attuned to the violence black Americans experienced in their home country. The following year, she joined a black women's group that supported the decriminalization of abortion and elimination of forced sterilization in order to improve the quality of life experienced by members of the African American community.[3] "I support the abortion campaign," she declared, "for reasons inherent in being a member of the black minority in racist America." Proclaiming abortion rights as a life-saving measure, Treadwell argued that "black women must consider the larger consequences (of abortion outlawed) in a society which is not only unwilling to provide a quality life for black children, but tries to destroy life for all black people."[4]

Treadwell's unexpected involvement in grassroots organizing typified the experiences of many women of her generation, drawn into a world of politics that redirected their careers and transformed their personal relationships. In 1973, she married Marion Barry, her partner and colleague in SNCC and Pride. They later divorced and Barry left Pride to pursue a storied career in municipal politics, but Treadwell continued her work as an advocate for the city's black residents.[5] Like many other middle-class black women galvanized by the era's social change movements, she poured her energies into fighting racism and poverty, remaking America's democracy, and acting on her belief that the poor could become agents for political and social change.

Treadwell's activism also reflected the way that the black freedom movement nurtured the political involvement and leadership of women, even as it sometimes failed to link racial and sexual oppression. Through SNCC, Pride, and numerous community development and antipoverty programs, women campaigned to address the intertwined problems of racism and poverty. The activities in D.C. resembled those in other cities across the United States, where the Congress on Racial Equality (CORE), the Urban League, the NAACP, settlement houses, and other groups worked for economic development and to combat high rates of incarceration, police brutality, joblessness, dislocation caused by urban renewal, and inadequate public services.[6] Two groups of women joined these efforts: Treadwell and other middle-class black and white activists who staffed civil rights and antipoverty initiatives, and poor women who joined and led programs within their communities. Each group of women understood and confronted the problems that African Americans and poor people experienced in different ways. Their activism was linked, however, by the cross-class settings in which they organized and through which they experienced a growing sense of their importance.

Even as poor and middle-class women acted collectively to combat racism and poverty, in the mid-1960s these movements did not directly attack gender discrimination within D.C.'s political organizations or the larger society. Instead, black freedom activists and antipoverty workers stressed male political and economic dominance both as a means to strengthen African American communities and a symbol of racial liberation. Particularly as the decade progressed and the call for civil rights gave way to the demand for Black Power, organizations such as Pride and SNCC promoted men's leadership of families, neighborhoods, and institutions as a means to strengthen black communities. Federally funded antipoverty initiatives, enacted on the local level by activists committed to community betterment, similarly operated within a framework that assumed men's proper place as breadwinners and family heads. By linking racial liberation to men's economic and political power, the solutions proposed by SNCC, Pride, and other groups ignored the ways that sexual oppression exacerbated poverty and resulted in particular expressions of racism. Yet despite the biases that shaped these efforts, women activists gained experience, skills, and a sense of gender solidarity that became the basis for later initiatives more directly attuned to ending sex oppression.

Inaugurating a Mass Movement

Throughout the twentieth century, African American residents of Washington had maintained a persistent struggle to end racial discrimination and to increase their political power. After World War II, the pervasive practice of racial segregation in D.C.'s neighborhoods, public accommodations, and workplaces became embarrassing to a country engaged in a contest with the Soviet Union for control of the hearts and minds of the world's developing nations. Within this Cold War context, Jim Crow in the capital city exposed the United States to charges of hypocrisy arising from the contradiction between its democratic rhetoric and the reality of segregation.

Capitalizing on the opportunities created by international attention and the strength derived from a growing black population, after World War II civil rights activists pushed to end legal segregation.[7] In the area of education, District residents, supported by NAACP lawyers, successfully argued in court that no D.C. laws required segregated schools and, furthermore, any such laws would violate the Fourteenth Amendment to the Constitution.[8] Other activists set up the Coordinating Committee for the Enforcement of D.C. Anti-Discrimination Laws to force compliance with two statutes from the 1870s that outlawed racial discrimination in the capital. Disregarded for decades, the laws still remained on the books, mandating that access to public accommodations could not be denied on the basis of race or color. The Coordinating Committee also tested the legality of racial segregation in the city's restaurants, using negotiations, picket lines, and then lawsuits when African American customers were refused service. These efforts resulted in a 1953 Supreme Court decision, affirming that the nineteenth-century laws remained valid. But although District activists laid the groundwork to eradicate segregation in the schools and in public accommodations, the practice remained customary in the city's workplaces and neighborhoods.[9]

Building on the unfinished work undertaken in the 1950s, CORE and SNCC entered Washington's black neighborhoods after 1960, conducting parallel fights against racial discrimination and to increase opportunities for African American workers. Like other national organizations with chapters or headquarters in D.C., SNCC and CORE chapters divided their energies between local and national campaigns, generating visibility for Southern civil rights actions and organizing residents to address their own concerns.[10] Before long, however, both groups concentrated on mobilizing District residents to express publicly their outrage at government neglect, their exclusion from jobs and housing, and other violations of their rights. Both groups were committed to the tactic of nonviolent protest and encouraged mass participation as a necessary means to exert political pressure and nurture political consciousness. Racially integrated until the mid-1960s, the organizations nonetheless emphasized black self-determination and prioritized expanding African American political power.

University students and young adults formed the core of SNCC, coming together to plan protest activities that would lead individuals from all parts of the black community to overcome internalized racism and take action to improve their communities.[11] In Washington, Howard University's Nonviolent Action Group (NAG) functioned as a SNCC chapter from 1960 until SNCC opened a D.C. office nearby three years later. NAG initially focused on reforming conditions on campus and getting students politically involved, but activists also campaigned against racial discrimination locally and nationally in conjunction with CORE and other organizations. About fifty people participated in the group, developing organizing skills and political consciousness that many subsequently transferred to positions as SNCC field secretaries and leaders.[12]

Many Howard students in the early 1960s found the campus surprisingly conservative and disconnected from the political campaigns that swirled beyond its boundaries. Howard University faculty, staff, and students had played critical roles in supporting the desegregation campaigns of the 1940s and 1950s and this activity, along with the prominence of its many distinguished African American scholars, had earned the university a reputation as a center of black learning and political struggle. But even after 1960, when vibrant political movements sprang up at other historically black universities, Howard's administration attempted to suppress student protest. The university refused to officially recognize or support NAG. Deferring to parents who sought assurances about their children's safety and to the federal government that funded school operations, Howard's administration tried to focus students' attention on the social, intellectual, and professional opportunities their education would afford.[13]

Men and women took part in NAG in equal numbers, assuming similar roles and displaying comparable outspokenness and courage. But women experienced distinctive barriers to their activism. Stokely Carmichael (who later adopted the name Kwame Toure) had attended Howard from 1960 to 1964, where he had helped to formulate NAG's approach during discussions with faculty and at conferences with prominent black leaders. Carmichael remembered that although the university's administration generally had discouraged political activism, the campus climate particularly had stifled women's involvement. Curfews represented one such obstacle, requiring women to be safely ensconced in their dorms at night but leaving men free to walk on and off campus. In practical terms, the curfew made it difficult for women to attend evening meetings or late-night bull sessions with professors and male students or to travel to events held away from Howard. Justified as protecting women who might be vulnerable to attack, these restrictions nonetheless reinforced the idea that proper women must abstain from sexual and political activity without encouraging similar restraint by men. In addition to formal policies, campus mores dissuaded women's activism by perpetuating expectations that women should be fashionable but conservative in appearance and assume a "ladylike" manner that eschewed matters political and intellectual. As members of the campus community and the larger black society whose norms Howard perpetuated, NAG men were not concerned with the impact of university culture on their female counterparts. Instead, when NAG pressed the university's administration to eliminate the nighttime restrictions as part of its broader effort at campus reform, the group treated the issue more as an insult to men's access to women than a restriction that discouraged women's activity.[14]

Even if women did not directly confront practices that restricted their mobility or perpetuated their complacency, the university policies nonetheless cultivated female activists' conviction that the campus and black community needed to change in order to promote racial equality. Despite the administration's attempts to squelch female students' activity, Howard women still found ways to act on their political beliefs. Paradoxically, the curfew may have unwittingly fostered women's political involvement, turning their dormitories into places where they could exchange ideas, discuss their grievances, and coordinate activities.[15] As women's political consciousness grew, they expressed it both in individual and collective ways. Bill Hall, who later worked with SNCC, became involved with NAG because his girlfriend insisted that he join her on the picket lines. Stokely Carmichael's girlfriend, Mary Felice Lovelace, who joined NAG at his urging, challenged Howard's policies after the university threatened to expel her from her dorm for wearing an Afro. Although members of the administration considered her hairstyle scandalous and inappropriate for a woman student, Lovelace insisted on her right to make a political and cultural statement in support of black liberation.[16] By thus merging the personal and the political, NAG activists shaped relationships to support their fight against racism and bourgeois notions of respectability that hindered women's protest activities.

In 1963, SNCC opened a Washington office to coordinate fund-raising, publicity, and lobbying of the federal government on behalf of its Southern projects. The creation of the D.C. office occurred at a period of growth and change in civil rights activism, as SNCC concentrated on planning for Freedom Summer, when it would organize the Mississippi Freedom Democratic Party, a bid by black Mississippians to become delegates at the Democratic National Convention. The Democrat's rejection of the MFDP's challenge to the state's delegation, and the apparent betrayal of white liberals who supported President Johnson, came as a blow to those who worked hard to win a different outcome. At the same time, the passage of the Civil Rights Act in 1964 and the Voting Rights Act the next year presented the possibility of shifting attention from desegregation and voting rights to other issues. Finally, SNCC's efforts in Mississippi and other rural locales, where the group had concentrated prior to 1965, had demonstrated the inseparable nature of political and economic oppression.[17]

Stokely Carmichael's election to chair SNCC in the spring of 1966 signaled the organization's emerging emphasis on Black Power, a slogan that promoted African American identity, self-determination, and political independence. Black Power was not synonymous with racial separatism, but white staff gradually left SNCC during these years, turning their attention to other issues: stamping out racism in white communities, protesting U.S. involvement in Vietnam, and organizing for women's liberation. Acting in accord with its new philosophy, the organization shifted its resources toward urban areas with large black populations located within and outside the South.[18] During this period, too, a small group of women, led by Casey Hayden and Mary King, initiated discussions of sexual oppression within SNCC and the broader society. Although some white women appreciated how SNCC had fostered their confidence, they also perceived that SNCC minimized their contributions by relegating them to secretarial positions, failing to have women chair meetings, and expecting women in leadership positions to defer to men for final decision making. Many African American women, in contrast, disputed white women's complaints and found SNCC's culture conducive to their participation and leadership.[19]

Within the context of these debates about SNCC's future, Washington chapter members attempted to address the interlaced political and economic repression the city's black residents suffered. Under Marion Barry's direction, the number of paid staff increased, supported by the work of volunteers. Barry prioritized dramatic, short-term activities that would instigate residents of the large city to work on their own behalf. This approach, he admitted, contrasted with SNCC's typical philosophy of "base building then action," but Washington's size and diversity made it "difficult to build a city-wide base on a single problem."[20] The D.C. chapter also embraced opportunities to promote intraracial cooperation and unity. The Washington staff told SNCC's national office it planned to "establish a program which will mean that Black people will talk and work with other Black people to develop Black consciousness and awareness which will unite Black people and enable them to transform this unity into power—power that can be used to change the conditions in which Black people live."[21]

In January 1966, the D.C. SNCC office launched its first campaign, challenging a proposed rise in the cost of bus fares. The action represented the kind of catalytic event SNCC favored to build momentum across the city. SNCC circulated a petition that approximately 10,000 people signed, registering their opposition to the proposed change, followed by a one-day boycott. The day of the boycott, SNCC staff and volunteers stood at bus stops, discouraging people from riding, and directed commuters to cars that could provide alternative transportation. When nearly 90 percent of the regular riders stayed off some routes, the transit company lost approximately $18,000 in revenue and postponed the fare increase.[22]

SNCC's bus boycott diverged from those that took place previously in Montgomery, Alabama, and other places where residents refused to ride in protest of the unfair treatment of black riders. The D.C. effort promoted the economic concerns of the city's black residents who relied on public transportation and could ill afford even the five-cent proposed increase. Overall, about 17 percent of the city's total population lived in poverty on annual family incomes below $5,000. African Americans, who made up 70 percent of the city's population, also suffered twice the rates of poverty as their white counterparts (see table 1.1) With the bus boycott, therefore, SNCC effectively began to articulate economic concerns as part of its racial liberation agenda, recognizing that racism and economic inequalities could not be separated in Washington, where pronounced disparities in poverty separated black and white residents.

After the boycott, SNCC quickly turned to three other issues that related to economic disparities, albeit in less direct ways: electoral rights, the war in Vietnam, and police brutality. Viewing D.C. voters' partial disfranchisement

Table 1.1. Percentage of selected population groups below poverty level in 1969

All persons	17.0%
African Americans	19.5%
White	10.0%
Female heads of families	29.0%
Children under age 18	23.0%
Persons over age 65	21.0%

Source: *1970 Population of the Census. Subject Report: Low-Income Areas in Large Cities* (Washington, D.C.: Government Printing Office, 1973), 833.

as a restriction on black power, SNCC tried to rally support for instituting a popularly elected local government and voting representation in Congress. Barry argued that with increased political power, Washingtonians could free themselves "from our enemies," most of whom he considered responsible for some form of economic-based repression: "the people who make it impossible for us to do anything about lousy schools, brutal cops, slumlords, welfare investigators who go on midnight raids, employers who discriminate in hiring, and a host of other ills that run rampant through our city."[23] SNCC's attention to the war in Vietnam and police brutality at home also highlighted black men's particular vulnerability to violence and death as a result of their race and their economic status. Rejecting SNCC's original nonviolent philosophy, the group argued that police treatment of African Americans constituted a form of genocide that warranted a defensive response. "We will not allow the genocide of Black people to go unanswered," SNCC announced. "We will protect ourselves for survival and existence. The only power that Gestapo cops respect is 'equalized' power. Blacks, we will match power with power." Despite the militant rhetoric, the committee concentrated on collecting statements from black men who claimed to have been arrested without justification or who alleged mistreatment at the hands of municipal law enforcement. Finally, the chapter also called on local citizens to resist the draft and protest U.S. involvement in Vietnam.[24]

Like SNCC, Washington CORE channeled nonviolent direct action toward ending racial discrimination. Nationally, CORE chapters proliferated outside the South, and the group was best known for two sets of Freedom Rides intended to desegregate interstate public transportation, one in 1947 and one in 1961 that several NAG activists joined. Washington's CORE chapter, founded in 1958, struggled through bouts of inactivity until 1962 when Julius Hobson took over. Hobson, whom *Ebony* magazine dubbed "the angriest man in Washington," was a World War II veteran originally from Birmingham, Alabama, who was now an economist for the federal government. A longtime member of the NAACP and assorted civic organizations, Hobson took the helm of CORE determined to end racial discrimination in housing and employment.[25]

With more than 20,000 unemployed persons in the city, nearly three-quarters of them black, District residents desperately needed more jobs.[26] Operating in a manner similar to its forerunner, the Coordinating Committee for the Enforcement of D.C. Anti-Discrimination Laws, CORE attempted to negotiate with private employers to hire black workers and, when needed, increased pressure with picket lines and boycotts. But unlike the earlier committee, CORE perceived that it wielded more power by instigating protests and raising a public outcry rather than hammering out individual agreements with employers and landlords. Thus, CORE acted as a "gadfly," using public visibility to arouse residents to join future protests and to press for change.[27]

CORE's victories revealed the efficacy of such techniques. Between 1960 and 1964, according to one account, a successful CORE campaign against the D.C. Transit Commission led to the hiring of the city's first black male bus driver, and the group coordinated more than eighty picket lines at retail stores in downtown Washington, opening up jobs for more than 5,000 black women and men. These activities "darn near changed the complexion of the shopping area," one resident observed. To eliminate housing discrimination, CORE members picketed at the homes of property owners who excluded black tenants. A 4,000-person march through the city finally led to the passage of a nondiscrimination order for District homes. CORE also launched a campaign against the segregated restaurants that lined nearby Highway 40 in Maryland, bringing in more than 1,000 college students (including NAG members) to conduct sit-ins until dozens of restaurant owners agreed to serve African American customers. With seventy-five to one hundred active members, black and white, men and women, the group could draw even larger crowds of people to walk picket lines, make phone calls, and coordinate rallies.[28]

In Washington, as elsewhere, women constituted a significant proportion of those working with both CORE and SNCC. A March 1964 list of active members of CORE included more than one-third women, a proportion roughly equivalent to the gender breakdown of the SNCC chapter. The internal dynamics of the two organizations differed greatly, however, in ways that affected women's experiences. SNCC emphasized consensus and discussion within the group and devised practices meant to nurture widespread participation and develop local leaders, approaches that welcomed women's participation.[29] In contrast, CORE adhered to a more traditional structure, with elected officers and written bylaws. Within this hierarchy, turmoil often erupted and women struggled to gain recognition.[30]

Julius Hobson, who chaired CORE until the fall of 1964, held tight reins on the chapter, and his means of maintaining control stirred controversy and disunity. Hobson's treatment of Roena Rand, who would become the only African American woman elected to chair the chapter, especially provoked complaints. During the spring of 1964, Hobson expelled Rand for alleged disruptive behavior, canceled an employment campaign that Rand coordinated at a grocery chain, started another against the D.C. public schools, and refused to allow people to offer dissenting opinions at meetings. Rand fought back by appealing to CORE's national office, seeking to unseat Hobson for violating the chapter's constitution. Members rallied to the defense of the two tussling leaders, with more women than men opposing Hobson's authority to make such decisions. Ultimately, the national office reinstated Rand and expelled Hobson, but the dissension led many members, including Hobson, to break ties with the group.[31]

Without Hobson and his supporters, the remaining CORE members concentrated on the problems of the city's poor residents. In a move symbolizing its new orientation, CORE relocated its office from northwest D.C., where it had enjoyed close proximity to SNCC and Howard University, to the southeast area across the Anacostia River, where most of the city's public housing was located. This move was accompanied by shifting priorities, and the chapter began to agitate for subsidized, low-income housing and organized a demonstration against a highway construction project that threatened to break up a black neighborhood. CORE members also chained themselves to the entrance of a local junior high school to protest the run-down conditions at the school. At the end of 1964, CORE opened a Freedom School in Anacostia, offering afternoon courses in African American history and citizenship, as well as training in barbering, boxing, leatherwork, and typing. Like SNCC, CORE viewed these programs as a path to personal transformation for community members and a way to stimulate long-term change. An apparent success, this project eschewed CORE's more provocative role in favor of an ongoing program geared toward political and economic empowerment.[32]

Hobson's expulsion not only occasioned this shift in CORE's approach but also temporarily opened opportunities for women's leadership. In December 1964, women won five of the eight elected positions in the chapter and in June of the following year, Roena Rand took over as chair. As CORE's head, Rand gained greater visibility, and she led a citywide committee investigating a racial disturbance at a local amusement park.[33] But the promotion of women within Washington CORE quickly fell off as the chapter adopted a more explicit Black Power philosophy. The most vivid example of this transition occurred in 1966 when members elected a slate of officers composed entirely of African American men except the recording secretary. Richard Anderson, who replaced Rand as the group's chair, declared upon accepting the position, "CORE will not automatically turn the other cheek when violence is attempted against the personal rights of colored people. CORE will continue to solicit participation and patronage of all segments of the community . . . but its efforts will be directed toward developing the political and economic strength of the most disadvantaged segment of the community." Another CORE member indicated that the group's new philosophy encouraged residents to "Be Proud That You Are a Black Man."[34]

CORE members must have been deliberate about their choice to express black empowerment in masculine rather than gender-neutral terms, just as they calculatedly began to talk about rejecting nonviolent principles. Indeed, the group might not have intended such language to belittle women's roles or imply a change in women's status. Yet when combined with CORE's rejection of women's leadership, expressions of Black Power perpetuated men's prominence at women's expense. The use of rhetoric that equated masculinity with racial pride and assertiveness promoted men to the vanguard of the movement and pushed women to the margins. In addition, conceiving racial liberation as an expression of manliness justified outrage and a refusal to compromise when exhibited by men, but Rand's expulsion suggested that disruptive behavior was unacceptable from women.

In many ways, D.C. SNCC compared favorably to CORE in terms of the positions available to women and the treatment they received. Betty Garman, the chapter's coordinator of federal programs in 1965 and 1966, found that women enjoyed responsibility and good treatment in SNCC.[35] Women worked behind the scenes, coordinating campaigns, fund-raising, participating in mass protests, typing and running the office, and managing education programs. Sharlene Kranz and Tina Smith staffed the SNCC office, conducting clerical work, ordering supplies, answering the phone, and facilitating the activities of the other staff and volunteers. The clerical tasks they performed fell within women's traditional domain, but also put them at the center of the flow of communication, receiving and disseminating information within the office. Similarly, Robin Gregory, a Howard student, worked in the SNCC office during the summer of 1964. Serving as a liaison between Washington and Mississippi, Gregory received reports by phone from SNCC volunteers in Mississippi and conveyed information to the office of the U.S. attorney general. Mary Treadwell chaired the fund-raising committee, gaining pledges of money to support the activities of the local chapter and SNCC's Southern projects. Both women and men worked outside the office, interacting with residents and drumming up participation in the chapter's projects.[36]

As these examples demonstrate, administrative titles did not necessarily indicate the degree of one's power or influence. Women and men assumed leadership and responsibility in many ways, all important to the chapter's functions. Washington SNCC vested women with authority over many aspects of the chapter's activities, but generally placed men in titular leadership assignments where they communicated with the media and negotiated with business owners and political leaders on the group's behalf. Washington SNCC never selected a woman to head the chapter, nor did women represent SNCC on citywide committees. The local media responded by complimenting men for the group's activities. Of Marion Barry's role in the bus boycott and other activities, the *Washington Afro-American* noted that "his success . . . should not be underestimated. His tactics may be abrasive, his ideas may at times appear irrational, but while others talk, Barry is at least doing something." Such praise gave Barry single-handed credit for movement accomplishments, ignoring the contribution of SNCC organizers who helped to pull off the bus boycott and the thousands of riders who stayed off the buses.[37] Most SNCC organizers threw themselves into their work because of their commitment to racial liberation and community empowerment, not because they sought personal fame. But even if most SNCC organizers did not pursue public visibility, the types of recognition given men and women mattered, because the face and voice that the group presented to the larger public helped shape residents' reactions to SNCC and nurtured individuals' confidence that they could step into roles as community organizers and leaders.

By 1966, opportunities for women in the SNCC chapter began to change as the group shifted ideologically. Three women who had been active in SNCC for several years—Tina Smith, Sharlene Kranz, and Betty Garman—all resigned early in 1966. This turnover came about for a combination of reasons. Kranz, who was white, departed for a paid job with the local antipoverty agency, the United Planning Organization (UPO). Drawn into the black freedom movement in 1963 as a suburban Maryland high school student, Kranz subsequently worked with SNCC as both a volunteer and paid employee. Although Kranz left because she needed the salary UPO could pay, she also feared that SNCC was on the verge of collapse.[38] Other SNCC staff felt pushed out, repelled by what they considered Barry's undemocratic means of running the group. Garman, a white activist who had worked with SNCC since early in the decade, believed the chapter no longer valued her contribution. Garman's race and prior intimate relationship with Barry no doubt influenced her sense that it was time to move on.[39] Barry had declared that white activists could continue to assist the D.C. chapter but they would be discouraged from local organizing. Garman agreed that SNCC's white staff should concentrate on organizing white communities to support the black movement, but she disliked Barry's style of leadership, which she characterized as authoritarian.[40] Tina Smith expressed similar doubts. A black Washingtonian who had served as the chapter's office manager since the summer of 1964, she grew concerned that the national organization did not sanction some of the chapter's activities. Moreover, she considered Washington SNCC's new programs geared to furthering the political careers of individuals rather than furthering the organization's important work.[41]

Thus the new directions that both CORE and SNCC pursued between 1964, when they shifted to local concerns, and 1968, when both groups effectively dissolved, directly influenced women's roles and contributions. In both groups, women generally experienced new constraints with the embrace of Black Power philosophies and the concurrent adoption of new agendas. Arguably, the issues that SNCC took up in 1967 and 1968—the draft and police brutality—put men at the center of SNCC's agenda, a charge that white women would later articulate about the antidraft movement. But the divergent experiences of SNCC and CORE activists defy easy generalizations about the nature of women's participation in the black freedom movement and suggest the importance of organizational philosophy, structure, and leadership in determining the treatment of members. Individual personalities and relationships certainly mattered as well. Women in CORE had encountered an uncomfortable environment under Hobson's leadership and, after a brief respite when female leaders emerged, the group's adoption of Black Power rhetoric further constrained their activities. Like CORE, SNCC typically assigned formal leadership roles to men. But the local SNCC group largely avoided rhetoric that equated masculinity with liberation, and women continued to play important roles until the chapter closed down.

Community Growth and Change

SNCC's and CORE's attempts to address the political and economic demands of black residents dovetailed with fruitful efforts by neighborhood centers, settlement houses, churches, and reform organizations to organize neighborhood women. Just months before passage of the 1964 Civil Rights Act, President Lyndon B. Johnson gave these institutions a new weapon when he declared a "national war on poverty." This multifaceted attack on persistent deprivation in a land of plenty combined direct aid programs with initiatives to expand access to employment, health care, and education. The 1964 Economic Opportunity Act created the Office of Economic Opportunity (OEO), an agency authorized to fight poverty by supporting local initiatives. Although hampered by insufficient resources, the OEO legitimized struggling poor people throughout the country. The United Planning Organization (UPO), the agency that administered OEO funds in the D.C. metropolitan area, allocated more than $112 million to local antipoverty projects over a five-year period. Disseminating money through the UPO and to private agencies circumvented the congressional committees that otherwise controlled the city's budget, and thereby gave residents, African American leaders, and black-run social service agencies greater power to identify community needs and funding priorities.[42]

The notion of collective involvement and citizens' empowerment philosophically and practically connected the civil rights movement and the community development projects. The two movements also shared success in mobilizing women to take action to address community concerns, albeit without an explicit analysis of women's particular vulnerability to poverty. Because the federal government mandated that projects funded through the OEO and its Community Action Program include low-income constituents in program development and governance, black women would have a meaningful impact by virtue of their prominence in Washington's population[43] (see table 1.2). Following a government directive to activate the "maximum feasible participation" of poor people, by 1968, more than 1,500 low-income Washingtonians served on policy and advisory boards for community action programs, neighborhood advisory groups, and the UPO's Board of Trustees.[44]

One particularly energetic effort emerged in southeast D.C. This part of the city, also known as Anacostia, changed dramatically between 1960 and 1970. Washington's overall population shrank during this decade, but Anacostia's population expanded by nearly 23 percent; the school-aged population increased by 78 percent; and the racial makeup shifted from 60 percent

Table 1.2. Numbers of D.C. residents with income below poverty level (1970)

Men over age 16	27,989
White	7,086
African American	20,211
Women over age 16	47,928
White	10,669
African American	36,688
With children under age 17	20,755
In labor force	15,913

Source: *1970 Population of the Census. Subject Report: Low-Income Areas in Large Cities* (Washington, D.C.: Government Printing Office, 1973), 834, 838–39.

white to 90 percent black. By 1968, the southeast area contained more than two-thirds of all D.C.'s government-subsidized apartments, prompting one *Washington Post* writer to label Anacostia the "city dump of housing."[45] As the demographics shifted in the southeast, those receiving public assistance formed the largest proportion of residents in these housing complexes. Many residents were black families headed by women who lacked options in the District's expensive and still largely segregated housing market. The rapid population growth strained city services and public programs. Local schools stretched beyond capacity, and officials' fears of unrest heightened when riots broke out in other cities and black activists replaced the rhetoric of nonviolence with calls for Black Power.[46]

The same conditions of social disruption that led officials to nervously anticipate violence in this section of the city also motivated activists and reformers to create programs for the southeast residents. Multiple projects converged at Southeast Neighborhood House (SEH), a neighborhood agency that had served D.C.'s poor black population since the 1920s when it was established by Dorothy Boulding Ferebee, a physician affiliated with Howard University.[47] Settlement workers had created after-school, recreation, and nutritional programs for children and senior citizens, to "promot[e] . . . health, happiness, welfare, intellectual, social and spiritual development" of neighborhood residents.[48] Sewing clubs, mothers' and fathers' clubs, and other groups for adults also had met regularly in the settlement house. In the 1950s, the SEH made space available for staff from a black-run Planned Parenthood clinic to hold community education programs and distribute birth control supplies and information. And when CORE began its Freedom School in 1964, it held classes at the SEH.[49]

After years of operating on a shoestring, access to federal funds for community organizing projects rejuvenated the SEH. Poor women and OEO-paid organizers now interacted through campaigns for economic justice and welfare rights that brought residents into direct confrontation with municipal authorities who controlled housing, access to health care, recreation and job opportunities.[50] Specifically, SEH developed a community action program that encouraged grassroots leadership and gave citizens the dominant voice in determining policies and programs that affected them.[51] Using a $133,000 grant from the UPO, in 1965 the SEH hired antipoverty workers, many nearby residents, "to go door to door in the fight against poverty." This group included six men and seven women—eleven African Americans, ten of whom were formerly unemployed, and the majority occupants of public housing. Whereas previous employees of the settlement house had been professionally trained to work with impoverished populations, a situation that perpetuated class distinctions between clients and servers, the new practice represented potential control by the poor over programs that affected them. As community insiders, resident organizers realized that their insights and experiences counted as a form of expertise equally important to that of social workers and others who had received formal preparation and credentials.[52]

Neighborhood residents already donated time and energy toward improving the area, but as antipoverty employees, SEH organizers enjoyed opportunities to work for a larger social cause and to receive a paycheck for work they already performed on a voluntary basis.[53] Before assuming her new job, Lois Wilson had served as president of the tenants' council in the housing project where she lived and she had volunteered her time running programs at SEH and a local Planned Parenthood clinic. Other new employees at SEH were more directly influenced by desegregation campaigns. Urged on by her father, a former backer of Marcus Garvey, Theresa Jones had become politically active in high school when she joined struggles to desegregate the District's public schools. Later, Jones had helped organize tenants of her apartment complex to negotiate with the National Capital Housing Authority (NCHA), the agency that managed public housing in the city. Jones and her neighbors had demanded that the NCHA make sensible improvements to their apartments, arguing, for example, that the housing agency's decision to install wooden screen doors rather than more durable metal doors saved the agency money but cost residents who paid for frequent replacements.[54]

Spurred on by the SEH organizers, Anacostia residents revitalized tenant councils and started initiatives that would expand their access to resources. Residents of one housing complex lobbied to bring in a new, conveniently located supermarket, while those at another formed a tenants group and established their own antipoverty center. Others created a cooperative laundry, with residents becoming co-owners by buying two-dollar shares in the business.[55] The SEH soon hired a second team of organizers who focused particularly on Barry Farms, a public-housing complex that typified the plight of the poor in Anacostia. Built in 1942, Barry Farms consisted of approximately 440 apartment units housing more than 2,600 people who lived on some of the lowest incomes in the city. By the 1960s, numerous problems plagued the complex, including dilapidated buildings, rats, and lack of convenient access to public transportation. Because few recreation facilities were located close by, young children played in the unpaved streets where the absence of stoplights caused certain danger. Older children resorted to vandalism, further degrading morale and worsening conditions. For several years, a tenants' council had met intermittently with housing management to seek improvements, but without broad support, the council had wielded little power.[56]

The "Target Team" hired to work in Barry Farms consisted of nine men and one woman, a composition that differed from other SEH organizers in several important ways. Whereas most of the organizers hired by SEH in 1965 came from the surrounding area, the Target Team included people selected for other reasons. Among them, Dorothy Burlage, a white Texan, had belonged to Students for a Democratic Society, the Southern Student Organizing Committee, the Northern Student Movement, and SNCC before moving to D.C. With extensive political experience and a deep commitment to social change, Burlage applied the lessons of the southern civil rights and New Left movements on behalf of Washington's poor citizens. Lacy Streeter, from North Carolina, had spent more than a year organizing black residents in rural Virginia before moving to the city. He later directed UPO's programs for youths and ex-convicts. Pharnal Longus, a D.C. native, had attended nursery school at the SEH and later earned a social work degree from Howard University. He turned to community organizing out of frustration with the welfare system's treatment of its clients, and headed up the Barry Farms initiative. John Kinard came to D.C. after working on economic development programs in Africa. The organizers shared an analysis of the social structures that supported poverty, a commitment to community transformation, and a critique of the role that social welfare agencies, including settlement houses like SEH, could play in that effort.[57]

The Barry Farms team consisted primarily of men, in contrast to the equitable gender split in the first group of SEH organizers. Pharnal Longus, the director of the Barry Farms organizing staff, deliberately selected men because he believed they would most effectively persuade and motivate the area's female residents. Longus also criticized the previous efforts of neighborhood women who had organized tenant councils and other groups. These women, he charged, had concentrated on developing relationships with community residents and attempting to address individual problems rather than promoting collective action.[58] Longus's preference for male organizers was shared by other antipoverty staff who often downplayed women's facility for using personal relationships as a foundation for political organizing. The director of one antipoverty program in northwest D.C. initially hired male civil rights activists, hoping that rhetoric emphasizing racial unity and pride would attract neighborhood residents to new community programs. The organizers discovered, however, that women had an easier time canvasing neighborhoods and convincing residents to talk about poverty than did their male counterparts. Antipoverty workers attributed this phenomenon to women's greater degree of patience and ability to establish new relationships and put people at ease. These explanations perpetuated stereotypes about women's nature, as did the explanation that women cared more about pragmatic, everyday problems related to children and families while men emphasized politics. But male antipoverty organizers nonetheless conceded women's effectiveness in mobilizing local residents for action.[59]

By convincing Barry Farms residents to become more involved in solving the problems of their community, Longus considered the SEH project a way to create "strong, large, militant community organizations (independent from Southeast House), pushing for economic and social power."[60] Or, as Dorothy Burlage put it, the organizers' "plan was to work ourselves out of a job with one group, then start with others and repeat the process." These objectives went beyond the belief that maximizing participation of the poor would increase residents' participation in economic opportunities. Instead, the Target Team emphasized that if people mobilized first to address their neighborhood concerns, they would grow confident enough to work together to tackle larger political problems. To prepare residents for activism, the organizers coached them in research and taught them about the functions, structures, and operations of government agencies as they braced for possible confrontations with public officials. From these activities, new leaders quickly emerged to replace the paid organizers.[61]

Although they intended to provide residents with the skills and support needed for initiatives to emerge from the neighborhood, the SEH staff realized that local women already possessed numerous useful skills. Some strong male leaders lived in the neighborhood, but area women moved to the forefront thanks to their passion and energy. Women's organizing spirit was grounded in their history of voluntary activism and nurtured through their relationships with friends, family, neighbors, and fellowship in church and education-related groups. Women's readiness for community work also related to their economic status. Whereas men's work schedules and fear of losing jobs might have prohibited their participation in protests, unemployed women did not face such constraints. It also helped that women tended to be home when organizers visited during the day. Female antipoverty activists built solidarity and commitment to action by mobilizing networks and skills they had developed earlier through tenant organizations and activities such as arranging church suppers or petitioning for school crossing guards.

Ironically, the very structure of the housing complex likely assisted organizing: because families lived in close proximity, women knew their neighbors and could discuss political issues as a community, and they could share child care when they went to a protest or demonstration.[62]

Among the many neighborhood groups formed as a result of antipoverty campaigns in southeast D.C., the Barry Farms Band of Angels became one of the most effective. The group emerged in 1966 after the NCHA announced plans to spend money on improving the Barry Farms complex. Worried that the NCHA did not share their priorities, the Band of Angels sought to represent the tenants' interests and direct the agency's attention to the leaky plumbing, rats and roaches, faulty furnaces, and falling plaster they confronted every day. Threatening to organize a sit-in at NCHA offices if the agency failed to consult them, the tenant group pressured director Walter Washington to examine conditions at Barry Farms in person. After the visit, the NCHA director reallocated funds from exterior improvements to interior repairs in the apartments and quadrupled the money available for renovations. The group's pressure also resulted in monies for pest extermination and enhancements to the area streets.[63]

The activities of all the neighborhood groups were limited, however, by the strictures set by funding agencies and sponsors, a situation that clearly affected the employment programs that UPO backed. Many of these programs perpetuated a family wage model that ignored the large numbers of single women in the city's poor population and offered few opportunities for citizen input into how such initiatives developed. The UPO Pre-Vocational Center in southeast D.C. supplied job training and placement for young men, many of them high school dropouts with criminal records. In its first year, the center registered 1,250 men who participated in programs for an average of three months before finding permanent employment, entering training programs, returning to school, or joining the armed services. The center's predominantly male staff prided itself on furnishing a "father image" for the young men, a significant benefit for boys raised in homes without adult men. They emphasized "character building, and teamwork, and citizenship and self-reliance and responsibility and dependability."[64] The UPO training program fell far short of meeting the vast needs of Washington's unemployed men; nonetheless, it did offer hope to some. Unfortunately, though, the UPO training program excluded the mothers and sisters of the program's enrollees, even though data collected by federal researchers indicated that, relative to their male counterparts, female-headed households were approximately four times more likely to be poor than those headed by men. When it came to developing priorities in the War on Poverty, however, the statistical reality succumbed to traditional beliefs about gender roles and families.[65]

The occasional UPO employment programs that were geared to women tended to reinforce sex stratification in the paid workforce and thereby to perpetuate generally lower rates of pay for women. One program aimed to upgrade pay, status, security, and skills for domestic servants, an occupation that would not substantially improve the financial resources of low-income families or offer women opportunities to advance. Other UPO-funded initiatives for women included programs to train typists and nurses' aids. Summer vocational workshops for teenagers offered sex-segregated career training: classes in auto mechanics, carpentry, metal- and woodworking, electricity, and upholstery for boys, and classes in sewing, office work, cooking, printing, and music for girls.[66] SEH staff and female residents of the surrounding neighborhoods set up another project, a sewing cooperative, training women to make clothing and home accessories. The cooperative nature of this program promised women more power over their working day and salaries than if they worked elsewhere. The women planned to seek contracts with government agencies and private shops to sew uniforms, draperies, and other products, but the program faded without adequate funding.[67]

Of course, poor women supported vocational programs for men and young people, and Barry Farms residents had articulated similar priorities. But many activists and antipoverty workers criticized this pattern of neglecting women's economic situation. Women needed resources to develop job skills and achieve financial security. Poverty programs taught men skills like carpentry and auto mechanics, but, one antipoverty employee complained, "bright women . . . had been kicked out of school, had no family support, and no manpower training program was teaching them anything—except typing." Within the UPO, some staff shared the dissatisfaction at the neglect of women workers, including one employee who was fired for complaining to a news reporter about the scarce funding for vocational programs for women but the simultaneous availability of money to combat poverty through birth control. Women's organizations expressed similar concerns about government priorities when it came to treating the sources of women's poverty. The D.C. Commission on the Status of Women, set up to study the legal, economic, and social condition of Washington women, identified education as a critical aspect for women for work. The commission pushed the city's public school system and the U.S. Labor Department's Manpower Training Program to open centers where Washington women could seek counseling about education, training, and employment. Members of the National Organization for Women, formed in 1966, also turned their attention to the issue. In 1967, a NOW task force issued a report that faulted federal antipoverty programs for paying insufficient attention to women and for offering training only in cosmetics and clerical fields, areas that would not pay adequate salaries or foster future achievement. Unlike the Commission on the Status of Women, however, NOW restrained from recommending specific initiatives that would fill the gaps left by local and federal programs.[68]

But despite the criticisms directed at the antipoverty programs' priorities, the emphasis on men's employment generally mirrored the emphases, if not the motivations, of the city's black liberation groups. Marion Barry and Mary Treadwell started Pride, Inc., in 1967 with backing from the U.S. Department of Labor to hire 500 young men for summer jobs cleaning the city's alleys and streets. Government sponsors hoped these jobs would avert racial disturbances like those that recently had plagued Detroit, Watts, and other cities. Over the next several years Pride spun off several subsidiary projects: Pride Economic Enterprises purchased and operated a range of profit-making ventures, including gas stations and a landscaping business, staffed by young men; P. I. Properties bought and managed low-income housing complexes; and Youth Pride provided vocational training for teenagers and young adults. Pride's projects represented an attempt to help young men find employment and to bolster the economic clout of the city's black residents. But Pride's initiatives also continued to promote men's economic empowerment without parallel attention to women's needs.[69]

Civil rights and antipoverty organizers did, however, criticize UPO for suppressing black activism and discouraging black residents' participation in relief programs.[70] Some activists characterized the UPO as a "passive" organization that worked against the interests of the black community by dissuading political militancy and "keeping oppressed people looking to their oppressors for the solutions to their oppressions." Julius Hobson and Marion Barry both objected that the local antipoverty agency spent too much money on salaries and administration, creating professional opportunities for middle-class workers at the expense of tangible gains for the poor.[71] Ironically, however, some of the SNCC activists who criticized the antipoverty programs also worked for them or received UPO funds to start new initiatives. After all, antipoverty programs provided one of the few paid jobs for community organizers, forcing some to place financial need above political ideals. Furthermore, the UPO-funded projects exceeded the civil rights organizations as a catalyst for developing local leaders and opportunities for residents, especially women, to have a say.[72]

The Legacy of Antipoverty and Civil Rights Movements

Even as the War on Poverty succumbed to the war in Vietnam and dissension splintered SNCC and CORE, activists from civil rights and antipoverty movements remained central to struggles for social change, acting as community organizers, business owners, cultural workers, neighborhood representatives, and elected officials. Men and women from SNCC, CORE, and the SEH, along with thousands of others touched by these movements, attained influence within programs to benefit low-income and black Washingtonians. One local journalist credited the UPO-funded community programs with teaching residents how to fight the government and precipitating a "massive transfer of power in Washington" that gave blacks "a measure of mastery over local political affairs."[73] In Barry Farms and other locations where antipoverty programs took root, women especially benefited from the attention of organizers. Women's efforts resulted in tangible improvements in the apartments and neighborhoods where they lived and enhanced their sense of community and power. By gaining a commitment to each other and steeling their nerves, women's civic participation and political leadership grew. Through repeated confrontations with government officials—such as those who managed the housing authority—women's fear of retaliation diminished, freeing them to mount further protests when officials ignored their demands.[74]

Transformed through the process of political participation, both male and female activists rejected conventions that reinforced passivity and powerlessness. They embraced and passed along values of democracy, civic participation, and community. At the same time, however, gender stereotypes partly limited women's positions within social change organizations. Hobson and Barry used the networks and renown they built in the 1960s as the foundation for future political careers that exceeded those of female colleagues. Julius Hobson's reputation as "the angriest man" in the city cemented his position as an activist committed to fighting racial discrimination. In the city's first election since Reconstruction, Hobson won a seat on the Board of Education in 1968. He ran unsuccessfully for office twice more, finally winning an at-large city council seat in 1974, a post he held until his death in 1977.[75] Marion Barry was elected to the school board and the city council every year from 1971 until 1978, when he became Washington's second popularly elected mayor. Each man clearly possessed exceptional political skills, especially Barry, who repeatedly rebounded from scandals that blemished his later mayoral career. But Barry's and Hobson's successes also illustrated the importance of their grassroots activism to the celebrity that helped win them public office.[76]

In contrast, most women worked with minimal public recognition on the front lines of movements against poverty and racism. Whereas some women in other SNCC chapters chafed at being relegated to what they considered secondary status, Washington women publicly raised no such complaints. Many experienced positive feelings generated by political work undertaken within a community of similarly committed colleagues and they reveled in the discovery of newfound skills and opportunities to perform meaningful work. Sharlene Kranz held a clerical position in the SNCC office off and on until 1966, when she left for a similar but higher-paid position at the offices of UPO. Kranz never felt marginalized by her $10-a-week clerical job; rather, she welcomed the opportunity to use her typing skills on behalf of a cause to which she was deeply committed. Tina Smith, who also left SNCC for similar but better-paying jobs, nonetheless maintained her connection to the group and in 1979 went to work at city hall for the new Barry administration.[77] Dorothy Burlage felt similarly empowered by her experiences working with the Barry Farms Target Team. Despite her status as the only woman and one of the few white paid organizers, she appreciated serving as an "equal member of a team." When organizing poor women, Burlage considered sexism of secondary importance to the problems created by racism and poverty. Consequently, when other activists began to discuss feminism and how to improve women's experiences within radical movements, she felt no incentive to join them.[78] Even those who, like Mary Treadwell, highlighted the ways that sex oppression exacerbated problems in African American communities continued to maintain close working relationships with male activists and to work for programs like Pride that emphasized vocational opportunities for men. Yet, as Treadwell demonstrates, women could and did emerge from SNCC with skills, networks, and analyses that they used on behalf of subsequent organizing efforts that sometimes included an explicit analysis of women's roles.

Meanwhile, in Anacostia, women continued to exert pressure through collective action, gradually taking on leadership positions at the SEH and in neighborhood groups. Like their middle-class counterparts, some low-income women directed their skills and contacts into new forms of political involvement and paid employment in UPO-funded programs or at the antipoverty agency itself. Lois Wilson, who had supported SEH programs as a volunteer before she was hired to work as an organizer, subsequently coordinated arts and cultural programs at the settlement house. After her work as a SEH organizer, Theresa Jones was hired by UPO and sought professional training for a career in social services. She later represented her neighborhood at national African American political conventions, the local Constitutional Convention (another step toward D.C. home rule), and on municipal committees. In 1969, the mayor appointed Jones to the citywide Commission on the Status of Women, and in 1978, she sat on a task force to coordinate the transition when Marion Barry became the mayor.[79] But most women remained "outside the system," working on a grassroots level to push for policies and practices that would better their lives and those of their children. Some turned to gender-specific concerns such as welfare reform, women's employment, and reproductive rights, targeting needs left untouched by these earlier efforts and, in that way, influencing the agendas of feminists and black freedom activists.

Participants in 1960s community development initiatives and civil rights activities neither adopted the language or ideas of feminism nor articulated self-defined "women's rights." But by making women visible in the public arena, these campaigns established the legitimacy of women's political involvement; generated a sense of solidarity that fused racial, economic, and gender identity; and shaped women's expectations about their participation. Individual activists cultivated skills as community mobilizers, demonstrating the effectiveness of a very personal form of organizing, and created networks that supported later campaigns related to women's issues. In addition, community development and civil rights movements contributed to a shift of political power within Washington as common citizens exercised an increasingly important voice in municipal government. The focus of settlement houses, civil rights organizations, and community development centers realigned to form an infrastructure supportive of social change efforts. But at the same time that these efforts improved some of the conditions under which poor women lived, they resulted in only a limited assault on the economic and social forces that pushed women, particularly African American women, into poverty. For this reason, the work left undone by community development efforts became an agenda for future efforts.

2

Defining Welfare Rights

When Southeast Neighborhood House workers convened meetings of Barry Farms apartments' occupants, Etta Horn heard about many problems—run-down homes, rats, lack of recreational facilities, invasive welfare investigators—that resembled her own. Finding that antipoverty organizers and her neighbors shared a commitment to fighting these indignities, Horn joined the Barry Farms Band of Angels and targeted welfare reform as a solution to many hardships that plagued her community. During the next decade, Horn drew on her experiences as a recipient of public assistance and resident of subsidized housing, leading a fight to make antipoverty agencies and public housing officials more responsive to poor women's needs. Connecting with other welfare recipients across the country, Horn became a founding member of the National Welfare Rights Organization (NWRO) and one of the first officers of that organization, thereby helping launch a movement of recipients of public assistance—mostly African American women—who demanded better benefits, improved treatment, and a greater voice. By the early 1970s, Horn's commitment to securing welfare rights incorporated explicitly defined women's issues, including reproductive rights and sexual violence, and she frequently participated in women's organizations and feminist events.[1]

The mother of seven children, separated from a husband with whom she had sworn never to reunite, Horn understood the dilemmas many women faced in applying for public assistance. On the one hand, with only an eighth-grade education and poor health that had forced her to quit doing domestic work, Horn stood little chance of finding a reasonably paying job. Welfare, therefore, presented the only realistic way to provide for her children. On the other hand, Horn resented welfare's prohibition on two-parent households receiving relief and its failure to provide sufficient funds to buy wholesome food, medicine, furniture, and clothing. Along with others in Washington, she had endured humiliating late-night visits by welfare investigators who showed up at her apartment without warning to discover whether any man, or men's belongings, were housed within. These inspections enraged her but she feared if she complained, the welfare department would revoke her funding.

Participation in antipoverty activism and then the welfare rights movement changed Horn's conception of the rights and responsibilities connected to motherhood and citizenship. As a member of the PTA and her church, Horn had tried to better her family's and community's well-being, but also conform to society's expectations for women's behavior. Once she joined with other welfare activists, Horn embraced civic participation as a central component of her maternal role. Attending meetings and protests sometimes meant shirking her familial responsibilities for the sake of broader ends. Acting to reform the welfare system, in addition to volunteering at her church and her children's school, she could improve the lives of other women and children.[2]

Under the banner of the welfare rights movement of the 1960s and 1970s, Etta Horn and thousands of women mobilized to mitigate the effects of poverty and to assert the public's responsibility to assist poor women in the work of mothering. As they did in antipoverty campaigns, black women dominated the rank-and-file of welfare rights organizations. And like civil rights and antipoverty campaigns, the welfare rights movement expanded popular definitions of rights by stressing participatory democracy. Low-income women—mainly recipients of Aid to Families with Dependent Children (AFDC)—demanded increased funds and insisted that by exercising self-determination and influencing policies, they would become better mothers and turn welfare into a more meaningful form of assistance.

Welfare rights activists also created an agenda that put women's issues—work, motherhood, and sexuality—at its center. Their demands accentuated women's vulnerability to poverty and pointed out the ways society denigrated mothers, particularly unmarried African American women. Welfare activists reinforced women's importance to family life and they generally avoided criticizing men, but they simultaneously challenged these roles by rejecting stereotypes that stressed mothers' passivity and assignment to a domestic sphere. In this way, they promoted a view of welfare mothers as politically active women, entitled to a public voice and empowered to act for the sake of their children. As they opposed efforts to force poor women into jobs without addressing the need for child care, welfare rights activists also highlighted the tension between women's roles in the home and in the workplace.

By critiquing society's treatment of mothers and women workers and questioning standards of sexual morality, welfare rights activists raised issues that would be incorporated into the growing feminist movement. These concerns became the basis for interactions between welfare activists and members of other women's organizations who sought to win greater independence for women in the public and private arenas. But even as welfare rights and feminist activists collaborated and drew from each others' ideas, welfare rights activists maintained a distinct perspective that reflected the ways their race and class shaped their experience. Pursuing an agenda that recognized the intertwined nature of race, class, and sexual oppression, welfare rights activists pushed other feminists to redefine women's liberation by taking into account the views of low-income women. In this way, welfare rights activists contributed to a movement against sexual oppression that gained momentum in the late 1960s.

"Mother Power"

Spurred by antipoverty organizing in southeast D.C. and across the city, Etta Horn and other women formed the Washington Welfare Alliance, composed of AFDC recipients who sought to interject their views into a national effort to reform the welfare system. The group's agenda prioritized poor people's need for "more money, more dignity, and more justice." By mobilizing low-income women from throughout the city, the Alliance could provide women with opportunities to express their frustrations and receive support from knowing that others shared their concerns. In addition, the Alliance could use women's complaints and knowledge about the workings of the welfare system to create a mass movement to transform public assistance.

Washington's welfare recipients lived in dire conditions that public assistance did little to alleviate. In 1970, the average annual income of D.C. families receiving welfare was only $1,409, an astonishing 53.7 percent below the poverty level designated by the federal government. Indeed, the welfare department acknowledged that regular monthly welfare checks issued in 1970 were calibrated to cover only 85 percent of 1967 living costs. Black families, who made up the majority of the city's welfare recipients, suffered disproportionately, with approximately 56 percent falling into poverty as compared to only 13.7 percent of white families. Many of these families contained workers whose low salaries nonetheless qualified them for relief. Single-parent families, most of them headed by African American women, faced the worst misery, with 66 percent collecting assistance insufficient to meet the government's recognized poverty level. As a result of their limited budgets, these families lived crowded into dilapidated apartments without adequate food, clothing, and household goods, not to mention air conditioning, automobiles, and telephones.[3]

In addition to demanding larger public assistance grants, members of the Welfare Alliance wanted respectful treatment by welfare employees and an end to regulations that seemed punitive rather than helpful. Lack of job training programs limited recipients' ability to get out of the system, and scarce affordable day care restricted women's ability to work and look out for children. Welfare employees treated benefits as a privilege to be earned through chastity and compliance rather than an entitlement determined by economic need. Some welfare policies negatively affected women's freedom, such as efforts to rout out men living with unmarried AFDC recipients and to coerce women to use contraception or undergo sterilization. To address these concerns, the Alliance demanded official recognition to bargain, negotiate, and represent AFDC recipients on policy boards.[4]

A year after the Alliance began, it affiliated with the newly formed National Welfare Rights Organization (NWRO). The NWRO was founded in 1967 when welfare activists from throughout the country, including Etta Horn, responded to a call from George Wiley, a CORE organizer. Along with Wiley, the organization was directed by paid staff and representatives from local chapters across the country. Tens of thousands of welfare recipients, primarily AFDC recipients, affiliated with the national group. NWRO sought to build an interracial mass movement of welfare recipients, yet most members were black women although white women made up the majority of the welfare rolls. Thus, in design and structure, the NWRO was a black women's organization, although founded and led by men.[5]

The Washington Welfare Alliance, now renamed the Citywide Welfare Alliance (CWA), served as the District's first official representative to the national body. The Alliance expanded rapidly, adding groups across the city and becoming larger and more geographically diverse than SNCC or CORE. In January 1968, the NWRO recorded five D.C. chapters, each averaging twenty-five members; eighteen months later, nineteen groups from Washington, totaling approximately 850 members, belonged to the national organization. By July 1970, the District's membership stood at approximately

1,300 people in twelve groups. In October 1971, thirteen neighborhood groups made up the D.C. Family Rights Organization, which had replaced the CWA as the city's NRWO affiliate. These groups represented many neighborhoods, with members hailing from the Mount Pleasant, Shaw, Adams Morgan, and DuPont Circle neighborhoods in the city's northwest district in addition to those living in housing complexes such as Barry Farms in southeast D.C.[6]

Reflecting their presence in the population of D.C. welfare recipients, African American women headed most of the city's welfare groups. Several of them also held national positions in the NWRO, including Etta Horn, who became vice chairman in 1967. Between 1967 and 1970, she sat on the National Coordinating Council that directed the NWRO and chaired a committee that coordinated a campaign to win individual recipients credit at major department stores. The year after Horn left the National Coordinating Council, Elizabeth Perry served on that body. The head of the Near Northeast Welfare Rights group, Perry raised her eleven children in poverty after a disability forced her to resign her position with city government.[7]

NWRO chapters in Washington independently developed their programs and raised money, although D.C. chapters collaborated on both citywide and national campaigns. Indeed, a significant amount of cross-fertilization occurred between the local and national-level movements. Washington women's presence on national committees kept the local groups connected to the priorities set by the NWRO and to the agendas developed in other locales. In addition, NWRO located its headquarters in the District, and staff of the national organization often helped coordinate local events and prepare Washington women for new activities. NWRO staff also called on D.C. activists to represent the national movement, arranging their testimony before Congress or in other forums where issues affecting all welfare recipients would be presented or deliberated. The overlap between local and national levels of NWRO, therefore, gave Washington activists unusual opportunities to broadcast their concerns but, at times, the activities of the national office overshadowed the demands of District residents.

Washington's peculiar form of local governance also created a complex structure within which welfare activists fought for reforms. Because the District of Columbia's budget was set by federal politicians rather than local officials, an additional layer of bureaucracy complicated welfare activists' ability to demand reform. Local welfare bureaucrats and municipal officials often deflected activists' demands by pleading their own lack of control over the welfare budget or by implying that welfare activists were only following orders from NWRO's national office. City welfare department employees also used the District's lack of home rule as a way to pressure welfare activists to moderate their demands and their strategies. The inflammatory language and direct-action tactics that activists employed heightened the conflict, authorities claimed, and they recommended that activists adopt more polite means to express their plight and win sympathy.[8] But working within the constraints of the city's governance structure, welfare activists often found only mass protests won the attention of officials and welfare department administrators. Indeed, welfare recipients believed they had no choice but to use militant tactics, arguing that "the only way we can shake them [city welfare administrators] up and get anything accomplished is to have a riot. Before that, they can't do anything for us."[9]

Besides responses meant to dissuade welfare mothers from using militant tactics, policy makers and bureaucrats attempted to impose a structure that restricted other aspects of women's behavior. This control was often expressed through stereotypes about poor women, especially black mothers, that guided policy makers. Some members of congressional budget committees ignored or insulted D.C. welfare activists, not encumbered by a concern with winning their vote. Senator Russell Long, chair of the Senate Finance Committee, the body that oversaw appropriations to the District, was outspoken in his disdain for welfare activists. On one occasion, Long hinted that CWA members might better spend their time doing "useful work" or "picking up the litter in front of their homes" rather than trying to influence public policy.[10] He also outraged welfare activists by calling them "brood mares" and "bums" who raised "all sorts of mischief" when they should be working. Their protests, Long threatened, would only work against their cause by angering senators who controlled welfare legislation.[11] Senator Robert C. Byrd, chair of the Finance Subcommittee most directly responsible for the District's appropriations, implicated poor black women in his fight against welfare, sexual immorality, and crime. Pushing for a new publicly funded birth control program for D.C. welfare recipients, Byrd argued that fighting "a war upon the evils of illegitimacy" would free society from the burden of high rates of crime, violence, and welfare dependency. Byrd's and Long's statements reflected popular characterizations of poor black mothers that exaggerated their supposed character flaws—sexual immorality, aversion to work, and lack of cleanliness—and demonstrated how such beliefs influenced public assistance budgets and programs.[12]

On the national level, too, elected officials, welfare bureaucrats, and activists sought to reform welfare within the context of a debate about the state of African American families set off, in part, by the 1965 publication of

Daniel Patrick Moynihan's report, *The Negro Family: The Case for National Action.* Moynihan, then assistant secretary of labor, argued that black poor and working-class families were coping with a new pathology, reflected in increasing rates of birth outside of marriage and welfare dependency. The report acknowledged some government responsibility for the downward spiral of black incomes, but placed responsibility on the shoulders of women. Arguing that women had surpassed men in gaining access to jobs and schooling, the report called attention to the negative impact of women's success, especially the disintegration of family life caused by so-called matriarchal patterns of behavior that increased women's authority and deprived men of their proper respect. Some African American activists used these ideas as a call for racial unity. An editorial in the *Washington Afro-American* explained, "For generations the American economic system has used the women of our race to help displace and demean the colored male to the point we have practically developed a matriarchal society which strips the male of his manhood and self respect. . . . Since the days of slavery, the male has been put out to work to earn enough money so his sisters could go to school and acquire the education and skill by which she could contribute to the financial advancement of the family. The male . . . bore his unpleasant burden without protest even when this handicap spilled over into his political life where his brilliant wife or sister was given the political plum which he thought he might have gotten." This explanation provided a theoretical foundation to support a range of initiatives to establish patriarchal authority in African American families, including the creation of jobs programs for black men. Moreover, the "black matriarchy" thesis turned motherhood into a destructive force in African American society and cast black women's political assertions into a questionable light.[13]

The Moynihan thesis and stereotypes about black women's character failed to mesh with the experiences of welfare activists, but nonetheless affected the agenda and ideas that welfare rights activists devised. In particular, social and governmental attention to African American families forced welfare rights activists to defend their position as mothers and to explain their demands within the context of their maternal role. In this regard, welfare activists faced a challenge similar to black women earlier in the century who worked to improve their communities despite popular conceptions of their immorality. Mobilizing on the basis of motherhood, these activists had explained women's public work and protected their respectability by depicting mothers as "naturally" hardworking, pious, nurturing, sexually restrained, and motivated by a greater good.[14] Welfare rights activists of the 1960s also operated within a culture that made it hard to establish their moral authority but they refused to conform to ideals of selfless motherhood requiring them to deny the reality of their lives. AFDC recipients' status as mothers raising children without male support—because they had never married or were separated, widowed, deserted, or divorced—drew public attention to the sexual activity or immorality that allegedly had brought them to that state. Unlike earlier generations, welfare activists spoke forthrightly of sexual harassment and their desire for intimate relationships rather than renouncing their sexuality. Finally, building on the black freedom movement, welfare activists used the tools of direct action—boycotts, sit-ins, and mass demonstrations—forms of protest that took them into the streets and sometimes led to their arrest. Through such demonstrations, welfare activists put themselves on display and directly confronted policy makers', politicians', and other activists' ideas about motherhood.

The slogan "Mother Power," appearing on signs at marches, conveyed the multiple notions that motherhood could be the basis of power, that mothers were powerful, and that the protestors needed power as mothers.[15] In public statements at protests, interviews with reporters, and welfare rights publications, activists stressed that motherhood granted them a source of moral authority and responsibility. The image of women with children at demonstrations and meetings served to remind the public of the reasons they fought for reform. By focusing attention on their status as mothers, welfare activists suggested that their demands were not selfish but rooted in their commitment to their children's well-being. Motherhood rhetoric also became a potential foundation for solidarity with groups of women who might otherwise perceive little commonality with welfare recipients. Just as calls for "Black Power" became the basis for racial pride and cohesion that could undergird a new political consciousness, so calls for "Mother Power" could be used to rally women. Finally, welfare activists opposed policies that limited their parental authority, making it difficult to act according to their understanding of their families' best interests and compromising their freedom to establish relationships with men and control their own reproduction. "Mother Power" thus represented a form of women's liberation, centered on demands for self-determination and assertions that women's role should encompass both the public and private realms.

In one expression of their maternal concerns, D.C. welfare activists contrasted their devotion to their families to the federal government's willingness to risk lives, particularly those of black men, in Vietnam. Welfare rights activists sprinkled their public statements with references to the wastefulness of the war. Protestors appeared at demonstrations holding signs urging "welfare not warfare." At a 1967 "mother's march," numerous speakers declared that war costs were depriving children of food and criticized the government for establishing more rigorous criteria for assessing women's qualifications to receive public assistance than it did for determining men's eligibility to be drafted for military service.[16] By linking opposition to the war abroad to demands for welfare reform at home, welfare activists contrasted their own commitment to the well-being of their community and nation to the priorities evidenced by the country's political and military leaders. The implication that welfare recipients were more moral than those who set the nation's priorities also refuted the stereotype of sexually immoral black mothers.

Invocations of "mother power" represented more than a rhetorical strategy, however, and the concept formed the basis for welfare activists' claims regarding the rights that mothers should possess, regardless of their race or economic status. The freedom to determine how to balance motherhood with other responsibilities constituted one of their chief demands and one of their primary complaints about the regulations governing welfare. Welfare reforms enacted by Congress in 1967 as part of its amendment of the Social Security Act, for example, included a so-called Work Incentive Program (WIN). The WIN mandated that women with school-aged children find work or enroll in a job training program in order to continue to receive AFDC; as incentives, the legislation made some funds available for day care and let women keep their monthly welfare benefits along with their salaries. The legislation also leaned on states to regulate the personal lives of welfare recipients by not providing funding to cover increases in public assistance because of children born to unmarried mothers or poverty following divorce or desertion. At the same time, the legislation increased the power of states to remove children from "unsuitable" homes and provided more money for foster families and institutions that housed such children.[17] The changes were justified as a way to reduce welfare rolls by pushing poor women to find alternatives to public assistance and by discouraging women from having large families. But the amendment also threatened women's autonomy by requiring them to look for work and to adhere to particular standards of moral and family life lest they lose their children or their public assistance.

Welfare activists resented the new legislation for impinging on their privacy and authority and for threatening the well-being of their families. Although they supported steps to make job training programs and day care accessible to women who wanted to work, activists feared the consequences of forcing women into the paid labor force. Taking action in response to the legislation, in August 1967, D.C. activists joined numerous protests against the welfare bill, including a mock hearing at the Capitol where hundreds heard testimony about the potentially devastating impact of the bill. A "Mother's March on Washington" followed, ending with pickets in front of the U.S. Department of Health, Education, and Welfare. A month later, welfare activists from around the country again convened in Washington to protest the legislation, staging a sit-in at the Senate Finance Committee hearings and vowing to stay until the committee heard their protests. At these protests, welfare activists likened the new legislation to slavery, terminology that highlighted the racial dynamics at play and reinforced the view that what legislators considered work "incentives," women interpreted as forced labor that would ultimately harm, rather than benefit, their families.[18] In addition, Etta Horn insisted that the Social Security Amendment would lead poor children to starve and their mothers to riot, thus spreading unrest beyond their families.[19]

Even after the Social Security Amendment was signed into law at the start of 1968, the CWA continued to fight the new regulations by reaching out to new allies who would sympathize with poor women's efforts to care for their families. In early spring, Etta Horn, as the CWA's chair, requested representatives from a dozen women's and religious groups in Washington to attend a meeting to show support for welfare activists' efforts to "reverse these totalitarian—and probably unconstitutional—amendments." In her invitation, Horn highlighted the perceived coercive and antichild aspects of the legislation that made mothers find low-paying jobs and forced their young children into inadequate day care facilities or foster homes. During the meeting, welfare activists also railed against other ways the welfare bureaucracy restricted their freedom, especially threats by some welfare caseworkers to rescind benefits if women joined political protests.[20]

The CWA's invitation to representatives of other national women's groups constituted an attempt to build solidarity and sympathy on the basis of women's status as mothers. But this strategy did not obscure the ways that welfare activists' views of their rights differed from middle-class women. Representatives of the local League of Women Voters, who were invited to CWA's spring meeting, had consistently advocated for welfare reform. In the early 1960s, the LWV chapter had studied the city's welfare system, concluding that it was overburdened and underfunded, and they tried to leverage their political influence to push for increased allocations and reformed procedures at the welfare department. In articulating their support for welfare reform, LWV members had expressed little solidarity with welfare recipients on the basis of sex, but had argued that reform would cut crime, minimize family breakups, and prepare welfare recipients for economic independence.[21] When Congress passed the Social Security Amendment, the LWV urged officials to create child care facilities to serve the families of women who would be affected by the new programs. As they had before, league members responded to the new legislation by emphasizing the negative impact on families and, by extension, the civic community. Testifying before Congress, LWV representatives argued that "lack of adequate available day care for children is the cause of many women being thwarted in their desire to become more effective breadwinners, parents, and participants in community life."[22] This conclusion hinted that welfare recipients were inherently better citizens and parents when they were paid employees; getting women into the work force, therefore, served the public good.[23]

The bias toward viewing work as a positive benefit to families and society also shaped the response of the National Organization for Women. NOW had formed in 1966, only two months after NWRO, and had prioritized eliminating inequalities in women's economic opportunities, focusing especially on the workplace as an arena where women were denied opportunities comparable to men. The D.C. Capital Area Chapter of NOW, which organized in 1967, had attempted to address such inequalities by protesting sex-segregated help wanted ads in newspapers and boycotting corporations that failed to hire or promote women.[24] NOW's Bill of Women's Rights, issued in 1968, stressed that "the rights of women in poverty to secure job training, housing and family allowances in equal terms with men must be secured by revision of welfare legislation and poverty programs which today deny women of dignity, privacy and self-respect." Its Bill of Women's Rights specifically condemned work requirements. It would be "punitive, undemocratic and un-American," NOW stated, "to deny welfare mothers of the *option* of choosing whether to work or stay home with their children."[25]

Obviously, AFDC recipients, LWV and NOW activists, and government officials who backed the law differed in their views on the proper political role of welfare recipients, especially mothers. No one disputed that for AFDC recipients being good mothers constituted a primary responsibility, and all parties assumed that child rearing fell primarily to women. Yet activists and bureaucrats disagreed over both the definition of a good mother and what that role required. In the language they used and the policies they crafted, government officials implied that good women should not burden society with children born outside of marriage; barring that, good mothers would value paid work over continued public assistance, keep their homes clean, and adhere to the policies and decisions made by officials, administrators, and social workers. NOW and LWV objected to compulsory work if Congress failed to take other steps to ensure care for children and to improve living conditions in poor families. NOW and LWV refrained from the derogatory stereotypes at play in congressional deliberations, but failed to acknowledge the role of racism in determining welfare policies and contributing to black women's poverty. NOW and LWV also provided little support for welfare activists' other demands, not publicly backing campaigns to expand the size of welfare benefits and avoiding public comment on aspects of the legislation that attempted to control welfare recipients' sexual or political activity.

In contrast, welfare activists highlighted the racist, elitist, and sexist motives of lawmakers. Referring to work requirements as a form of slavery, activists played up the dynamics involved when white elected officials proscribed mandatory work for poor black women. To welfare activists, the coercive nature of the new legislation, combined with existing policies in effect on the local level, also demonstrated middle-class attempts to circumscribe and control the lives of low-income people. Fighting to influence welfare policy, activists challenged the presumption that middle-class professionals, whether in welfare agency offices or the halls of Congress, should have authority to interfere in the lives of poor women. Instead, welfare activists fought for recognition that, like other Americans, they had the right, and the capability, to make decisions related to their own and their families' well-being. Poor women should not be deprived of such freedom as a result of their race, sex, and economic status. "Whatever the middle class person says about welfare doesn't count," Washington activist Annie McLean contended. "He doesn't know it like we know it, because we live with it." Nor would middle-class people put up with the harassment that welfare recipients experienced, McLean alleged. Horn summed up the new legislation as a violation of poor people's rights: "We're branded as illiterate, immoral, poor housekeepers—you name it, they've got a label for it. Our kids are dying for this country, but we're not supposed to demonstrate, and now they tell us we have to work even if we don't want to."[26]

Besides fighting the Social Security Amendment, welfare activists challenged other regulations intended to restrict their sexual activity. In the District and eighteen states, a substitute parent regulation, the "man-in-the-house" rule, denied AFDC funds to children in families where a male partner presumably contributed support. The regulation also disqualified aid to children whose mother formed a long-term relationship, regardless of whether the man had any legal responsibility to the family. Even more offensive to welfare activists, the substitute parent rule authorized unscheduled searches of recipients' homes and uninvited examinations of their private lives, a practice that local welfare bureaucrats defended in order to discourage welfare "cheats" and to channel public monies only to the deserving. Devoting more and more resources toward inspections, the department increased its investigative staff from five to seventy-five people over the period 1961–67. Welfare staffers conducted nighttime visits of recipients' homes, hoping to catch male visitors or find men's belongings. Investigators also interviewed friends, neighbors, relatives, and ministers; snooped in bank accounts; talked to moneylenders; and scanned insurance company records for evidence of unreported income.[27]

Welfare bureaucrats saw searching recipients' homes as a way to cut down on fraud, but activists believed the practice violated their rights for the sake of compelling their dependency and chastity. At least one Washington woman who barred welfare inspectors from her home was subsequently denied public assistance, an incident that undoubtedly compounded women's fear of retribution if they challenged the agency's authority.[28] Recipients also considered the "man-in-the-house" provision a form of punishment for women who attempted to establish two-parent households. Women objected to the welfare department's far-reaching control: one activist from the Washington suburbs likened it to "a jealous husband" who required women to "justify their existence to caseworkers, friends, family, and 'public opinion.'" More graphically, another Washington woman captured the abusive qualities of what she called a "mother-fucking system" that "screws mothers and children financially, emotionally, systematically, daily." Similarly, Johnnie Tillmon, the first chair of NWRO, compared AFDC to "a super-sexist marriage. You trade in *a* man for *the* man. But you can't divorce him if he treats you bad. He can divorce you, of course, cut you off any time he wants."[29] Ironically, some of the women had terminated marriages for this kind of behavior and thus resented the city agency's policy.

Welfare activists used the courts and mass demonstrations to fight the regulation. In 1967, welfare activists picketed at the house of a welfare department administrator, turning the tables by violating his privacy in order to express the anger they felt when welfare investigators barged into their homes. Others joined a class action suit to challenge the District's policy. Two women went to court alleging that recipients could never give "voluntary" consent to home inspections when they thought that turning away investigators could lead to a loss of their checks.[30] Finally, in June 1968, the Supreme Court ruled in an Alabama case, *King v. Smith,* that such practices violated federal welfare policy and that in the future, male inhabitants would not be assumed to be providing income. Although the Court's ruling specified that welfare recipients' relationships would not become the grounds for automatic termination of a family's assistance, the decision left welfare departments with a rationale for carrying on home inspections. By invalidating the denial of funds only in cases where a man held no legal ties to a family, *King v. Smith* allowed welfare departments to cut off AFDC when an able-bodied natural or adoptive father was legally responsible for supporting his children.[31]

Washington welfare officials worried that the Court's decision would increase the number of families eligible for public assistance without a corresponding growth of funds. Strapped by the size of its total budget, the D.C. welfare department announced in 1969 that, despite the court's ruling, it would continue to review "facts on financial resources, family composition, and living arrangements."[32] Washington's AFDC recipients hailed the Court's decision as a victory in their struggle for privacy and stability because it increased their chances to marry and move off the welfare rolls, and they considered the local agency's plans to continue searches a grave misuse of funds.[33] With the Supreme Court's decision on the side of welfare recipients' privacy, other supporters emerged to call for the cessation of home inspections. The *Washington Afro-American,* the city's black newspaper, editorialized that welfare investigations left poor families "stripped of all dignity, rendered into nothingness. . . . Because people are poor . . . is no reason to say that they have to submit to invasions of their privacy, that no one else would submit to. . . . Perhaps if enough people raise their voices the Welfare Department can be persuaded that it should give less attention to snooping, and more to helping people build decent lives."[34] Members of the D.C. City Council also took action, contending that home investigations represented an unsuitable use of resources and requesting that the Senate's District Appropriations Committee shift funds from investigatory functions into direct relief.[35] But the Congressional Appropriations Committee still pushed for home inspections, assuming that the dramatic growth in D.C.'s welfare rolls stemmed from cases of fraudulent eligibility.[36] Even though they claimed insufficient resources to increase public assist grants to recipients, federal and local officials continued to funnel money into investigations.

Welfare is a Woman's Issue

By the end of the 1960s, Washington's welfare rights movement began to gradually shift its guiding tactics and ideas. Mass protest diminished when activists adopted new methods they considered more effective or appropriate in light of the movement's successes and the increasingly conservative climate. This change was accompanied by some activists' pursuit of political and employment opportunities that siphoned off energy previously devoted to the welfare rights cause. Finally, the growing feminist movement locally and nationally presented welfare rights activists with potential new allies and frameworks for understanding the causes of poverty and its impact on poor women.

These changes were occasioned, in part, by the disappearance of many of the victories earlier won by welfare rights activists. When the Supreme Court ruled in 1971 in *Wyman v. James* that "welfare officials could insist on the right to inspect recipients' homes and cut off aid to those who refused," the decision represented a significant reversal of activists' hard-fought right to privacy.[37] Bolstered by the Court ruling, D.C. welfare officials expanded examinations to include thousands of families it suspected received AFDC benefits larger than their entitlement. The investigations uncovered less fraud than the department expected—of 1,951 cases investigated by the end of 1971, 128 (6.5 percent) proved ineligible for AFDC, 348 (17 percent) were found to be receiving overpayment, and 197 (10 percent) were underpaid. Congress responded by dropping eight million dollars from the 1972 D.C. welfare allocation, yet the remaining budget included money to hire forty-five new investigators.[38] That same year, D.C. authorities cut programs that could have opened avenues of possible employment, including a job training program for welfare recipients run by the D.C. Manpower Administration that had experienced overwhelming use. Capping the reversal of earlier welfare reform, in July 1973, the Department of Human Resources reported that the welfare caseload showed signs of slowing down, after rising at a rate of 10,000 people a year since 1970. This lessening did not represent falling poverty rates but rather, according to department spokespeople, reflected the effectiveness of new procedures meant to identify "ineligibles" and to encourage potential applicants to seek paid work instead of public assistance. The decline in welfare rights organizing also contributed to falling numbers of welfare applicants compared to the high levels seen in the late 1960s.[39]

These changes altered the relationship between welfare activists and city administrators; they became less adversarial as they joined to oppose fiscal and programmatic cuts instituted at the federal level. In this regard, Washington resembled other cities across the country where dwindling funds for antipoverty initiatives, Nixon's welfare reform plans, and Supreme Court rulings that limited welfare rights all pushed welfare rights activists to substitute cooperation with local welfare bureaucrats for the direct action that prevailed in the 1960s.[40] The D.C. Family Rights Organization, for example, coordinated hearings where welfare activists, city officials, and welfare administrators spoke out against a proposed $32 million public assistance cut contained in the city's 1972 budget.[41] Several years later, thousands of activists rallied in support of local welfare officials accused of accounting discrepancies and mismanagement, including their failure to process hundreds of welfare applications filed years earlier.[42] Declining use of mass action no doubt also stemmed from both earlier victories and failures that made it difficult to sustain activists' involvement. The continued struggle to increase benefits probably exhausted some activists, while effective challenges to objectionable policies, such as the "man-in-the-house" rule, also may have made it difficult to prolong the anger necessary to feed the movement.[43]

Lessened antagonism made for more peaceful tactics, but welfare rights moved off the front pages of Washington newspapers and protests moved from the streets into government buildings. Furthermore, testimony at hearings involved smaller numbers of participants than mass demonstrations, thereby requiring the mobilization of fewer women. As before, local welfare rights groups objected to the renewal of home searches, but they expressed their concerns through meetings with the head of the District's Department of Human Resources rather than through mass demonstrations. For its part, the agency recognized the importance of listening to representatives of the recipients, even if only to avoid having activists take their complaints to the streets. Women achieved their goal to play a part in setting policies and negotiating with authorities, but only within a context where their demands were expressed in the more orderly fashion preferred by bureaucrats and where they collaborated with a welfare department weakened by funding cuts and a hostile Congress.[44]

Some welfare activists, like earlier antipoverty and civil rights movement activists, parlayed skills and public profiles into paid positions as social service workers, appointments to local social service agencies' boards, and political positions. Inclusion on these bodies fulfilled welfare activists' demand that those with personal knowledge of AFDC hold responsibility for its administration and for oversight of programs used by welfare recipients. Etta Horn went from "being a no-nonsense street leader of the forlorn and destitute . . . [to] become a no-nonsense administrator," in the words of a *Washington Post* reporter. In a 1975 newspaper profile, Horn pointed out that "out of the advocacy movement have come a number of leaders who are making a substantial contribution to their communities." Running two child care centers in southeast D.C., Horn provided a free service for children living in low-income, female-headed homes. Through this work, she continued to try to improve the economic circumstances of women by caring for young children while mothers worked, looked for jobs, or attended vocational training programs. By providing care for children, Horn could support women who opted to move into the workforce, but without perpetuating the coercive aspects of the 1967 WIN.[45] Other activists developed advocacy centers, work programs, and child care facilities to provide care and recreation for neighborhood young people and create jobs for adult women.[46] And some welfare activists moved into political arenas, attending the Democratic National Convention in Chicago in 1968 and the National Black Political Convention in Gary, Indiana, in 1972, where they joined local businesspeople and representatives of a variety of political organizations and social service agencies. These activities did not represent diversions from their interest in welfare reform but chances to insert welfare activists' perspectives and expertise into debates about other matters.[47]

As welfare rights activists expanded their efforts beyond the welfare reform movement, they also linked to the broader women's movement by taking action on a range of issues that related to poor women's lives and demands. In 1969 and 1970, members of the CWA fought to expand women's access to safe contraception and abortion and supported efforts to end sex discrimination. This shift occurred for three reasons: NWRO's overtures to other women's groups as part of a broader effort to reach new allies, the increasing visibility and availability of feminist groups that shared an interest in economic issues, and an internal struggle for control of NWRO. Although few welfare activists publicly proclaimed that they were feminist, they adopted practices and advocated principles that demonstrated their commitment to the ideals of women's equality and women's liberation.

On the national level, making connections to a larger women's movement became a more prominent strategy for welfare activists after 1970, when the NWRO struggled to stay afloat in the face of internal and external pressures. In order to increase the organization's power and credibility, Wiley sought to open the NWRO to other groups of low-income Americans, particularly unemployed fathers and members of America's working poor. Wiley also pushed to establish alliances as a way to maintain the strength of the welfare rights movement, inviting speakers from a variety of organizations to speak at NWRO conventions and join NWRO events.[48]

But Wiley's direction also caused conflict regarding NWRO's governance and priorities. Since its inception, low-income black women had predominated in the NWRO membership and on the National Coordinating Council and Executive Committee that governed the organization. But the mostly middle-class, white, male staff held the power to make hiring decisions, allocate resources, plan programs, and devise strategy. Some individuals on the paid staff, like the welfare bureaucrats in Washington, considered recipient-activists incapable of leading the organization.[49] The recipient-activists who made up NWRO's membership and sat on its committees, however, believed that the black women's perspectives should take precedence. In 1972, welfare recipients took over the leadership of the organization, replacing George Wiley and many of the middle-class professionals who had staffed NWRO. Johnnie Tillmon from Los Angeles, who had helped found the NWRO in 1966 and who had sat on the Executive Committee for many years, succeeded Wiley as executive director. Once women assumed leadership of the organization, they increasingly connected to the growing women's movement rather than to the movement for economic justice. With Tillmon at the helm, NWRO's Executive Committee soon issued a "Women's Agenda" that explained how welfare and poverty were women's issues, and they began new procedures influenced by feminist ideas. Tillmon published this analysis in an article, "Welfare Is a Women's Issue," in the spring 1972 inaugural issue of *Ms.* magazine. In contrast to writings by white feminists that made middle-class women's experiences the norm, Tillmon's analysis suggested that welfare recipients best understood why women needed liberation. She argued that "for a lot of middle-class women in this country, Women's Liberation is a matter of concern. For women on welfare, it's a matter of survival." As one step toward that liberation, Tillmon insisted that women's unpaid labor in their homes and families must be recognized as work for which women should be paid. Women of all economic and occupational statuses would benefit from such a step. Arguing that "no woman in this country can feel dignified, no woman can be liberated, until all women get off their knees," Tillmon claimed a place for welfare recipients at the center of the feminist movement.[50]

Within Washington, a similar transformation occurred at the same time that the District's welfare rights movement crested, with activists extending their influence beyond the movement against poverty and into other women's campaigns. In the early 1970s, welfare rights activists began to talk about welfare as one of many social, political, and economic forces that constrained women's lives, and they demonstrated a willingness to identify male supremacy, and not individual politicians or bureaucrats, as responsible for their oppression. In a 1970 proposal requesting funding to start a child care program, for example, CWA members pointed out the problems caused by a society that devalued women by refusing to recognize motherhood as a form of work deserving compensation and requiring training. Society's assumptions resulted in men's lack of responsibility for child care and perpetuated women's unpaid labor, the proposal concluded.[51] Etta Horn, who had become known as "*the* welfare lady in D.C." appeared often at events organized by various women's and feminist organizations. She testified about constraints on poor women's reproductive rights at a forum organized by local feminists, and she sat on a D.C. Commission on the Status of Women panel discussing women and violence. Other local women testified before Congress in support of family planning, stressing the importance of programs giving poor women the ability to control their reproductive decisions. And welfare activists joined and helped coordinate events that brought together women to protest U.S. involvement in Vietnam and to demand an end to the war.[52] Through such activities, welfare rights activists educated audiences about the particular needs and views of poor women and connected welfare reform to other important issues.

At the same time that welfare activists became involved in these other issues, feminist groups began to create opportunities for further interaction. In general, second-wave feminists had maintained affirmative but loose connections with the welfare rights movement, showing less interest in pressing for welfare reform than in educating middle-class women about poverty and fighting employment-related issues. NOW's task force on women and poverty had represented an early effort on the part of that group to address women's poverty and propose ways to minimize gender-based economic inequalities. These proposals had made it into the Bill of Women's Rights that NOW issued in 1968. But NOW's stance in support of welfare reform never translated into any significant activity around that issue, instead prioritizing work-related concerns that more directly affected the group's membership. Members of NOW's National Capital Area Chapter focused on compelling employers to comply with legislation outlawing sex discrimination in employment. The group also supported the creation of day care facilities and labor organizing. These concerns touched on ways to improve women's working lives and the benefits they derived from employment, but did little to address the concerns of unemployed women or those in low-wage, menial jobs excluded from collective bargaining agreements.[53] But in 1971, four years after the chapter formed, it began a task force on Women in Poverty with the goal of educating members about the links between sexism and poverty and expanding the numbers of low-income women represented in the group. The task force brought welfare rights activists to speak at NOW gatherings, and articles about poverty occasionally appeared in the chapter's newsletter, the *Vocal Majority*; otherwise, the chapter took little action.[54]

Along with members of the D.C. chapter of NOW, other middle-class feminists analyzed welfare and educated their constituencies about the subject. A monthly D.C. newspaper, *off our backs,* that began publication in 1970, carried occasional interviews with welfare activists and regularly reported on the activities of Washington's welfare rights groups. Similarly, the *Vocal Majority,* newsletter of the D.C. chapter of NOW, printed articles about welfare and the experiences of poor women. Few of these analyses were written by or for welfare recipients, but represented the perspectives of more affluent women, albeit some who had worked as organizers in poor communities.[55] In addition to reporting on the activities of welfare rights organizations, the essays that appeared in feminist publications seemed aimed at generating sympathy for welfare recipients among middle-class women. They did so by stressing similarities in women's struggles and minimizing the differences resulting from economic status.

In one article, Marilyn Salzman Webb, a journalist and prominent participant in Washington's women's liberation and antiwar movements, addressed the double standards that pervaded the federal government's assistance programs. In "Welfare for the Rich," which appeared in *off our backs* in July 1970, Webb pointed out that U.S. corporations received huge subsidies from the government but welfare activists were denied opportunities to buy furniture and goods not covered by food stamps. Another article, "Mama's Welfare Blues," by Nancy Young of a NWRO chapter in suburban Washington, appeared in *off our backs* in November, 1971. Here, Young accentuated the commonalities between welfare recipients and other women who experienced discriminatory and dangerous treatment from health care professionals. "Welfare mothers face the same problems with delivery of medical services that middle-income and even affluent women have to cope with," Young stated, "finding a doctor who will take new patients; waiting; alienation from the experts treating them; the heavy hand of the drug companies; the lack of nutrition and preventive health information; and the passing of the housecall." Young's article simultaneously acknowledged women's differing economic experiences and argued against their relevance: in effect, she normalized middle-class women's perspectives.[56]

Welfare activists conceived of the links between poverty and other women's issues in ways that differed from the middle-class feminists described above and they resented other activists' attempts to speak on their behalf.[57] Nonetheless, feminists' analyses of welfare provided some foundation on which welfare activists could establish cooperative alliances. In 1972, a group called Friends of Welfare Rights attempted to build an alliance between welfare activists and middle-class women in order to foster understanding of the ways that women of all classes suffered as a result of their inferior status. Through this partnership, the organizers hoped, welfare mothers would come to understand "that they are on welfare because they are women," and middle-class women would "recognize the welfare mother's plight as an essential issue in the struggle for women's rights." In practical terms, the new alliance proposed to fight for women's common goals, including twenty-four-hour child care centers and equal educational and employment opportunities. Finally, the goals included creation of a permanent Friends group that would provide resources and support for the D.C. Family WRO. These stated goals reflected an uneasy merging of feminist and welfare recipient viewpoints. Child care centers and expanded educational and work opportunities would certainly benefit women and, some feminists believed, paid employment promised to liberate women from the home and their domestic role. But as they had since the start of their movement, welfare activists rejected the imposition of work requirements. They considered compulsory work bad for their families and antithetical to their demands to determine what was best for their children. Moreover, they insisted that motherhood represented an important form of women's work, albeit one that offered no monetary compensation, and that most other institutions (e.g., child care centers) could not do the work of mothering as well as women themselves could. Welfare activists' distinct definition of women's liberation, therefore, emphasized self-determination and stressed that women's economic independence should not rely on paid employment outside the home but should be available through other means.[58]

An article by Washingtonian Marie Ratagick from the Mount Pleasant Welfare Rights Organization further explicated these arguments. Her 1973 *Ms.* essay explicitly described the links between welfare and women's rights. "We in the Women's Movement," she explained, "have realized that welfare is a woman's issue. That realization was forced on us because 85 percent of the welfare recipients in the country are women and dependent children, but only now are we beginning to see the fundamental power system that oppresses women most—but also oppresses others." She conceived of economic justice, particularly women's financial independence, as a key component of their liberation, but instead of seeking only to transform the welfare system, Ratagick brought a gender analysis to the institution of marriage and to the larger economy. The monetary and familial problems faced by welfare recipients—challenged to take care of their children when forced to find paid employment and support their families with minimal paychecks or public assistance monies—resembled the situation of all women who worked outside the home for meager wages and without adequate child care facilities. Given these realities, work would not liberate women if they were denied access to day care and high-paying jobs. At the same time, she gave economic issues a central place in women's liberation efforts. Women of all economic backgrounds and occupations should act collectively to free their sisters from dependence on men in the form of "prostitution by marriage or other bought-and-paid-for relationships."[59]

As Ratagick reflected on her three years of experience as a welfare rights activist, she emphasized how sharing information and companionship with other women had transformed "a group of desperate, lonely welfare mothers" into "a sisterhood." When the welfare bureaucracy intimidated her, she found strength from other women and, conversely, the courage to "storm the gates for my sisters."[60] Deborah Smith, another member of the Mount Pleasant Welfare Rights Organization, similarly stressed the value of "sisterhood" as an outcome of women's discussion of welfare problems and solutions. As Smith wrote in a letter to the NWRO paper, the *Welfare Fighter,* "one rule in developing groups with real feelings of sisterhood is that members are never wrong . . . the regulations are usually against us and we should try in every way to help sisters do what they need to do." But as women united, they needed to avoid antimale attitudes. Expressing a sentiment voiced by other African American women, Smith warned that "you have to guard against letting sisters and brothers talk against each other," so that women's solidarity did not provoke antagonism between women and men.[61]

Ratagick's and Smith's statements reflected the emergence of feminist sentiments and perspectives within the welfare rights movement. Earlier welfare rights activists, nurturing a sense of community from their position as mothers, had seized opportunities to define maternal responsibilities and rights on their own terms. Feelings of sisterhood established among women activists the understanding of economic barriers that women faced, and analysis of the intersecting burdens of gender, race, and class that black women bore reflected the growing importance of the feminist movement that had emerged by the end of the 1960s. Welfare activists did not simply adopt middle-class feminists' analyses but shaped understandings of women's oppression that reflected their experiences and their goal of greater autonomy in work, family, and sexuality. Although welfare activists' analysis of women's oppression converged from the perspective of middle-class feminists, the questions that welfare activists raised about the social value of mothering, the importance of paid work, and women's right to make decisions about motherhood, sexual morality, and labor would resurface in the feminist struggles of the next decades.

3

Washington Women's Liberation Movement

In early 1968, Marilyn Salzman Webb had begun meeting with a small group of women who wanted to understand how society perpetuated women's secondary status and how women activists could find meaningful work without abandoning their radical political ideals. Webb, a member of Students for a Democratic Society (SDS), an antiwar activist, and a journalist, was joined by other white women, many of them newcomers to the District who were active in black liberation and New Left campaigns to dismantle America's racist and capitalist system.[1] For many, the gatherings provided their first opportunity to discuss positive and negative aspects of their roles in these movements. Recognizing the important contributions that women had made to campus-based movements, antipoverty programs, and antiwar activities, the women nonetheless shared feelings of anger and confusion at male colleagues' expectations that women would make coffee and meals, type and do office work, and have sex in order to demonstrate their radicalism. Questioning how SDS, SNCC, and other radical organizations could attack some forms of oppression yet reinforce others, discussants sensed still-unfulfilled possibilities for personal and political change.[2]

These meetings in Webb's apartment formed the nucleus for a broader movement against sex-based oppression that began to emerge in the late 1960s. Aware that their experiences in black liberation, antipoverty, and antiwar campaigns reflected inequities that remained stubbornly entrenched in American society, women tried to articulate theories and devise actions that would unite them in a collective movement for their own freedom. In so doing, they sought to make their own condition primary. Women's liberation, or radical feminism as it was also called by its participants, encompassed a multifaceted movement to destroy the institutions responsible for women's oppression and to bring about a society in which men and women could assume new roles without the constraining influences of capitalism, racism, and sexism. In this way, the liberation of women formed an essential part of the larger struggle for peace, equality, and justice. Although they recognized that African American women and women in Vietnam, for instance, faced distinctly oppressive circumstances, nonetheless they argued that sex primarily determined an individual's place in society. Women's subordinate status under a system of male supremacy resulted in similar struggles and provided a potential bond to unite women across race, class, and region. These bonds could be nurtured within women's liberation groups and coalitions where women activists could come together to support each other through the process of self-discovery and personal growth, with the goal of developing institutions to facilitate broader changes.

Radical feminists, like participants in the New Left, welfare rights, and the civil rights movements, considered personal and political transformation inherently linked. Personal transformation constituted the first step in building a mass movement to change society. In order to gain insight, courage, and a sense of community that would stir them to action, women needed to reject conventional ideas about their roles and expectations, coming to understand how their experiences represented common limits faced by all women. This process of self-discovery could be fostered by group discussions and participation in local projects and direct action protests that would simultaneously arm women with resources to help them destroy the institutions that supported their oppression.

Radical feminism in Washington, D.C., eventually engaged thousands of women in efforts to analyze their condition under patriarchy and articulate ideas about how to eradicate women's secondary status. Radical feminists created the D.C. Women's Liberation Movement, a citywide organization to coordinate the movement's many activities. The DCWLM joined the city's NOW chapter, the District of Columbia Commission on the Status of Women (later called the Commission for Women), chapters of the NWRO, other Washington groups that pressed to end sex discrimination and to mobilize women's energies around sex-specific causes. But the DCWLM differentiated itself from these other groups by its pragmatic and ideological connections to the New Left, seen especially in members' adherence to the idea that the country's economic, political, and cultural institutions—for example, organized religion, families, and capitalism—perpetuated social inequalities.

Whereas NOW, the Commission, and NWRO concentrated on political and legal reform, radical feminists believed that women's liberation would only come as a result of overthrowing these institutions and replacing them with nondiscriminatory and nonhierarchical structures. According to the DCWLM, such reformist approaches would benefit some women—especially those who enjoyed race and class privilege—at the expense of others. But despite ongoing links to the New Left, women's liberationists' criticism of that movement's failure to address sex-based inequalities propelled them to balance their commitment to women's liberation with continued struggle against American racism, capitalism, and imperialism. On this balance hung radical feminists' ability both to distinguish their movement from so-called liberal feminism and to stake their claim as radicals dedicated to fighting multiple forms of oppression through a movement for women's liberation.

Thus, in its broadest interpretation, radical feminism potentially incorporated all who shared the goals of women's liberation and social revolution. In practice, however, radical feminists typically were young, white, and middle-class, united by a collective identity as radicals. As women's liberation grew, participants discovered that their self-avowed radicalism proved a difficult foundation on which to build a movement that professed solidarity with women worldwide. Even on the local level, where radical feminists concentrated their efforts, Washington activists were challenged to theoretically and practically position themselves as simultaneously separate from, yet connected to, women from across the political spectrum and leftists who put attacks on racism, economic inequalities, and American involvement in Vietnam before women's liberation.

Movement Beginnings

Radical white women in Washington had begun to discuss organizing a women's movement distinct from the New Left and antiwar campaigns in preparation for the Jeannette Rankin Brigade, a women's protest against American military involvement in Vietnam. Convened in D.C. in January 1968, representatives from civil rights and pacifist women's organizations coordinated the Brigade, including members of the Women's International League for Peace and Freedom (WILPF) and Women Strike for Peace (WSP). Brigade organizers invited Webb and other women who occupied prominent positions in SDS and other New Left groups to take part in the event. Rankin, the first woman elected to Congress and the only representative to vote against U.S. involvement in both world wars, was chosen by Brigade organizers to symbolize the distinct role that women could play in opposing military engagement. Promoting Rankin as a pacifist and embracing a stereotype that emphasized women's opposition to war on the basis of motherhood, the peace activists, like welfare rights activists, attempted to unify women around their maternal roles. The Rankin Brigade organizers encouraged women to gather on Congress' opening day, wearing black, the color of mourning, to demand that Congress end the war.[3]

During the January protest, Marilyn Webb and other Washington activists met with about fifty women from across the country to reflect on the roles that they currently played in the antiwar and draft resistance movements and to envision how they might change those roles. These activists embraced the Brigade's broad antiwar message but disagreed with the tactics and symbolism used. For one, they criticized the Brigade leaders for targeting Congress, a body they considered powerless to stop the war, and for failing to recognize the full extent of the United States' imperialist might. The radical women voiced even more vehement objections to a view of women promoted by the Brigade coordinators that stressed women's roles "as wives, mothers and mourners; that is, tearful and passive reactors to the actions of men." Instead, Webb and other radical women advocated the importance of "organizing as women to change that definition of femininity to something other than a synonym for weakness, political impotence, and tears."[4]

Declining to join the formal programs, Webb and others used the occasion of the Rankin Brigade to organize their own protests and to lay the groundwork for future activities. Between 200 and 500 activists, led by New York Radical Women (NYRW), gathered near Arlington National Cemetery to symbolically bury the "traditional" American woman. NYRW, formed the previous fall, included members who urged the formation of a new radical women's movement separate from the New Left.[5] The women encircled "a larger-than-life dummy . . . complete with feminine getup, blank face, blonde curls, and candle," resting on a funeral bier draped with curlers, garters, and hair spray. A eulogy pointed out how the use of feminine stereotypes, such as those around which the Brigade organized, reinforced the image of women as powerless and passive. They stressed the need for women to act militantly, as exemplified by the banner "Don't Cry: Resist!"[6]

The mock funeral directly countered the views of liberal, pacifist women, but mainly the group emphasized the need to transform women's positions within the New Left. Many women belonging to SDS, for example, felt aggrieved at the ways the organization's men treated them. Despite its commitment to democracy and its support for the Vietnamese liberation movement and the African American freedom struggle, many SDS members had vigorously resisted women's attempts to change the organization. Between 1965 and 1967, SDS women had repeatedly objected to sexism in the New Left by speaking out at conferences and writing angry articles insisting that men address the problem of male chauvinism within the movement. Just months before the Brigade and in the face of widespread opposition, women's efforts bore fruit when SDS members passed a statement supporting the concept of women's liberation.[7]

When they came to the Brigade, therefore, Marilyn Webb and other women had accumulated several years of experience confronting chauvinism within SDS. They also shared an idea of forming an independent women's movement and an analysis that supported women's liberation as part of a broad movement for justice. Given the opportunity to gather without men to discuss the larger movement, the Brigade participants concluded that their roles in New Left and antiwar organizations had exemplified their position in the larger society. Confined to office work and background roles, they had felt discouraged from expressing their views and holding leadership positions. "Our position vis-à-vis the anti-draft movement is clearest of all," they surmised. "Men can refuse induction, burn draft cards, etc., but all women can do in opposing the draft is to aid and abet." Thus, it was necessary to "organize for our own equality within this broader struggle." They concluded that "no people could be free, that social change could not come, until all people were free." That meant, they argued, that the New Left could not be considered truly revolutionary if it did not promote the liberation of women.[8]

From the Rankin Brigade grew the women's liberation discussions that brought Marilyn Webb together with other women to form the D.C. Women's Liberation Movement. Over the first year, the movement remained small in terms of numbers, but closely tied to New Left and antiwar activities in D.C. and elsewhere. Members initially concentrated on formulating a theoretical and tactical basis to explain why women's liberation was needed and how such a movement could be built. The need to create local groups that could prod women to self-awareness and action became evident. But at the start, outreach to draw in large numbers of women did not constitute a concern.

Instead, the Washington movement coalesced around a core group of women from New Left, draft resistance, and antiwar groups, benefiting from personal networks and underground publications that spread news of DCWLM activities. Several local newspapers, including the *Washington Free Press,* the *D.C. Gazette,* and *Quicksilver Times* announced women's liberation projects and printed articles detailing the new movement's ideas. SDS, which had struggled to establish a presence in the District, yielded some members to the new women's group. Heidi Steffens had helped organize SDS chapters within the metropolitan area, including one at her own school, American University. Cathy Wilkerson was active in SDS for several years, moving to Washington in 1968 to open a regional office and set up chapters at local universities. She soon left the city and later joined the Weathermen, one of the groups formed when SDS splintered in 1969.[9] Other women, among them Charlotte Bunch, Betty Garman, and Marcia (Kopit) Sprinkle, had experience working with black liberation and antipoverty groups, heeding the message of SNCC to concentrate their political skills on organizing against racism within white communities.[10]

The Institute for Policy Studies (IPS), a think tank that backed the work of radical scholars, policy makers, and activists, also provided immeasurable assistance to the new movement. In fact, the IPS surpassed other left, antipoverty, and civil rights organizations in terms of its tangible contributions toward getting the Washington women's movement off the ground. Most of the early participants in the DCWLM had personal or professional connections to the institute, a circumstance that reinforced their view of women's liberation as a radical movement and embedded the new movement into personal networks centered around the IPS. In addition, the institute provided meeting space, office supplies, and seed money to support many initiatives and encouraged Charlotte Bunch, who was on the payroll, to organize feminists on a national level.

But as was the case with the New Left in general, the IPS also facilitated the growth of women's liberation in inadvertent ways. The institute made money and assistance available, yet its staff trivialized women's grievances, thereby compounding the urgency women felt. Many women complained that a sexist atmosphere permeated relationships among IPS's staff, fellows, and affiliates.[11] In addition to demonstrating pervasive views about women's roles and capabilities, the attitudes expressed at IPS no doubt demonstrated leftists' anxiety that the women's movement would negatively affect their own movement and their personal relationships. Cathy Wilkerson expressed the dilemma of many women who attempted to establish a new movement but retain commitments to the larger struggle. "The men in our organizations demanded that we assert and re-assert constantly our loyalty to them, and not to the independent women's groups," Wilkerson recalled.[12] Forced to justify their movement, radical feminists had to articulate a worthy political rationale and risk jeopardizing personal relationships with New Left men.

Despite the failure of some IPS staff to support women's activities, with the institute's financial support, Washington women organized two national conferences in 1968 that proved critical to the growth of radical feminism. A small group of about twenty women gathered in Sandy Springs, Maryland, during the summer of 1968, followed by a larger conference near Chicago several months later. The meetings brought together women who joined similar organizing endeavors in other locales, thereby reconnecting old friends and building new networks among radical women from across the country. In addition, the political exchanges made at these gatherings helped legitimize radical feminism in the minds of participants and provided women's liberation activists information about activities under way across the country. Conference attenders presented papers explaining the roots of women's oppression and introducing new ways of thinking about building a women's movement. Some of these papers made their way into newsletters and newspapers published by the emerging women's groups. Wary of political alliances that might ending up dismissing or marginalizing women's liberation, conference participants moved toward declaring their support for, and their independence from, New Left and black liberation movements. These conferences also represented the only attempts to form a national movement. Rather than trying to connect women's liberation into a single national organization or to develop ongoing conferences or other mechanisms for regular contact, women's liberation would take the shape of a confederation of independent, local groups, loosely tied through personal relationships and supported by a vibrant independent media that reported on activities and disseminated ideas throughout the country.[13]

By the end of 1968, then, the DCWLM had established a small membership, strongly affiliated with local radical groups and linked to women's similar efforts in other locales. The local movement remained exclusive, however, drawing in women who already subscribed to similar ideas about revolutionary change. The DCWLM's concentration on mobilizing radical women generally downplayed the goal of building a mass movement within the city, instead preferring to strengthen connections among those who already shared a commitment to transforming the political and social structure of the United States. This emphasis on limiting organizing to women who held similar political views and experiences insulated activists from the conflicts they faced when asserting the importance of women's liberation within the larger radical struggle. Such separation also offered radical feminists emotional and physical space to begin to lay the intellectual groundwork for a larger mass movement that would come later.

Growth and Change

As the Washington women's liberation movement evolved, it explored new directions that tested its relationship to the larger New Left and to other women's organizations in the District. By the summer of 1969, between thirty and fifty women regularly joined DCWLM discussion groups, and many more took part in other activities. Without any procedure for joining or dues to pay, women flowed in and out of the various project and discussion groups, as determined by their particular interests.

For the most part, the DCWLM's activities emphasized women's self-transformation through learning about the broader contours of gender roles in society. In an article, published in the spring of 1969, Marilyn Webb articulated the group's insights. The article's title, "Woman as Secretary, Sexpot, Spender, Sow, Civic Actor, Sickie," summarized the roles women most commonly occupied. By serving and entertaining men, by viewing consumer goods as the key to winning men and satisfying their families, and by volunteering their labor, women contributed to the smooth operations of capitalism. Yet, as Betty Friedan had argued in her 1963 book, *The Feminine Mystique,* when women accepted only these positions, they experienced emptiness and unhappiness. But social constraints made it difficult for women to act otherwise. Women who repudiated their assigned roles were labeled "sick" and pressured to conform. Moving away from the position taken by Friedan and the National Organization for Women, Webb argued that attempting to use the vote and electoral politics to end women's oppression would be futile because private corporations controlled the economy and therefore had power over how everyone worked and lived. Instead, only a cultural revolution that destroyed the economic structure could effectively end women's oppression.[14]

Another publication, "Women: The Struggle for Liberation," written and distributed by the D.C. women's liberation group and the D.C. chapter of SDS, echoed Webb's arguments. The pamphlet's authors asserted that women's oppression stemmed from their role as a surplus labor market and their unpaid work raising children and keeping households.[15] Media, especially advertising, reinforced women's limited economic roles by perpetuating the view that women were passive and could find fulfillment only through motherhood and relationships with men. This analysis was backed up by participants' personal experiences in the working world, where they found few professional jobs available to them, despite their college degrees. Those women who managed to find employment commensurate to their education nonetheless expressed discontent with "the conflicting *obligations* women are taught to live with—mother, wife, worker . . . and the psychological havoc these contradictory roles wreck on us." Living in the District, where so many professional positions required working for the federal government, created additional dilemmas for committed leftists, a personal and political conflict that some DCWLM members resolved by quitting their jobs or crafting unusual positions, such as the job-sharing arrangement worked out by Marilyn Webb and her husband. These decisions undoubtedly freed time for movement work but also demonstrated their relative privilege compared to other women whose families depended on their paid labor.[16]

In order to generate an anticapitalist, antipatriarchal revolution, according to the DCWLM, women needed to attack policies and institutions that perpetuated women's lack of autonomy and control. Reflecting the particular concerns of the middle-class white women in Washington women's liberation movement, Marilyn Webb considered women's main obstacles to be "abortion laws, low wages, hiring discriminations, Bridal Fairs, Wall Street, [and] Virginia Slims ads." She urged women to take action by establishing new institutions—child care centers and abortion referral services, for example—and pressuring employers and the government to take over these services.[17]

Along with structural changes, Webb and other Washington radical feminists concentrated on generating women's transformation through self-reflection and revelation. To support this process, radical feminists concentrated on developing new forms of political organizing and adopting techniques for direct action protest that had been popularized by other movements. As a result, consciousness-raising groups became the most widespread DCWLM activity. The practice called for women to disclose their personal experiences within small, nonhierarchical and nonjudgmental groups. By speaking of their lives as daughters, wives, mothers, activists, and consumers, women would recognize common patterns and identify the collective nature of their experiences. Women's feelings of anger or fear could offer hints about cultural expectations and pressures that limited their opportunities. In addition, giving voice to their feelings and experiences helped women grow confidence and trust in each other, thereby laying a foundation for collective action. By making women's experiences central to their analyses, consciousness-raising participants asserted that women possessed a better knowledge about their lives than other so-called experts. Finally, the nonhierarchical structure of consciousness-raising groups mirrored radical feminists' vision of their movement and their long-term dream for an egalitarian society.

Radical feminists' practice of consciousness raising resembled methods used by welfare rights groups, albeit with some important differences. Welfare rights organizers recognized that poor women could acquire a sense of personal power when they recognized that the problems they endured were neither unique nor of their own making. As Etta Horn and other poor women activists showed, discussions of personal experiences generated ideas and personal bonds from which subsequent action emerged. In addition, welfare activists and women's liberationists both recognized women's personal experiences as the basis for claims of expertise and knowledge. Radical feminists formalized the process of consciousness raising in new ways, however. By naming the practice and formulating procedural guidelines, radical feminists elevated its importance. At the DCWLM-organized conference near Chicago in November 1968, New York activist Kathie Sarachild presented "A Program for Feminist 'Consciousness Raising'" that provided a blueprint for the process. As Sarachild explained, discussions of feelings were not trivial but constituted a step to other activities, including the development of theory and collective action. By sharing personal experiences—within their groups or by writing articles or pamphlets reflecting ideas spoken about within their groups—women would understand their lives in new ways and begin to institute changes necessary for a larger cultural revolution. Thus, consciousness raising could prepare women to fight oppressive forces at work in their own minds and in the larger world.[18]

In contrast, welfare and antipoverty activists sought to give poor women greater control over their lives and to increase the political power of poor Americans, but did not necessarily see nonhierarchical small groups as the foundation for this transformation. Nor did welfare rights and antipoverty activists consider separatism from men an essential ingredient for open and equal small groups. Finally, welfare rights and antipoverty activists often had the benefit of preexisting networks that brought them together and helped them establish personal and collegial relationships that facilitated their organizing. Their proximity as neighbors and their membership in churches and school groups provided a foundation of trust and reliance that emboldened them and cemented their commitment to collective action. Similar bonds existed among the small group of radical women, affiliated with IPS or SDS, who began the DCWLM, but as that organization grew, radical feminists turned to consciousness raising and small groups as the means to build community.

Mirroring the structure of consciousness-raising groups, the DCWLM was organized with the intent of generating personal and social change. Rather than replicating the structure of SDS or other groups, radical feminists self-consciously tried to build an organization that would provide opportunities for participants to share responsibility for assessing and running the DCWLM. Women rotated work in the DCWLM office, diffusing control and fostering collective ownership and direction. Representatives from each consciousness-raising group attended general DCWLM meetings in order to report on and coordinate their diverse activities.[19] In addition, this nonhierarchical, loose structure provided small groups with the flexibility to develop their own initiatives and encouraged a sense of equality that women lacked in their other political efforts. By avoiding putting individuals in leadership positions, the DCWLM could encourage women to take up all the tasks of coordinating projects and running groups. These included speaking to the media and at public events, putting out a newsletter, and responding to requests for information and assistance. Although many of the DCWLM's organizing methods succeeded in creating conditions that stimulated and supported feminist activities, the group's attempt to institutionalize equality was less effective. Some individuals still attained prominence as leaders, especially Marilyn Webb and Charlotte Bunch. Both enjoyed formal affiliations with the IPS, where they received office space and salaries that supported their movement work and where they could mobilize tangible resources to coordinate the women's liberation conferences. In addition, both wrote articles that associated their names with ideas developed in the context of group discussions, gaining them notoriety within the city and beyond.[20]

Still, the DCWLM contrasted with other D.C. feminist groups that adopted more formal structures. NOW's National Capital Area Chapter elected officers and designated leaders of its various projects. Similarly, chapters of the NWRO appointed women to head local branches and to direct specific campaigns. As an arm of city government, the members of the D.C. Commission on the Status of Women were appointed by the mayor. Eventually, consciousness raising spread to other women's groups, becoming a popular technique for introducing women to feminism and building bonds that would support women's activities.[21] Even after consciousness raising became diffused throughout the movement, however, the DCWLM stood out as the city's only feminist group explicitly committed to devising new operational structures as a foundation for empowering women. DCWLM members, therefore, looked at their modes of organizing as an essential marker of the kind of movement they hoped to build and as a sign of their distinctiveness from other women's groups.

Discussions and ideas generated within DCWLM small groups became the building blocks for activities aimed at promoting broad political change. The organization's projects aimed to draw in diverse groups of women: high school students, government employees, and radical black and other Left women who lived in the District and elsewhere were targeted. A feminist newspaper, *off our backs,* begun in 1970, exemplified the connections between personal transformation and collective mobilization the DCWLM hoped to inspire. The monthly production of *off our backs* presented an opportunity to translate feminist ideals into practice. Rotating responsibility for writing, layout, and other production tasks, the members of the *off our backs* collective demonstrated the essential nature of both intellectually challenging and menial tasks to the dissemination of feminist knowledge. In addition, *off our backs* offered feminist perspectives typically ignored or distorted in mainstream and underground media.[22] Circulated nationally, the paper reported women's liberation events and announced new publications and projects throughout the U.S., thereby supporting the creation of a mass movement. The paper also printed articles on a range of topics, including reproductive technologies, auto mechanics, health food recipes, child care, women's history, and the war, along with essays of a more theoretical nature. Finally, *off our backs* helped the movement in more tangible ways. In its first year of publication, the paper's office logged numerous requests for assistance from organizations involved in putting out similar publications and looking for people to speak and write about women's issues. The collective's office became an important space, hosting out-of-town visitors and Washington women who dropped by searching for like-minded activists.[23]

Other DCWLM activities directly attacked political and social structures that supported male supremacy. By so doing, they also connected radical feminists to the New Left and to other movements that emphasized direct action protest. Starting in the spring of 1969, members of the women's liberation group organized WITCH, the Women's International Terrorist Conspiracy from Hell. A loosely connected national organization that started in New York, WITCH members donned costumes and used guerrilla theater performances to raise public awareness of women's oppression.[24] As their first action, District WITCH members, dressed in black and hidden by masks, stormed the downtown offices of the United Fruit Company (UFCO), an international corporation with farms throughout Latin America. They chanted "United Fruit makes lots of loot" and put a hex on Chiquita Banana. The WITCHes protested the corporation's exploitation of workers, its monopolistic control of the banana market in the United States and Latin America, and the role of UFCO in supporting a CIA-backed overthrow of a democratically elected government in Guatemala in the 1950s. Later in the year, the women put on their costumes again to protest at the Justice Department at the start of the trial of men arrested for conspiring to commit a riot during the 1968 Democratic National Convention in Chicago.[25]

To outsiders, the invasion of the corporate offices and the protests at the Justice Department might have seemed tangential to women's liberation, but according to Heidi Steffens, a former member of the D.C. chapter of SDS, "Washington WITCH sees itself as the political action arm of the D.C. Women's Liberation groups." Steffens explained, "We act as political women attacking all aspects of capitalism; those which oppress all people, as well as those speaking directly to women. This action, and all WITCH actions, are conceived, planned and executed by women; they are actions of women acting as revolutionaries." Like Webb's assessment of the Rankin Brigade the previous year, Steffens stressed that through WITCH, Washington women could mobilize on their own terms, yet still remain connected to the New Left.[26] By targeting U.S. corporations and the Justice Department, women could fight a system that "provides us with meaningless work, tells us what to think, what to wear, how to live, what products we need, defines our friends and enemies—controls our lives, as well as the lives of half of the people of this world."[27] Besides expanding New Left thinking, the women's participation in WITCH suggested other benefits. Redefining witches historically as "heretics and the first guerrilla fighters," the group also claimed the mantle of revolutionary. This reclamation of the symbolism of witches, combined with the liberating force of anonymity, empowered women to take action. One witch reported, "Some girls have told me they get this great feeling of power when they're in the [witch's] costume and afterwards they feel like a different person."[28]

Women also chose other activities that would transform society but in a more gradual manner. A Children's House aimed to meet an immediate need for child care, thereby freeing women for political activities. But the child care center also aspired to the larger goal of overcoming rigid adherence to gender roles that limited men's and women's activities and programmed children to assume those same roles. Although outsiders criticized the women's movement as antifamily, radical feminists cared deeply about how to improve the lives of their own and others' children. Several analyses in *off our backs* compared the role of children to that of other minority groups in U.S. society. Despite being physically and emotionally dependent on adults, and therefore limited in their freedom, children presented a potential force for revolutionary change. If allowed to grow in a supportive and loving environment, children could acquire a commitment to justice that would lead them to attack social inequities. But if feminists did not organize revolutionary day care, then government, schools, or corporations would take on the task and build centers that perpetuated the status quo. Additionally, DCWLM members urged feminists to set up day care programs as a way to expand their movement by connecting to mothers who did not yet identify as feminist.[29]

Finally, Washington women's liberation got involved in some projects not because they would lead to a revolution but because they offered opportunities to back—and possibly influence—other women. For example, the DCWLM proclaimed its support for some demands put forth by the NWRO and occasionally joined local NWRO demonstrations and protests. In the fall of 1969, when members of DCWLM coordinated a demonstration during a large antiwar rally in Washington, they incorporated welfare rights activists' ideas about the connections between poverty and the federal government's spending into their own platform. Targeting the Health, Education, and Welfare (HEW) department, the women's liberation group claimed that, "by refusing to provide basic services to the mass of people here, it [the department] effectively runs a program of genocide in that it contributes to the early death of minds and bodies—particularly of women and third world peoples."[30] The next year, DCWLM and NWRO activists joined in another protest at HEW. During a sit-in at the office of HEW's head, they insisted that the federal government guarantee a $5,500 annual minimum income for a family of four (rather than the $1,600 proposed by the Nixon administration), and that the president call off the bombing of Cambodia and end the war in Vietnam. "Stop the war and feed the poor," their signs read.[31]

The DCWLM's support for NWRO's demands came despite differences in the two groups' constituencies and approaches. Welfare rights activists viewed their struggle to reform public assistance as a women's issue, albeit one inextricably linked to their class and race, and they aimed to reform the welfare system. Radical feminists generally rejected reform, fighting instead for a broad economic and political revolution through a multifaceted movement against sex oppression. Yet both groups identified common concerns around which they could coalesce. At the HEW protests, for example, radical feminists and welfare activists joined in protest to express their outrage at the spending decisions of the U.S. government, which they believed prioritized the war in Vietnam over the needs of poor families at home. The DCWLM's selective backing of NWRO demands, however, meant that despite their collaboration, the lines between the organizations—and the larger movements they represented—remained distinct. At the same time, by taking up

NWRO issues and joining welfare activists in sit-ins and other disruptive activities, DCWLM members accentuated their solidarity with poor and African American women and demonstrated their position as radicals.

Creating a Common Base

By the spring of 1970—at the same time that *off our backs* began production—Washington women's liberation participants looked both with satisfaction and criticism at the movement they had created. A four-part series of articles about the DCWLM that appeared in the Style section of the *Washington Post* called the Washington group one of the most active women's liberation organizations in the country. With more than 250 "hard core" participants, it was second only to Boston's in size. By that fall, the DCWLM encompassed approximately forty small groups focused on consciousness raising and other projects.[32] For veteran members of Washington women's liberation whose political backgrounds had been shaped in civil rights and the New Left, the struggle against racial inequality and capitalism remained central to their agenda and contributed to their self-identification as the "only really active radicals in town." Accordingly, even though their movement remained predominantly white, the lack of racial diversity among local women's liberationists did not alarm Bunch, Webb, and others, who appreciated black women's primary commitment to the struggle for racial equality. As one woman told a *Washington Post* reporter, "We'd like to have black women in our movement, but we understand it when they say they want to get the black movement together first."[33] Moreover, they showed concern for incorporating what they perceived as the main concerns of African American and poor women. African American women might elect to prioritize struggles for racial liberation over battles against women's oppression, but the women's liberation movement could still assert its potential relevance to those women who were not radical, white, or middle class.

As the movement expanded in 1970 and 1971, radical feminism extended beyond its association with any single ideology, organization, or group of adherents. Veteran members of the DCWLM experienced this growth as a destructive force responsible for disintegrating the relative consensus and the sense of community they had enjoyed previously. When most DCWLM members came from similar backgrounds—white, middle-class, heterosexual, and radical—a sense of unity had predominated. But as DCWLM activities attracted new members, lesbians, socialists, and liberal women introduced alternative priorities, analyses, and approaches that challenged prevailing ideas.[34] Conversely, some of the "new" women perceived that their integration into the DCWLM was difficult because those who made up the informal leadership—people such as Charlotte Bunch and Marilyn Webb—distrusted newcomers.[35] Frances Chapman, who helped produce *off our backs,* believed cliquishness within the DCWLM severely hampered the movement by curtailing open communication and relegating newcomers to positions with little influence.[36] Likewise, when Bev Fisher attended several DCWLM meetings during the summer of 1970, she perceived that "heavy politicos who had an analysis about the war, about imperialism, and about capitalism" dominated. Rather than return to DCWLM, Fisher helped start a women's liberation group at George Washington University.[37]

Although DCWLM activists experienced these tensions as part of a split between veteran members and newcomers, they also demonstrated an ongoing struggle to define the relationship of women's liberation to the left, black liberation, and larger feminist movements. The challenge of articulating organizational and movement boundaries intensified as other feminist organizations emerged that differed from the DCWLM in terms of theory and strategies. So-called liberal feminist organizations, represented most prominently in Washington by NOW and the Commission on the Status of Women, along with other organizations that represented more narrow constituencies of women, offered alternative ways of understanding the obstacles that women faced when pursuing autonomous and self-directed lives. Like the DCWLM, NOW and the Commission on the Status of Women cast a wide net, attacking multiple issues that affected women's lives and the opportunities available to them. And all three groups claimed to represent diverse women's interests, although middle-class women predominated in each group and the memberships of NOW and DCWLM were overwhelmingly white. Most clearly, the Commission and NOW differed from DCWLM in terms of stressing legal and statutory reforms that would improve women's lives. Whereas the DCWLM pushed to overturn America's economic and political structures in order to liberate women, liberal feminist groups showed more faith that these institutions could become vehicles to deliver equal opportunities. To the DCWLM, the other groups' willingness to let extant political and economic structures stand demonstrated their insufficient concern for the status and conditions of the country's poor and minority citizens. In addition, the DCWLM went beyond the other organizations in arguing that so-called personal issues, especially those related to sexuality and family life, reflected widespread cultural views about power and gender roles and therefore constituted legitimate grounds for political organizing.[38]

The DCWLM's struggle to devise and follow radical feminism's distinct agenda emerged repeatedly when its members collaborated with other women's organizations, such as the National Capital Area Chapter of the National Organization for Women (NOW) and NWRO. Joining occasionally in 1970 and 1971, DCWLM members agreed to work with activists whose demands for women's equality differed from the broader call for women's liberation. Despite their differences, DCWLM members undertook these activities convinced that they could persuade other activists to adopt their ideas and tactics and thereby spread their movement while expanding its scope and diversity. They found such alliances, however, typically offered more frustration than satisfaction and failed to bring them closer to their goal of recruiting women to radical feminism. Instead, cooperation with other feminist and women's groups blurred the lines that separated liberal and radical movements and caused DCWLM members to anxiously consider the negative costs of compromise.

In early 1970, members of DCWLM joined the Women's Strike Coalition to coordinate a citywide commemoration of the fiftieth anniversary of passage of the women's suffrage amendment. Betty Friedan, the departing president of NOW, originally proposed a countrywide work stoppage by women as one way to mark the event. Women's groups across the country followed up on NOW's initiative by forming coalitions to plan local events. In Washington, planning for the August 26, 1970, occasion involved women from the DCWLM; local chapters of NOW and NWRO; the Young Socialist Alliance (YSA); and two new groups, Federally Employed Women (FEW) and the Alliance of Union Women. Each organization arranged complementary activities for their own members and to send a message to the public and the federal government about the broad support the feminist movement enjoyed.

The Alliance of Union Women, made up of members of local and national unions, fought sex-based discrimination within the labor movement. The YSA opposed the war in Vietnam and advocated building a women's liberation movement that tackled both sex and class oppression. According to the YSA, the struggle for women's liberation would help break America's capitalist system. At the same time, women would only attain total liberation after a socialist revolution.[39] FEW, a national organization headquartered in Washington and with a D.C. chapter, represented women who worked for the federal government, the area's largest employer.[40] FEW educated its members on matters related to women's equality before the law and pressed to improve the benefits and opportunities available to female federal employees. Unlike YSA and DCWLM, FEW considered direct action inappropriate for its members, a position consistent with federal laws that prohibited government employees from striking. Shortly before the August demonstration, the organization's president stressed in the group's newsletter that FEW intended to "press the case of the woman federal worker in a dignified manner and strictly within the law." Reminding readers that FEW was not a direct action organization, she concluded "we fight with wits—not bricks—but we aim to win."[41] For August 26th, FEW planned a lunchtime rally across from the White House, coordinated by Tina Hobson, the wife of former CORE head Julius Hobson. Another partner in the jointly planned rally, the National Capital Area Chapter of NOW, hoped to call attention to the value of women's paid and unpaid work and to encourage Washingtonians to boycott *Cosmopolitan* magazine and three products (a brand of cigarettes, a dishwashing liquid, and a feminine hygiene spray) that allegedly used advertising that belittled and exploited women. Finally, local NWRO affiliates wanted to include welfare mothers' demands "for the right to hold jobs and earn equal wages" within the movement for women's equality.[42]

The decision to participate in the event challenged members of DCWLM to balance their desire to publicly express their views and thereby influence other women with their opposition to legislative reform as a means to end women's oppression. Only three months earlier, members of DCWLM had gone to Congress, testifying against the ERA as an amendment that might worsen women's lives, especially those of the working classes, by threatening protective labor legislation. The DCWLM opposition to the ERA put them at odds with the other organizers of the August 26th events. Members of NOW strongly supported the amendment and earlier in the summer had disrupted Senate hearings to press for consideration of the matter. Passage of the ERA also constituted a priority for FEW, whose newsletter regularly entreated members to contact their senators regarding the amendment. Despite disagreement over the ERA, Washington women's liberation decided to join forces with NOW and FEW and help coordinate the day's activities.[43] As Bunch recalled, "NOW defined itself as concerned with equal rights for women and had kept its distance from our radical brand of liberation. We too had kept our distance. But we joined in when NOW proposed major women's rights Marches for Equality in many cities on August 26, 1970."[44]

Ignoring the earlier smaller protests of Washington women's liberation and welfare rights groups, the *Washington Post* called the event "the first major demonstration of women's rights here since presuffrage days." More than 1,000 people marched throughout the city, 200 attended an ERA teach-in, and hundreds gathered for rallies in two public parks.[45] The mayor proclaimed August 26th Women's Day, and the city announced plans to monitor sex discrimination in municipal government.[46] At the rallies, a representative of NOW encouraged the audience to support the ERA but to recognize that sexist attitudes had to change along with laws. Another NOW speaker reminded women to use the power of their vote. A speaker from the Alliance of Union Women called on union members to pressure labor organizations to pay attention to women and to infuse "sisterhood into union brotherhood."[47]

Despite the predominantly white membership of the groups that organized the Strike Day, some African American women took the dais to address black women's role in the feminist movement. Evangelist Imagene Williams told crowds, "Being born black and being born a woman is a double putdown," and she targeted organized religion for its particularly egregious history of sex discrimination. Jeanne Walton of the Washington Teachers Union, a former member of the NAACP and CORE, argued that although "the women's liberation movement is not always relevant to black women," it nonetheless should concern them "because it's against a racist, capitalist system that oppresses all blacks, all women, and all workers."[48] At the same time, Walton urged black activists to prioritize the fight for racial freedom because the "black liberation movement can create a new system in which all people—black, white, yellow, brown—men and women—can live in dignity, neither exploiting nor being exploited, neither oppressing nor being oppressed."[49]

Other Washingtonians, however, disapproved of the march and other activities, insisting that women's liberation was a destructive force in society. Hecklers gathered at the edges of the rallies and lined the parade routes, shouting derogatory comments and voicing disagreement with the assertion that women lacked or deserved equality. WOMB, recently founded by women from the Howard University campus, urged a boycott of the day's events. Claiming from 200 to 600 members who had joined WOMB for the "education of the black woman politically and spiritually to aid in the liberation of all black people," the group encouraged African American women to turn their backs on the women's liberation movement. As WOMB president Roselyn Smith insisted, "Our fight is not with our black men but with the system." The day of the march, the *Washington Daily News* quoted other black women who indicated that they saw the march's demands as either irrelevant or ill-timed. One student told the paper that black and white women possessed distinctly different concerns: "The basic issue confronting black women is first of all remaining the backbone of her man," she said. "Our men don't have their rights. How are we going to start asking for our rights when our men don't have theirs?"[50]

Even the organizers of Strike Day, who shared a commitment to feminist change, did not agree about the best process for winning gender equality and women's freedom. In particular, DCWLM criticized their collaborators for focusing on issues that would most directly benefit their middle-class, white membership, even at the expense of other women. Similarly homogenous in the race and class background of its members, DCWLM nonetheless tried to speak for the interests of a broader constituency of women by promoting social transformations that would benefit all women. The ERA represented one issue that separated DCWLM from the other women's organizations. Whereas NOW and FEW advocated the amendment as a path to broader opportunities for women, Washington radical feminists did not equate women's liberation with legislative equality. Instead, the DCWLM charged, groups that prioritized winning the ERA primarily represented the interests of white, middle-class women. NOW, for example, could not build a broad women's movement when it failed to "consider genocide, welfare rights, the Black Panther Party and Gay Liberation as 'women's issues.'" Welfare rights activists' demands for a guaranteed annual income and affordable contraception, for example, needed to be added to the day's platform.[51]

Besides the ERA and economic issues, DCWLM members pushed their collaborators to recognize sexual orientation as an issue related to women's freedom. By the summer of 1970, NOW had earned a reputation for its hostility to lesbians, largely a result of Betty Friedan's charge that gay women formed a "lavender menace" that threatened to undermine feminism. Friedan's remarks did not typify the opinions of NOW's vast membership, but by virtue of her prominence, her views became associated with the organization's stance. In Washington, the movement's treatment of gay women particularly galled Joan Biren and Sharon Deevey, two lesbians who represented the DCWLM on the planning committee. Fighting to broaden the Strike Day's mission, Deevey and Biren successfully pushed to add a black lesbian and member of the Gay Liberation Front to the rally's lineup.[52]

Outspokenly critical of what they considered NOW's willingness to "accept a minimum position (which excludes our poor and black sisters)," DCWLM members were less clear about how to reorient the event to address broader concerns. Moreover, their efforts to "raise more radical political issues and relate to local D.C. black women," were confused and ineffective. For example, the DCWLM planned a Strike Day march to the city's Women's House of Detention in order to make the point that male supremacy imprisoned all women. Incarcerated women were all political prisoners, forced into crime or falsely accused of crime because their lack of opportunities left them subordinate to men; conversely, every woman was imprisoned by the oppressive conditions of patriarchy and capitalism.[53] Carrying banners proclaiming "Women Will Fight—Fight to Live" and "Free Our Sisters, Free Our Selves," a group of 100–200 women marched to the jail, threw rocks at the windows, tried to communicate with inmates who cried to be released, and then dispersed. The next day, a small group met to discuss the jail action and to plan a project to raise bail money.[54]

The group's protest at the detention center mirrored an analysis that *off our backs* had published earlier, but also seemed intended to accentuate the political differences between the DCWLM and other women's groups participating in the day's events. A Women's Jail Collective, formed as a result of the protest, claimed that the action "came out of our desire to express our strength and seriousness about our liberation struggle. We felt it was important to make women's strike day one in which we could grow and at the same time push political consciousness about women as prisoners."[55] But although the DCWLM attempted to express solidarity with poor and black women, the protest at the jail more sharply pointed out the shortcomings in radical feminists' efforts to speak on behalf of all women. Their political analysis linked the oppression experienced by incarcerated women to that shared by all American women, but theory did not create connections on a personal or pragmatic level. As DCWLM members conceded, they neither developed specific political objectives for the protest nor "seriously dealt with the lives of the women in the jails for whom we offered nothing concrete." Even the bail project they formed to assist in the release of female inmates was short-lived.[56]

Overall, the events leading up to and during the Strike Day reinforced disunity and highlighted the distinct ideas of the women who participated in planning the day's events. Discouraged at the prospect of changing the views and agendas of other women's organizations, DCWLM members reassessed their strategy of joining collaborative activities. They resented taking part in "an energy sapping alliance with organizations that risked the integrity of the women's movement by a timid process of organizing around the lowest common denominator."[57] DCWLM members perceived that NOW would not allow others to influence the program and demands; therefore, the Women's Detention House protest became the DCWLM's only chance to control the agenda (or the DCWLM thought they did—until the center's inmates challenged them to do more to help release them than simply proclaiming solidarity as sisters). Given this situation, DCWLM believed their own analysis became overwhelmed by their collaborators' willingness "to sell out large parts of the female society who were not media image wholesome:

white, heterosexual, middle class." Rather than promoting sisterhood, the DCWLM concluded, their collaboration with NOW was counterproductive: "The political goals of NOW legitimize the system we are trying to smash." In addition, DCWLM questioned the effectiveness of mass demonstrations; participants argued in *off our backs,* "for we know that women are not persuaded by listening to speeches, but rather by our example and personal contact. Energy wasted in working with groups with different priorities could instead be spent in organizing workshops which allow personal raps or actions which express solidarity with sisters."[58] Thus, by allying with groups with different and even contradictory goals, DCWLM members risked muting their own message and obscuring the differences between liberal and radical approaches.

NOW and YSA members, however, celebrated the day's positive outcomes, noting positively the large and diverse crowds. Affiliates of the YSA who gathered for a national conference several months later pointed to August 26th as an event that "helped to cut through the elitist myth that only a handful of middle-class women could understand and act against their oppression as women. Secretaries, high school women, Black women, women from all walks of life turned out on that day." Designing a blueprint for further women's liberation organizing, the socialists argued that "August 26, and the development of struggles for abortion law repeal and other feminist demands in states around the country, have provided an example of the real meaning of sisterhood—that is, the concept that women can unite as sisters on the basis of common struggle. Such actions are important in giving masses of women a sense of their potential power, in inspiring a sense of solidarity, and in demonstrating to women that their problems are shared by masses of others."[59]

Indeed, Washington's Strike Day did expand the city's feminist movement. At George Washington University, students became inspired to form a women's liberation group that would coordinate events on campus to raise awareness of the movement. Turned off by DCWLM, which they found dogmatic and unwelcoming, women on that campus nonetheless believed that the Strike Day had demonstrated the power of a unified women's movement and could serve as a model for future coalitions to fight for abortion and reproductive rights. Similarly, the local NOW chapter viewed the day enthusiastically and considered it a positive example of the combined power that women's groups could bring to collective struggle.[60]

In the end, then, for women's liberationists, the Strike Day raised many questions and doubts about the value of coalitions, particularly alliances with their liberal counterparts, and the efficacy of actions intended to mobilize large crowds. It also caused the DCWLM to question its attempts to speak for the interests of women not represented in the group, particularly the poor and African American women held at the detention center. Yet despite their vehement dismissal of coalition politics and cooperation with liberal feminists after August 26th, DCWLM continued occasionally to participate in events with NOW. In February 1971, for example, members of several local NOW chapters, the DCWLM, and a women's liberation group at the University of Maryland joined a demonstration organized by waitresses of a local restaurant chain who were protesting their skimpy uniforms and abusive treatment by management.[61] These alliances showed that at least some DCWLM members continued to see benefits in joining with other women's groups to address specific issues despite the compromises and moderation that cooperation usually entailed.

But the conflicts that emerged around the August 26th Strike Day also exposed tensions that soon led to the dissolution of the DCWLM and quickly reconfigured the feminist movement in Washington. Even among those activists who prioritized the fight to improve women's lives over other struggles, persistent polarization that contradicted feminists' notions of a unified sisterhood remained, and disagreements regarding ideology, agendas, and structure intensified as the movement grew larger in size and more diverse in political orientation. The solidarity that DCWLM members had initially gained through a common identity as radical women diminished, replaced by divisions about women's most dire needs, the roots of their oppression, and the legitimacy of organizing separately from the New Left. Partly as a result of these conflicts, the DCWLM office closed in July 1971, a year after the Strike Day. The notice of the office's closure in *off our backs* sadly recorded participants' feeling that the movement had lost direction: "The office collective is no longer interested in continuing to work on a project which doesn't seem to be going anywhere." No longer used on a regular basis (only the DCWLM health collective and the abortion counseling projects regularly occupied the space), the office folded in the wake of tension, dissent, and diffusion that characterized the feminist movement at the time. The absence of a women's liberation office left the radical feminist movement in Washington without a central core devoted to multi-issue organizing.[62]

Some women dropped out of the movement after the demise of the DCWLM, but other activists adopted new approaches for continuing the battle. Washington radical feminists increasingly tended to establish smaller groups and to initiate feminist projects that focused on single issues, such as reproductive rights, lesbian feminism, or sexual violence. Many of these groups affiliated under the auspices of the Washington Area Women's Center, a facility formed in the spring of 1972. Replacing the DCWLM as an umbrella organization, the Women's Center provided office and gathering space for feminist initiatives that fell across the political continuum. The single-issue approach reflected a move away from viewing women's oppression as a piece of the larger problems caused by male supremacy and capitalism that could only be eliminated through a larger revolution. Instead, the focus on reproductive rights or sexual violence tended to be more reformist than revolutionary, emphasizing changing laws and creating new services and women's institutions rather than dismantling existing economic, social, and political structures. Although disagreements about methods and analyses persisted, a narrower focus on single issues provided room for collaboration and, ironically, allowed for the incorporation of greater diversity of opinion and background.

4

Organizing for Reproductive Control

Women's access to safe and legal abortions and, more broadly, their right to freely decide when to become mothers, emerged as a central organizing issue for women in Washington in the late 1960s and early 1970s. Joining in a movement for reproductive control, activists from across Washington's liberal and radical political spectrum fought to secure legal, safe, and affordable abortion and contraception and to end involuntary sterilization. The D.C. Women's Liberation Movement and welfare rights activists, along with NOW, the Young Socialist Alliance, and other groups, united behind the movement's basic objectives. The reproductive rights coalitions that activists formed represented a rare instance of cross-racial, cross-class organizing around explicitly defined women's issues during this era. But even when women agreed that securing access to abortion and reproductive rights were central to women's liberation, activists visualized the barriers that restricted women's choices in distinct ways and they emphasized different approaches to political change. Through the campaigns and coalitions they formed, activists continually redefined the meaning of reproductive rights and connected their demands for reproductive control to movements for economic justice, black liberation, and women's liberation.[1]

Alice Wolfson, who moved to Washington in 1969, quickly became a central figure in the local fight to secure women's reproductive freedom. Along with other members of the DCWLM, Wolfson sought collective solutions to the health problems women experienced. A pediatric audiologist who was married to a physician, Wolfson brought personal and professional insight to the group's discussion of America's health care system. DCWLM members formed a women's health group where participants discussed their shared frustrations with the medical system. Many felt anger at the dismissive and condescending way physicians treated them and stifled in attempts to control their own health care. Matters related to fertility topped their list of grievances. At the time, no states allowed women unrestricted access to abortion, although the District's laws were some of the most liberal in the country, sanctioning so-called therapeutic abortions in order to preserve a woman's health and life. But even under these conditions, Washington women felt powerless and many had risked death to obtain illegal abortions or suffered side effects from ineffective or dangerous contraception. Without access to safe and legal forms of birth control, many DCWLM members struggled to make their own decisions about motherhood.[2]

In September 1969, participants in the DCWLM health group paired with members of the Citywide Welfare Association (CWA) to fight for improved medical resources. Specifically, they pressed to change the abortion practices of the city's only public hospital, the primary medical facility serving the District's poor residents. The women accused D.C. General Hospital of practicing economic discrimination by adhering to excessively restrictive criteria when determining women's eligibility for abortions. In contrast, more expensive private hospitals interpreted the city's abortion law more broadly and approved more women's requests for the procedure. The coalition attempted to meet with city health officials to discuss D.C. General's policies; after they were turned away, they responded by picketing the Public Health Department and staging a sit-in at officials' offices. These protests subsequently spun in several directions: legal action to force equitable compliance with the city's abortion statutes, public hearings on the issue of reproductive rights, and demonstrations during congressional hearings about the safety of birth control pills.

Within a year, campaigns for reproductive rights and safe abortions achieved greater prominence, pulling in liberal feminists, welfare activists, representatives of family planning organizations, and black liberation proponents. Throughout, Alice Wolfson made pivotal contributions: she organized picket lines, forced her way into meetings and Senate hearings, appeared on national television and radio shows, and published critiques of the medical profession. Wolfson's outrage grew along with her medical expertise and as she learned the ways that race and class differences affected women's ability to control their fertility.[3]

The pressure that Wolfson and other activists brought to bear changed how the District's laws were implemented even before the *Roe v. Wade* ruling granted women's right to choose to undergo an abortion.[4] *Roe,* the high court's 1973 decision, represented an important victory by making abortion legal, safer, and more widely available. The significant impact of *Roe* obscured, however, the broader issues that shaped how women articulated a reproductive rights agenda, including the challenge to define reproductive rights and to develop strategies to address a broad array of women's health concerns at the local level. Wolfson and other DCWLM members viewed women's control of their fertility—which they initially defined primarily as unrestricted access to abortion and safe, effective birth control—as a necessary component for women's liberation and they acted to ensure that such rights could be exercised. But through their attempts to secure these rights, and especially as a result of collaboration with other activists, women's liberationists expanded their conception of what reproductive freedom meant. In addition, through campaigns that lasted for more than a decade, feminists came to understand that poverty, racism, and sexism imposed multiple barriers to women's rights. Securing a legal right to abortion was vital to the movement, but activists discovered that this right alone would not ensure all women's control over their reproductive lives. Instead, feminists and their allies integrated the fight for improved health care for women, the battle for safe contraception, freedom from sterilization abuse, and the assertion of all women's right to bear children into the movement to secure women's right to reproductive control.[5]

Fighting for Women's and Community Control

Medical innovations, legal decrees, and federal government programs in the 1960s expanded the resources that made it possible for women to control their fertility. This shift began in 1960 when the U.S. government approved sales of oral contraceptives—the birth control pill—to U.S. consumers following a short period of testing on a small population of uninformed women in Puerto Rico. U.S. drug manufacturers rushed to market the pill and within five years of its introduction to U.S. consumers, the oral contraceptive became the leading method of birth control, attesting to women's desire for dependable and easy-to-use forms of birth control. The market for the new oral contraceptives widened further in 1965 when a Supreme Court decision, *Griswold v. Connecticut,* held that laws banning the use of contraception by married couples violated Americans' constitutional right to marital privacy.[6]

The *Griswold* ruling and the availability of the birth control pill provided new tools for public and private agencies that offered family planning services.

The Metropolitan Washington chapter of Planned Parenthood, which had operated two family planning clinics in the city since the 1930s, augmented its educational programs and health services by distributing contraceptive devices, typically birth control pills and diaphragms, to married women. More than promoting sexual equality, Planned Parenthood staff were committed to strengthening communities by promoting wanted children, healthy women, and stable families. Ophelia Egypt, a black social worker who ran a Planned Parenthood clinic in southeast D.C., encouraged residents' involvement in the administration of the facility's programs. African American women who lived near the clinic developed clubs for parents, distributed birth control information, and lobbied the city government to create maternity centers at the city's public hospital. Thus, the clinic encouraged community participation and control over family planning initiatives.[7]

With Planned Parenthood's assistance, Washington's Department of Public Health began to distribute contraceptive materials and information in 1964, using federal funds to provide free birth control for low-income women at the D.C. General Hospital and five health clinics located across the city. The funds came at the urging of Senator Robert Byrd, chair of the Senate subcommittee on D.C. Appropriations, who had pushed District health officials to dispense contraceptive information to welfare applicants.[8] Planned Parenthood staff assisted this initiative by training public health workers, physicians, and caseworkers to direct eligible women to the new services. Like the federal and city governments, Planned Parenthood staff agreed that birth control was critical in the battle against poverty. "To fight poverty without birth control is to fight with one arm tied behind your back," declared the executive director of the Washington group.[9] Senator Byrd even more directly saw birth control as a tool for decreasing poverty and cleaning up the city's black neighborhoods. According to the senator, birth control use would decrease illegitimacy and improve "parental responsibility," thereby lessening welfare caseloads and juvenile delinquency. But if illegitimacy in black families went unchecked, Byrd warned, "the burden of crime, riots and dole will ultimately become unbearable."[10]

The distribution of oral contraception, backed by the *Griswold* ruling, potentially increased family autonomy over fertility, but other actions threatened to lessen the control exercised by poor women. Namely, after 1965, the federal government began to sponsor family planning programs in the United States through War on Poverty initiatives. That year, for example, the federal government created the Medicaid program, a form of health insurance for low-income families. As part of the domestic War on Poverty, the Office of

Economic Opportunity turned its attention to the role that birth control could play in alleviating poverty within the United States, an initiative that differed from previous efforts to fund family planning programs outside the country through the Agency for International Development (AID). The OEO authorized the establishment and funding of family planning clinics as part of its community programs and, although OEO regulations specified that participation in family planning programs was voluntary, participation was also limited to women who were single or separated from their husbands. Amendments to the Social Security Act enacted in 1967 went further by requiring states to establish family planning programs, and permitted them to distribute grants to private agencies, including Planned Parenthood, that engaged in this mission.[11]

By yoking family planning to the fight against poverty, the federal government ensured wider availability of birth control within poor communities and implied that participation in antipoverty programs required women to use contraception. The connection of family planning and antipoverty measures also promoted differential standards of morality for poor unmarried women, for whom contraception was deemed socially responsible, and unmarried women whose financial means disqualified them from publicly funded programs and, hence, from legal contraceptive use. Because African American women of all income levels utilized public family planning services at greater rates than did white women—whether they were run by hospitals, family planning agencies like Planned Parenthood, or as part of other public health clinics—they experienced greater vulnerability to the priorities and regulations established by federal funders.[12] Indeed, federal funds were seldom available for family planning programs without some strings attached, and power dynamics created by racism and poverty compounded the pressure on poor women.[13]

Surgical sterilization represented the most egregious form of coercion in the federally funded family planning effort, with welfare recipients and poor women of color undergoing the procedure at much higher rates than in the general population. An estimated 100,000–150,000 poor women, nearly 50 percent of them African American, were sterilized annually in the early 1970s under the auspices of Medicaid or other federally funded welfare programs. Thousands of Native American women, by some counts as many as one quarter of women of childbearing age, were operated on without their knowledge or consent. Whatever their racial and ethnic background, women who depended on publicly funded health services possessed little recourse when physicians or social workers used deception or force to limit their fertility. Staff at one city hospital, for example, informed the head of a Washington welfare rights group that if she wanted an abortion she would have to submit to permanent sterilization; refusal would have sent her looking for other, more dangerous, ways to terminate her pregnancy. Other women consented to abortions after being threatened with loss of their welfare benefits, or were sterilized without giving their consent. By contrast, women who did not depend on welfare or Medicaid often struggled to find doctors willing to sterilize them at their request.[14]

The coercive uses of birth control and sterilization among black and poor women convinced many Americans that the government's family planning initiative was driven by racist intentions. Activists adopted the term "genocide" to describe what they perceived as the U.S. government's deliberate attempt to make birth control an instrument to promote a capitalist, imperialist mission in the world and white supremacy at home. In the summer of 1969, shortly before the DCWLM-CWA protests at the public hospital, Marilyn Salzman Webb, the journalist and member of the DCWLM, had published an article criticizing the worldwide population-control efforts of the Nixon administration. Webb accused the administration of backing family planning initiatives in order to curtail population growth in the Third World. Nixon and his associates, linking high population density with high rates of poverty, had justified these policies as an attempt to diminish poverty across the globe. But Webb countered that poorly distributed resources, rather than overpopulation, caused poverty in developing nations in Africa and elsewhere. Instead of fighting deprivation, aid to birth control programs promoted U.S. economic and political hegemony around the globe, Webb argued, while the federal government justified population control at home as a means to prevent social disorder. "Housing, education, ecology, and, indeed, our 'democratic' form of government would be threatened if babies continue to be born at the current rate in the U.S., particularly, it would seem, poor or black babies," Webb concluded.[15]

To Webb and other activists, tests of oral contraceptives on unsuspecting Puerto Rican women, incidents of U.S. welfare recipients sterilized without their knowledge or consent, and the prolific distribution of birth control in the Third World all added up to a targeted effort by the U.S. government to reduce population growth among selected groups. That these efforts concentrated on populations in places where mass movements were challenging the power of colonial or antidemocratic regimes seemed more than a coincidence. Family planning agencies including Planned Parenthood also came under suspicion for operating as an agent of the state rather than as a vehicle for women's liberation.[16]

Whether or not Webb accurately interpreted the U.S. government's motives, such ideas gained popularity at the end of the 1960s, especially among those activists who became outspoken critics of the alleged racist motivations behind government expenditures and policies.[17] An article in the Nation of Islam's official paper, *Muhammad Speaks,* argued that although sterilization clinics claimed to be "aiding the indigent," the obvious intention was "surgical genocide, as effective in a long term sense as Nazi Germany's gas chambers and with the same objective." Similarly, in 1969, the *Black Panther* newspaper described birth control as "nothing more than part and parcel of the anti-human practices of the fascist racist and U.S. government and their genocidal war effort."[18] The Nation of Islam and the Black Panther Party encouraged supporters of racial liberation to resist the government's genocidal efforts by increasing the size of their families. Promoting large families under patriarchal control, the *Black Panther* paper in January 1969 instructed black men to "educate your woman to stop taking those [birth control] pills. You and your woman—replenish the earth with healthy Black warriors." In other words, female activists could support the black freedom movement, and protect the African American community, by heeding male authority and rearing large families.[19]

The Nation of Islam and the Black Panther Party did not represent the perspectives of all African American activists—and the Black Panther Party's position on this issue even changed over time, eventually advocating birth control as an important tool for women's liberation.[20] Other black activists supported family planning programs and considered birth control vital to personal and family well-being. New York State Representative Shirley Chisholm, the first black woman elected to Congress, objected to any form of pressure that resulted in "compulsory pregnancy." Speaking in D.C. in 1970 at a conference at the Howard University College of Medicine, Chisholm advocated safe and sanitary abortions for women who wanted them. In addition to stressing the need for women's control of their reproductive decisions, she highlighted the risks that criminal abortions posed. Citing 80 percent of maternal deaths that resulted from illegal abortions, Chisholm asked "What could be more like genocide than that?"[21]

Bobby McMahan, Elizabeth Perry, and Beverly Crawford, members of the D.C. Family Rights Welfare Organization, also prioritized poor women's need for contraceptive access over the government's motives. Testifying in early

1970, when Congress considered legislation expanding the federal government's family planning and population research activities, they announced the welfare organization's support for an expansion in federal programs. Speaking as poor black welfare recipients, the three women conceded that many people in their community ascribed to the argument that the federal government hoped to reduce the African American population through its efforts. But they also backed family planning as a right that should be available to all women. "We think," McMahan testified, that "any woman, rich or poor, black or white, who wants to plan how many children she wants, and when she wants them, should have access to a comprehensive family planning service. . . . If the woman is pregnant and wants an abortion, we think she is entitled to have one."[22]

Suspicions about family planning were exacerbated as the legal structure that restricted abortion access began to fall. The increase in government-funded birth control programs, occurring at the same time that challenges to abortion laws grew, left many activists fearful that women might become more vulnerable to outside interventions. Among the most important figures in dismantling the city's abortion laws was Milan Vuitch, a physician who opposed the city's restrictions on where and why abortions could be performed. Vuitch refused to operate his medical practice in a secretive manner and, instead, allowed advocates to openly disseminate his name to women who wanted abortions. Arrested for his activities in 1968, Vuitch challenged the city's laws in court, arguing that the provision allowing abortions to protect a woman's health should apply also to her mental health.

A year later, in November 1969, a judge from the U.S. District Court of the District of Columbia ruled that the D.C. law was unconstitutionally vague in describing when abortion was warranted, making it difficult for physicians, hospitals, and law enforcement to determine if violations had occurred. Only a month earlier, a California judge similarly had found that state's abortion law to be unconstitutionally vague. In D.C., where only Congress held the power to amend the laws, the judge called for consistent application of the existing regulation. "It is legally proper and indeed imperative," the ruling stated, "that uniform medical abortion services be provided all segments of the population, the poor as well as the rich. Principles of equal protection under our Constitution require that policies in our public hospitals be liberalized immediately."[23] The U.S. attorney general's office appealed the decision to the Supreme Court, but in the interim, the ruling in *Vuitch* set aside the old law and created grounds for the city to implement new guidelines for Washington hospitals to follow.

Women's Coalition for Health and Abortion Rights

By invalidating the terms of D.C.'s restrictive abortion law and by urging the establishment of new regulations to ensure equal access, the *Vuitch* decision promised to increase the number of legal abortions performed in the city. This prospect alarmed city officials and public health administrators. But abortion supporters seized new opportunities to shape public policy as a tool for women's liberation and community empowerment.

Women affiliated with the DCWLM and the CWA introduced a new phase of the city's reproductive rights movement when they organized protests at the D.C. General Hospital in September 1969. Their campaigns transformed both the style and substance of the abortion movement. Calling for free medical care and abortion on demand, these activists exploited the ambiguity in the city's abortion laws to create a women-centered movement for birth control and abortion that relied on arguments and tactics earlier honed by welfare rights, antipoverty, feminist, and civil rights movements. Using mass protest and direct action strategies to pressure officials to change public policy, their pickets at the hospital represented the first mass demonstration against the city's abortion laws. By framing abortion within the context of women's quest for liberation and as part of a push for quality health care, they highlighted economic issues that determined women's ability to act in accordance with the city's laws. Yet the coalition brought into the open the differing views of women's liberationists and welfare activists regarding the connection between reproductive rights and women's liberation.

Members of the city's welfare rights organizations had not specifically tackled the lack of abortion access before the fall of 1969. But the problematic health care available to poor women and children had prompted Washington welfare activists to campaign against one hospital that refused to accept Medicaid payments despite its location in a primarily low-income area of Washington.[24] Members of the CWA also had prodded Congress in 1968 to improve health care access when setting the city's budget appropriations. In addition to following up on an issue of concern to its members, the CWA's attack on D.C. General in 1969 reflected that group's view that poor mothers were entitled to privacy, authority over their family, and autonomous decisions about motherhood.

For the DCWLM, the campaign at D.C. General represented both a continuation of previous activities and a new direction. In 1968, in the context of discussing women's health, members of the DCWLM had highlighted difficulties caused by limited information about and access to birth control and abortion. In addition, women's liberationists who counseled women who contacted their office seeking assistance in obtaining abortions heard stories about abortions occurring under terrifying, humiliating, and expensive circumstances. The most egregious abuses occurred when poor women went to D.C. General Hospital seeking safe and legal abortions, only to be turned away without adequate explanation and without time to pursue other options. Denied the opportunity to find a physician who agreed to perform a legal abortion, such women could bear unwanted children, try home remedies to induce abortions, or patronize the network of underground abortionists who often conducted the procedure in dangerous conditions and charged exorbitant fees.[25]

Alarmed by the accounts of women who had applied for abortions at the public hospital, members of the CWA and the DCWLM united to protest what they considered arbitrary and unfair implementation of Washington's abortion laws by D.C. General. Whereas physicians affiliated with the city's private hospitals might charge as much as $600 for an abortion, D.C. General charged little for services to low-income patients. But despite making abortions available at minimal cost, the hospital's rigorous policy for determining eligibility disqualified most women. In order to meet D.C. General's criteria, an applicant had to undergo evaluation by one of the General Hospital's four staff obstetricians and two other specialists who agreed that carrying a pregnancy would threaten her life or health. This policy disadvantaged women without the time and money to undergo the multiple examinations, denying them the ability to choose the doctors who examined them and to present their own rationales for their decisions. Even with the necessary documentation, the hospital inexplicably turned away women only to have them return for emergency care after they had tried other means to induce abortion. In addition, some D.C. General physicians insisted that poor women follow up abortions with sterilization, forcing them to relinquish the possibility of future children.[26]

Not surprisingly, disparate access carried significant consequences for women. In 1967, D.C. General doctors performed eight therapeutic abortions. Only doctors at Washington's four Catholic hospitals conducted fewer, whereas staff at two of Washington's private hospitals performed an average of 170 procedures each month.[27] The public hospital's policies failed to deter desperate women, however, and more than 500 women every year sought treatment at the facility for complications resulting from illegal and self-induced abortions. In 1969 alone, according to a report issued by the D.C.

City Council, the hospital admitted more than 900 women who fell ill after incomplete or illegal abortions. By conducting so few abortions, therefore, the public hospital actually exacerbated women's health and reproductive problems and increased its caseload.[28]

When two women were inexplicably refused abortions by the hospital, despite having met D.C. General's criteria, DCWLM and CWA members requested conferences with public health department and hospital officials to discuss D.C. General's abortion policy. After the administrators refused to meet, the women picketed the hospital. Gathering in front of the main entrance, more than twenty women called out for "free abortions on demand" and "free medical care for all."[29] The next day, thirty women and children barged into the office of the director of public health, who oversaw policies at D.C. General Hospital, staging a sit-in until he agreed to form a committee to recommend policy changes that would bring the hospital into line with the regulations imposed by other facilities. Once established, this committee included six members of the women's liberation group, three members of the CWA, and a slightly greater number of medical professionals and administrators. After meeting several times over the following months, the Department of Public Health's committee on abortion asked the health director to give D.C. General administrators permission to authorize all abortions unless medically harmful to the patient. The only objections to the recommendation came from a Catholic priest and physician who ran the obstetrics unit at Georgetown University's hospital.[30]

Throughout the fall, women activists also attempted to participate in hearings of a task force to study health resources in the city. The District's mayor, Walter Washington, had established the task force to reorganize the city's health department, designating a subcommittee to investigate conditions at the hospitals. When the subcommittee convened two days of closed hearings to gather information about D.C. General, welfare rights and women's liberation activists showed up and refused to leave the sessions until they expressed their grievances. Charging the task force with inappropriate secrecy, they argued that residents familiar with conditions at the hospital should be allowed to relate their experiences to the committee. Furthermore, they objected that male doctors rather than the women who depended on the hospital made up the majority of the task force members. Without input from residents who used public health facilities, and especially without adequate representation by women, activists feared the task force would downplay the serious health crisis facing the city. Disrupting the hearings by shouting out comments and questions, they demanded that the subcommittee address high mortality rates among infants and women in childbirth. Under pressure from the publicity created by the activists, the subcommittee chair invited the women to participate in future meetings, and the mayor appointed two CWA members to the group. In its report to the mayor, the task force concluded, "In the District of Columbia, legal abortions are almost totally unavailable to poor women because of the restrictive policy followed by D.C. General Hospital." Based on such evidence, the task force recommended that the mayor order the hospital to eliminate all restrictions and extend abortions to women upon request.[31]

The impact of the collaborative activities undertaken by the DCWLM and CWA can be measured in several ways. The tactics employed by the activists—picket lines, rallies, sit-ins—represented the continuation of methods previously used effectively by black liberation and welfare rights activists and expanded the repertoire of women's liberationists. In addition to asserting women's right to participate in policy setting, the coalition combated the silence typically surrounding abortion. Rather than treating abortion as a matter for discussion within the privacy of bedrooms or the confines of doctors' and clergy's offices, the welfare rights and women's liberation activists framed abortion as a woman's political due. Taking the issue to the public, welfare rights and women's liberation activists acted on their belief that shame—at poverty, welfare dependency, past mistreatment by physicians, or sexual activity outside of marriage—contributed to women's oppression. Coalition members overcame their own shame when publicly associating themselves with the movement and they hoped that their boldness would empower other women to join their movement.

Within welfare rights and women's liberation groups, the coalition provided an opportunity to act on critically important issues. Neither the CWA nor the DCWLM, however, intended to make the fight for improved health care and abortion access their primary focus. Instead, they viewed the hospital campaigns as one aspect of their ongoing struggles to win welfare rights and women's liberation, respectively. Only four days before the protests at D.C. General, welfare rights activists had picketed the welfare department demanding money for back-to-school clothing. During the fall, as DCWLM members fought to gain inclusion on the mayoral task force and met repeatedly with the Department of Public Health's committee on abortion, other women's liberationists took part in the WITCH protest at the Justice Department.[32] Even when joining to protest the hospital and the city's health care practices, welfare rights activists and women's liberationists established points of commonality but retained their larger—and separate—goals and activities.

In some ways, too, the coalition actually accentuated the different views of motherhood and fertility control held by DCWLM and CWA. To women's liberationists such as Alice Wolfson, free abortion on demand constituted a key element of women's liberation, a goal that also required eradicating sexism from the medical system and the larger society. Wolfson explained, "Freedom for women means the freedom for other forms of life work and identity than just the family."[33] In a similar vein, DCWLM member and journalist Judith Coburn maintained, "Women's liberation must fight to change society to allow women to make their own reproductive choices and whether or not to choose other careers than housewife and mother. For married women, this means round-the-clock day care centers at the place of work. For men, it means sharing equally the responsibilities of children, household, and conception."[34] Coburn's and Wolfson's statements suggested that DCWLM participants perceived women's roles as wife and mother as repressive, serving the interests of capitalism and patriarchy. In contrast, welfare rights activists embraced the identity of mother as a potential source of power and authority—when women possessed resources adequate to ensure the security of their families. But women's liberationists aimed to relieve pressures on women to marry and become mothers. With convenient and inexpensive access to abortion and birth control, they believed, women could freely make decisions about motherhood and achieve an essential step toward liberation.

Along with their concern for removing obstacles that prevented women's self-determination in reproductive areas, Wolfson and other women's liberationists viewed the problem of abortion access as a symbol of women's lack of control over their health care decisions. Doctors and hospital officials held inordinate power to determine the outcome of a pregnancy, but many, according to DCWLM activists, lacked compassion for women patients. One DCWLM publication, "Women and Health," reported that the doctor who headed the obstetrics/gynecology unit at D.C. General Hospital had allegedly stated that his staff avoided performing abortions because the procedure was "too boring." Believing such attitudes pervaded the medical field, women's liberationists concluded that widespread changes in the medical profession must accompany the movement to grant women's reproductive freedom.[35] Men vastly outnumbered women in the medical profession and business interests exerted too much sway over health care, feminists believed. Driven by the quest for profit, medical researchers who were funded by drug companies subjected women to new birth control pills before the risks had been sufficiently determined and information widely conveyed to consumers. Planned Parenthood contributed to the problem by funding contraceptive research and distributing unsafe birth control devices. Making abortion in particular and medical care in general freely available would eliminate the profit motive that resulted in a lack of excellent medical care for all Americans, especially those with little money. Indeed, DCWLM argued, even middle-class women lacked adequate health care because quality medical treatment "requires a system that is not based on profit for hospitals, doctors, drug industries, and private insurance companies. Health care must be seen as a national responsibility and it must be approached with a system of preventive as well as curative medicine." Thus, according to feminists, the battle for reproductive rights should be pursued as part of an effort to transform the country's health care system.[36]

Like women's liberationists, welfare rights activists understood that health care professionals exerted an extraordinary influence over women's reproduction. In contrast to the DCWLM, however, members of the CWA perceived that poverty and the structure of the welfare system posed the greatest obstacle to their reproductive control. The principle that women's receipt of public assistance funds should not restrict maternal rights was central to the welfare rights movement. Similarly, receipt of welfare or Medicaid did not prove a woman's qualifications as a mother. But women's economic status and the public assistance system limited how they could exercise their rights as mothers, affecting how well they could provide for their children's material needs and often forcing them to choose not to have or raise children. Within a political context where poor African American women were targeted as the reason for numerous social ills, the distinction between voluntary restrictions on contraception and coercion was ambiguous. Welfare activist Etta Horn characterized this situation as genocide: the medical system and, especially, the D.C. Department of Public Health, forced women into the abortion underground, while social workers at the welfare agency scared public aid recipients into using birth control. Furthermore, Horn argued, the ill health that had driven many women out of the labor force and onto public aid exacerbated the hazardous side effects of oral contraceptives. Whatever the political or economic motives that led public health workers and welfare caseworkers to discourage recipients' fertility, welfare activists insisted that impoverished women possessed the right to regulate their reproductive lives. As welfare activist Bobby McMahan put it, all women had the right to decide if and when they wanted children. Politicians might believe that welfare recipients demonstrated less concern for their families' well being than did more affluent Americans, but McMahan argued the reverse. "Poor people care just as much as the rich, if not more, about the welfare of their children. Poor people don't want their children to be destined to poverty."[37]

Thus, although members of all of the concerned groups agreed that restrictions on reproductive choice should be eliminated and that women must exercise reproductive control, they understood the problems in different ways. Women's liberationists emphasized the demand to terminate pregnancies, while welfare activists stressed the right to bear children. This difference in perspective did not make feminists' and welfare activists' demands incompatible, but did reflect how women's class and race backgrounds affected their experiences. Furthermore, the different perspectives represented by the two organizations limited their continued collaboration. White women in DCWLM acknowledged that the CWA taught them a lot about the conditions poor black women faced, especially how the government used reproductive control to conduct political and racial genocide. Yet DCWLM also conceded that it never "adequately resolve[d] the question of abortions as a means of genocide in the black community vs. the need for sanitary, free abortions for all, especially poor and black women. . . . We realized that we should not isolate the abortion issue from an overall demand to women's right to control our bodies, but this was not easy to carry out in practice and much of our work failed to get beyond these problems."[38]

These different emphases were accompanied by differences in approach. Whereas the CWA had called for legislative reforms that would restructure public assistance to better meet the needs of the country's poor, the DCWLM had prioritized changing culture over reforming laws or policies. Transforming consciousness about the existence of women's oppression, they reasoned, constituted one step toward a revolution that would bring equality to society, but reformist approaches would fall short of liberating women. The DCWLM's denunciation of reform may explain why Etta Horn contended that the coalition had not "really gotten together to work on abortion reform."[39] But the DCWLM gave pragmatic realities—including the predicaments women faced and the opportunities to influence public policy during a critical period—priority over their political ideals. As they described it in a pamphlet, organizing for abortion access required the group to "walk a fine line between continual struggle for ultimate freedoms and meeting some real and immediate needs at each step along the way." The fight to gain abortion rights, which they believed would address the urgent problems of illness and death caused by illegal abortions, could provide some short-term benefits until complete social and economic upheaval brought about women's true liberation.[40]

After women gained seats on the official policy-making boards of the city council and health department, the CWA and DCWLM sought new means to expand women's reproductive control. Moving away from the singular focus on abortion access, welfare rights and women's liberation activists both turned to push for reproductive freedom and safety by addressing women's need for safe birth control and to eliminate the particular pressures to terminate or avoid pregnancy that poor women endured. In general, despite their desire for more revolutionary change, DCWLM members focused on health care and abortion reform by way of the courts and Congress and consistently offered counseling to individual women. Simultaneously, welfare rights activists maintained their efforts to educate feminists about poor women's experiences and to highlight the coercive uses of birth control and abortion. Both groups continued to stress the disparities that marked women's ability to control their reproduction and to search for opportunities to express their demands and analyses to new audiences.

In the spring of 1970, DCWLM joined a suit to challenge D.C. General Hospital's criteria for determining women's eligibility for abortion. In response to the *Vuitch* ruling, D.C. General began to accept psychiatric evidence in order to assess women's mental health, but imposed stricter standards of evidence than private facilities in the city. As a result, the hospital lagged far behind other facilities in the terms of the numbers of abortions its staff performed, and women who seemingly met the hospital's criteria still found themselves inexplicably turned away.[41] A class action suit brought by the ACLU, which the DCWLM supported, tried to clarify the hospital's procedures and compel the facility to grant abortions without delay to eligible women. The suit clearly followed up on the DCWLM-CWA coalition's earlier efforts to make abortion available to low-income women on grounds similar to those available to patients able to pay for medical care, as demonstrated in a statement that the DCWLM issued opposing abortion, contraception, or sterilization used to oppress specific groups of people and affirming women's right to terminate unwanted pregnancies and to have children if and when they wanted them.[42]

Other DCWLM members acted on their concerns about the potentially harmful effects of birth control pills. After ten years of availability to U.S. consumers, research data on the detrimental physical and mental health complications of oral contraceptives suggested a need for further medical research. In 1969 and early 1970, the Senate's Small Business Subcommittee on Monopoly, headed by Senator Gaylord Nelson, convened hearings on the pill's safety. The DCWLM's Health Committee members had discussed their own experiences with the unpleasant side effects of oral contraception. Interested in learning more, Alice Wolfson and other DCWLM members decided to attend the Senate's hearings. As they sat in the chambers, they grew outraged at the voluminous evidence linking oral contraception to cancer and numerous other dangers. In addition, they objected to the absence of women researchers on the speakers' list and to the congressional committee's failure to solicit testimony from women who had used the pill.[43] Members returned to the hearing room the next day and brought the proceedings to a standstill by shouting out questions and comments from the floor. Their disruption halted the hearings, garnered national publicity, and won DCWLM an audience with Senator Nelson. After listening to their concerns, Nelson agreed to add "qualified" women to the witness list—researchers and women who had experienced severe complications as a result of the pill—but he refused to let DCWLM members question witnesses.[44]

The protests compounded radical feminists' distrust of the political system and of the efficacy of reform as a tool for women's liberation. DCWLM members' misgivings expanded further when, shortly after the Nelson subcommittee's hearings closed, the FDA weakened rather than strengthened the safety warning on oral contraceptive packages. Wolfson and other members of the DCWLM reacted with a sit-in at the office of Health, Education, and Welfare Secretary Robert Finch to protest the inadequate safety warnings and to demand that more explicit language be included in package inserts. The new FDA policy, according to Alice Wolfson, reflected the government's disregard for women's lives and health. The lesson from these encounters, Wolfson concluded, was that "if we are ever to have control over the institutions which govern our lives, women must band together and refuse to recognize a government policy that puts profit over people."[45]

As part of repudiating government authority in health care matters, in March 1970, the DCWLM organized their own hearings about the pill. More than 100 women gathered in a church to listen to personal testimony about women's health problems caused by taking oral contraception. One speaker accused drug manufacturers, advertisers, and physicians of prescribing and promoting oral contraception in order to turn a profit. "They never thought about what the pill would do to us women . . . it is genocide on Black people, poor whites, and women."[46] Other speakers warned of the many health problems associated with birth control—serious medical ailments that made its use ill-advised for women with some preexisting conditions. Among these groups were the many welfare recipients who, suffering from poor health that pushed them out of the job market, risked death if they used oral contraception. In alarm, Etta Horn insisted that better regulations should allow women to "decide what is done with their bodies." The hearings and publications that activists produced carried no official weight, but they contributed to the reproductive health movement by creating a forum for women to share their experiences, listen to research data detailing contraceptive risks, and create a public record of their concerns.[47]

Expanding the Fight

Between 1970 and 1973, welfare rights activists, radical feminists, and other women and men organized countless rallies and public meetings where they demanded women's control of their own fertility and improved health care for women. Across the country, state abortion laws toppled in response to suits brought by activists and reforms enacted by legislatures. New York led the way, passing legislation in early 1970 that made abortion legal during the first six months of gestation. Hawaii and Maryland quickly followed suit. For advocates of abortion rights, these state-level victories—and their sometimes insecure status—justified continued activity to overturn restrictive laws elsewhere. Abortion rights supporters also began to fight for legal repeal on the federal level, mounting a national campaign that would overlap state-level efforts.

In D.C., women's access to abortion expanded while public officials responded to popular pressure and tried to standardize the conditions under which abortions could be performed locally. Between the summer of 1970 and the fall of 1972, a series of public hearings demonstrated the degree of popular support for abortion access and convinced the city council to further extend the requirements determining when abortions could be legally performed.[48] In 1971, the council passed regulations allowing physicians to perform abortions at offices and clinics licensed for that purpose.[49] That same year, the Supreme Court ruled in the *Vuitch* case that the city's abortion law was constitutional, a decision that reversed the earlier judgment, but nonetheless accepted the argument that abortion for mental health purposes could be accommodated within the language of the law.[50]

The new *Vuitch* ruling and the city council's decision authorizing abortions in clinics and licensed physicians' offices made abortion services more widely available. By the fall of 1971, women could obtain abortions at four clinics located in the hospitals or independently run by reproductive health organizations. Four other organizations joined the DCWLM to provide information, referrals, and counseling about abortion. Planned Parenthood expanded services at its downtown clinic, offering pregnancy testing, abortion counseling, and prenatal adoption referrals. However, access to abortion continued to be uneven, with some hospitals and clinics refusing to grant abortions to women under twenty-one years of age without parental approval or to married women who did not have the consent of their husbands (even if the couple had separated). Women's ability to get abortions also varied depending on their economic resources, a condition Planned Parenthood tried to rectify by arranging loans for women who could not afford abortion services even at the $200 rate offered by most clinics.[51]

With the expanded visibility and legitimacy conveyed by the city council and Supreme Court actions, greater numbers of people were drawn into the local abortion rights movement, including representatives of organizations that previously had avoided taking a public stance on the controversial topic. More than in earlier campaigns for women's liberation or welfare rights, activists chose coalitions as the main vehicle for organizing activities and building public awareness about the need to expand abortion rights. The existence of three coalitions, formed in 1971, showed that winning women's reproductive rights represented a goal that united women who otherwise held distinct organizational affiliations and advocated contrasting views about women's liberation and social change. At the same time, the impulse to form three distinct coalitions, rather than one single umbrella organization, suggested the limits of unity and the difficulty of bringing together women with differing political philosophies and priorities to fight for reproductive rights. Alliances emerged, and folded, on the basis of participants' ability to develop consensus and compromise on tactics and priorities.

Typically, abortion rights coalitions framed their agenda around issues that seemingly all women shared rather than around demands that could be associated with particular groups of women. In the context of the growing national reproductive rights movement, this meant equating abortion rights with women's legal rights, and asserting abortion rights as the primary means to secure women's reproductive control. Articulating the right to legal abortion as the central demand of Washington's alliances, however, caused abortion supporters to downplay other barriers that restrained women's access to freedom of choice, including disparities in interpretation of the District's relatively liberal laws, and the problems of coercion that poor women of color experienced.

The difficulty that one new coalition, the Metropolitan Abortion Alliance (MAA), experienced in developing activities and sustaining consensus exemplified the challenges of linking activists with distinct ideas about women's liberation. The MAA formed in the spring of 1971 and included members of the DCWLM; representatives from the D.C. chapters of the Young Socialist Alliance (YSA), NOW, and FEW; members of a George Washington University women's liberation group; and supporters of Planned Parenthood and Zero Population Growth. The MAA initially agreed to promote three demands: (1) women's control over their own bodies; (2) free and safe abortions on demand, without involuntary sterilization; (3) and safe contraception for any woman who sought it.

Within months of reaching consensus on this agenda, divisions emerged over the strategy of arguing for abortion rights. NOW and YSA prioritized repeal as a goal, pushing to overturn restrictive abortion laws. In contrast, other members concluded that in D.C., where laws were relatively permissive, the worst abuses stemmed from poor women's inability to procure abortions in a safe, legal, and affordable manner.[52] Originally, the MAA had planned to publicize the "oppressive abortion policies" that denied women's control of their bodies by demonstrating in front of D.C. General. Harkening back to the DCWLM-CWA coalition's activities, this event would highlight the plight of the city's poor African American women. But at the last minute, YSA members relocated the rally to Lafayette Park, across Pennsylvania Avenue from the White House, a site that promised greater exposure and symbolically linked the MAA to a national cause. But the move symbolized a shift in attention away from local conditions to the national front, with legal repeal taking precedence over issues of access and implementation. In addition, the emphasis on repeal hinted at the MAA's attempt to articulate abortion rights as a demand all women shared, even those who might not identify with the problems of access that poor women experienced.[53]

Nonetheless, the Lafayette Park rally reflected the breadth and depth of the abortion movement on a national scale. Nationally known and local feminist speakers inspired the crowd with information about ongoing efforts to fight for abortion rights across the country. Jeannie Reynolds of the MAA and the local NOW chapter explained that two local groups were bringing legal suits using two different tactics: one challenging the tax-exempt status of the Roman Catholic Church because of its lobbying activities opposing the abortion movement, the other seeking to declare the city's abortion statute unconstitutional. A law student reminded the crowd that free abortion on demand would prevent the deaths of poor women who died as a result of having sought illegal abortions. Tina Hobson, the wife of former CORE director Julius Hobson and a representative of FEW, asserted that the meager benefits available to federal employees limited women's reproductive freedom by denying maternity leave and failing to make day care available. Finally, a high school student spoke of the difficulties faced by young women who became pregnant.[54]

About 200 people attended the rally in Lafayette Park, a turnout that disappointed organizers, but still exceeded numbers present at previous abortion rights demonstrations in the city.[55] The rally also solidified many activists' support for the focus on legal repeal and mass demonstrations as strategies to secure abortion rights. Jeannie Reynolds encouraged NOW's members to look beyond the small crowds at the Lafayette Park rally and commit to an ongoing fight. NOW should continue to participate in abortion rights demonstrations, Reynolds argued, and should create ways to organize the "energy and interest" evidenced by its members.[56] Another activist appealed to readers of *off our backs* to get serious about supporting "the most important issue in the movement." Calling on women to mobilize into "an organized fighting force," she argued that "sit-ins, protests, demonstrations of all kinds and more rallys [*sic*] are necessary to build sisterhood and an unshakable solidarity."[57]

The MAA disbanded shortly after the Lafayette Park rally, done in by conflict over strategy and focus. Another coalition, spearheaded by the local branch of the Women's National Abortion Action Coalition (WONAAC) soon took its place. The D.C. chapter of WONAAC formed in the summer of 1971, fighting to repeal abortion laws across the country and challenging local abortion practices. WONAAC was founded by YSA members who considered abortion of "central importance because as long as women are denied the right to control their own bodies, they cannot control their lives. At some time in her life, virtually every woman feels the threat of an unwanted pregnancy, and thus every woman has a stake in repealing the abortion laws." Strategically, the YSA argued that the abortion movement should abandon the earlier call for "free abortion on demand," a slogan that focused attention on medical services, and instead focus on women's legal right to abortion. The issue of abortion law repeal could form the center of a nationwide campaign with the participation of masses of women who might feed into a larger movement to transform America's political system.[58]

In keeping with YSA's philosophy, WONAAC primarily organized mass protests in support of repealing abortion laws. The group's position attracted many adherents, including the local chapters of NOW and FEW. By the fall of 1971, WONAAC had become the most visible abortion rights organization in the city. The D.C. branch joined a class action suit to protest the waiting period proposed by the city council and held public gatherings where women spoke from firsthand experience about back-alley abortions, sterilization, and local abortion regulations.[59] In November 1971, it coordinated the first national abortion rights demonstration in Washington, bringing more than two thousand activists to the Capitol and inspiring antiabortion activists to hurriedly put together a competing protest for the same day. WONAAC's agenda also called for an end to forced sterilization and the elimination of restrictive contraceptive laws, arguing that "restrictive abortion laws provide the basis of legalized murder of thousands of women. Involuntary sterilizations are the price poor women are often forced to pay in order to obtain safe, legal abortions." But these demands were always secondary to the fight for abortion law repeal and never became the focus of WONAAC's campaigns.[60]

Prominent local figures, including Bobby McMahan from the NWRO and Mary Treadwell, formerly of SNCC and now an executive director of Pride, Inc., publicly supported WONAAC. For African American women like Treadwell and McMahan, the coalition offered a place to join the fight for abortion law repeal but still advance a distinct perspective. WONAAC formed a Black Woman's Task Force and in Washington, black women's abortion groups were organized at American University and Howard University. These groups simultaneously provided affiliation with WONAAC, but also conveyed recognition that African American women faced particular dilemmas in the quest for reproductive control.[61]

Indeed, Mary Treadwell kept African American women's distinct concerns at the forefront when she spoke at a press conference that WONAAC organized in October 1971 to announce the founding of its Black Women's Task Force. Treadwell argued that racism in America convinced her of the necessity of abortion law repeal. "The legislators of this country are overwhelmingly white and overwhelmingly male," Treadwell pointed out. "While rejecting legalized abortion," she argued, "these very men sit in hypocritical splendor and refuse to provide an adequate guaranteed annual income for these children born to women without financial and social access to safe abortion. While rejecting legalized abortion, these very men refuse to fund quality, inexpensive pronatal and post-natal care to women without access to abortion . . .[and] refuse to fund quality education and training for the children of women without access to abortions."[62] In addition to highlighting the ways that racism and poverty limited women's reproductive control, Treadwell addressed black liberation activists on the issue of genocide. She argued that African Americans needed to understand that compulsory pregnancy, whether coerced by the government or by liberation activists, denied women's rights and damaged black communities. "Black women," she insisted, "particularly need this personal freedom to be able to fulfill themselves sexually without fear of conception. The outside pressures of this society wreak enough havoc within the black home and the black unit. It is unspeakable that legislated, racist pressures should accompany the black woman to her bedroom and creep insidiously into the center of her bed."[63]

Unlike Treadwell, other abortion supporters rejected WONAAC's approach. The organization's affiliation with the YSA led members of the DCWLM to question the sincerity of WONAAC's support for feminist demands and its role in the dissolution of the MAA. This distrust stemmed from the presence of men in socialist groups and from feminists' perception that WONAAC's attempts to organize women actually masked an effort to enlarge the socialist movement. In addition to suspicion about WONAAC's motives, some former participants in the MAA argued that YSA's single-issue focus on abortion law repeal would not lead to women's liberation.[64] Accusing WONAAC of pandering to the status quo by focusing on repeal, these former MAA members charged that making abortion legal would not make it accessible. "As long as hospitals and clinics can charge exorbitant rates and set their own policies . . . [WONAAC's] so-called 'right-to-choose' will be out of reach of poor women, especially Black and Latin American women."[65] WONAAC's approach also angered Healthwitches, a group with ties to the DCWLM that offered abortion counseling and referrals. Healthwitches objected that WONAAC's single-issue focus on abortion would not lead toward the larger goal of women's liberation; instead, the group anticipated that the movement would disintegrate after that goal was won. In addition, they noted that repealing abortion laws would not make abortions affordable to poor women or give women more control over their bodies. Poor women would still find abortions out of reach and "there would only be one more surgical experience available to us in impersonal hospitals and clinics." A better approach, the Healthwitches insisted, would incorporate the fight for abortion access into a movement to create alternatives to abortion (free prenatal care, free childbirth) and extend health care to every member of society.[66]

Reproductive Rights after *Roe v. Wade*

The 1973 Supreme Court decision upholding women's access to abortion on the grounds of privacy changed the nature of the movement for reproductive rights. The decision affirmed the legality of women's right to choose abortion during the first trimester of pregnancy. An article in *off our backs* called the decision a "significant first start in a continuing struggle for the right to choose." By making abortion legally accessible, the ruling represented a significant victory. But the terms on which *Roe* articulated women's legal right to abortion—in consultation with their doctors, during the first three months of pregnancy, and on the basis of their right to privacy—left ample room for opponents to limit the scope of the ruling. In addition, *Roe* did not secure women's access to abortion free from economic want, nor did the decision address other obstacles that prevented women's reproductive freedom, including the practice of involuntary sterilization.[67]

Antiabortion forces mobilized in response to *Roe,* seeking ways to roll back the rights it recognized. Within a year of the ruling, ten antiabortion bills and two constitutional amendments had been introduced in Congress. Many locales simply resisted compliance with the ruling or restricted the conditions under which abortions were available.[68] Regulations that exploited economic inequalities proved especially effective. The Bartlett Amendment was introduced in 1974 as part of the annual appropriations bill for the Departments of Labor and Health, Education, and Welfare. Under the amendment, none of the money allocated to HEW could be used to pay for or to promote abortions. More specifically, the amendment sought to ban the use of Medicaid payment for abortions, to restrict abortion counseling by any agency that received federal funds, and to prohibit medical schools that received funds from HEW to teach abortion techniques. Congress reconsidered the bill every year until it passed in 1976 under the sponsorship of Senator Henry Hyde.[69]

Opinion polls attested that a vast majority of D.C. residents supported legal abortion rights, some of whom mobilized to prevent Congress from further limiting abortion or declaring the procedure unconstitutional. Others, such as women formally affiliated with DCWLM's counseling service, continued to offer information and referrals to local women.[70] But activists put little emphasis on building alliances and coordinating mass protests. Instead, local feminist organizations used their publications to disseminate information about attacks on abortion rights and the deaths of poor women who could not obtain legal abortions. *Off our backs* reported regularly on congressional and state-level campaigns to restrict the scope of *Roe,* and NOW's newsletter urged readers to let elected officials know that they opposed new limitations. Members of the local NOW chapter used their location in the capital as a base while Congress deliberated restrictive abortion laws, organizing petitions and letter-writing campaigns, testifying at hearings, and lobbying elected officials from critical states. D.C. NOW members were deliberate in their strategies, picking ways to register their opposition that would depict feminists in a favorable light. As one NOW member explained, "Our tactics have to be different from the past. We should be in contrast to Right to Life. We want to show Congress that we have thought this out, that we're not a fringe group. Fanaticism . . . [is] not appreciated on the Hill. Instead, we ask Congress to look at the pros and cons rationally." But although NOW and other feminists' tactics were meant to appeal to elected officials by emphasizing publicity through feminist publications and by minimizing the use of mass protests, activists ensured that smaller numbers of women knew about or cared to join campaigns to fight the Bartlett and Hyde amendments.[71]

Moreover, activists painted the attack on abortion rights in this later period as solely a danger to poor women of color rather than the first shot in a campaign intended to deprive all women of reproductive rights. African American women moved to the forefront of the movement against the proposed amendments, revealing their particular stake in maintaining the right to abortion. In the fall of 1974, "black middle-class Washington women" in the newly formed National Black Feminist Organization lobbied members of Congress against the Bartlett Amendment. They were occasionally joined by representatives of the NWRO. Telling reporters that because most of the Washington residents who received Medicaid benefits were black women, the women argued that they had "to fight for our sisters." The *Washington Afro-American,* which had paid little attention to the topic of abortion before 1973, now spoke against the Bartlett Amendment on the grounds that it discriminated against the poor. Warning that the amendment would send many poor black women "back to the bootleggers and hustlers who promise a complete abortion, no ill effects and no infections," the paper applauded the "ladies" who got out to lobby against the amendment.[72]

Mary Treadwell remained an outspoken advocate for abortion rights and black liberation. In 1975, she testified in Congress against the proposed constitutional amendment to prohibit abortion. As she had argued earlier, Treadwell indicated that abortion was essential to the well-being of black women and children. In order to provide secure, loving homes for children, poor black women needed access to safe, affordable, and legal abortions and better family planning services so they could avoid unwanted pregnancies.[73] Treadwell emphasized these same themes in a letter to the *Washington Star* in 1977. The Hyde Amendment would force women to seek abortions in "the back alleys of our country." Berating opponents, she reasoned, "If just one fourth of the financial resources and fervor which are being used by those who are against abortion had been directed to a working pro-life situation," many African American women would be spared death and young people promised a future free from want.[74]

Despite the energetic efforts of Treadwell and other black women activists, the assault on abortion rights moved forward. Indeed, the tactics and arguments that feminists and other supporters of abortion rights used probably mattered little in the face of the mounting antiabortion movement and increasing conservatism of the times. The approaches taken by abortion supporters in Washington in the years after *Roe* provide evidence, however, of the exceptional nature of the coalitions that formed to press for reproductive rights between 1970 and 1973. Before the *Roe* decision, many feminists saw the reproductive rights campaign as an opportunity to broaden the movement's base by drawing in women who had rejected feminism for ideological or political reasons. Concentrating on reproduction and, by extension, women's health, motherhood, and families, feminists had articulated concerns that presumably all women shared regardless of race, economic means, or sexual identity. The presumed overlap between women's reproductive and health care struggles provided an impetus for white feminists to form alliances, reaching out to welfare rights and black liberation activists. In Washington, African American women and welfare rights recipients had responded affirmatively, publicly supporting reproductive rights and linking that movement to campaigns for economic justice and black liberation. But the victory that *Roe* conveyed, although limited, broke the fragile alliances that formed to support abortion rights and relieved activists from the difficult work of coalescing.

The associations that African American women perceived between poverty, racism, and women's lack of reproductive control provided the motivation to protest the Bartlett and Hyde amendments and other attempts to restrict women's access to abortion. Feeling a sense of connection to the struggles of their "sisters," Treadwell and other African American women stressed the life-and-death issues at stake in abortion debates and brought necessary attention to the lives of poor African American women. Black women's activism also challenged white feminists' supposition of women's commonality by reminding the public about the different circumstances under which women lived and organized politically. By emphasizing poverty and the quality of life in black communities, these activists sidestepped charges that abortion and other forms of birth control endangered African American solidarity and liberation. Positioning themselves squarely on the side of black liberation, they commanded awareness for the distinctive rights due to African American women.

5

Women and Black Liberation

On a fall evening in 1974, more than 800 people crowded into a Howard University auditorium to listen to a presentation on "The Role of Black Women in the Struggle." Taking the podium, Dr. Frances Welsing, a psychiatrist and professor at Howard University School of Medicine, denounced feminism for threatening African American demands for freedom. "I don't feel oppressed by any black man. What white women are struggling for is an equal chance to engage in the oppression of non-white people," Welsing insisted. To advance racial equality, men and women needed to assume distinct roles. Welsing explained that men must shoulder positions of authority because "women are not as strong as men, and there is no way that women could stand up to an all male white army." Instead, women should use their persuasive powers, including withholding sex, until men "decide to take the lead in the black movement." In contrast, Amina Baraka, a leader in the Newark, New Jersey–based Congress of Afrikan People (CAP), held that women's fight against oppression was "inseparable from the struggle to overturn capitalism." Women could play an integral part in CAP's programs and in the larger struggle, as shown by their recent efforts to establish a National Organization of Afrikan Women. While not the main thrust, women's liberation would follow a socialist revolution. The final speaker, Joyce Johnson, a member of the African Liberation Support Committee from North Carolina, asserted that the secondary status black women assumed in racial liberation struggles reflected sex roles found in the larger society. Implying that such practices impeded the cause of African American freedom, Johnson advocated an end to sex stereotyping. "We need every black man and woman on the front line in the struggle against imperialism and racism. Everybody," Johnson urged, "men as well as women, must take care of the children, be able to cook the food and clean the house."[1]

The presence of this gathering at Howard University revealed a vast change from the concerns expressed by NAG members a decade earlier. Whereas students affiliated with NAG generally gave little public attention to gender roles evident in the black freedom movement, the 1974 panel announced that these issues were central to the liberation struggle. The ranging opinions expressed by the speakers demonstrated vigorous disagreement surrounding the connection between feminism and black liberation. Activists might differ over women's proper roles, but the questions raised by women's participation in black liberation campaigns no longer went unnoticed. Throughout the 1960s, African American women had proven their importance to the freedom movement by challenging racially discriminatory institutions, coordinating and attending protests, and helping to create resources to support political struggles. When a new phase of the movement emerged in the late 1960s, women's positions shifted, sometimes becoming more marginal, as was the case in Washington's CORE chapter, where women's status declined with the adoption of ideas that explicitly equated freedom with manhood. Nonetheless, legions of black women remained committed to working through mixed-sex organizations where they pushed against sexism and tried to garner attention for the particular forms of oppression they experienced.

The increasing emphasis on black masculinity that emerged within some parts of the black liberation movement combined with the growing visibility of feminist demands, framing African American women's challenges to sexism and racism. Whether organizing in support of abortion rights or to eradicate sexism within the workplace, by the late 1960s, many black women contended that they could address women's specific concerns without betraying the black community.[2] According to a nationwide poll conducted in 1971, not only did a majority of African American women and men support women's liberation, but they were more likely to do so than their white counterparts. Sympathy for feminist demands was not unequivocal, however, as Inez Smith Reid, head of the D.C.-based Black Women's Community Development Foundation, discovered when she interviewed black female "militants" from across the country in 1971. Her respondents insisted that women needed better economic and employment opportunities, but feared that the women's movement would co-opt the black freedom struggle and undermine relationships between black women and men.[3] In other words, black women and men championed some forms of gender equality but feared feminism's potentially divisive impact.

The roots of this distrust derived from African Americans' firsthand experiences and observations. Few explicitly feminist organizations in Washington made black women feel welcome; consequently, these groups remained overwhelmingly white. White feminists' attempts to speak on behalf of all women, invoking a metaphorical sisterhood of struggle, provoked angry accusations that they exploited the black liberation movement by capitalizing on its ideas and piggybacking on its activities. As one black activist put it, among her African American friends, "those who are not turned off by the concepts of Women's Liberation are turned off by the reality of encountering the white members."[4] White women's liberationists' actions prompted many African American women to repudiate feminism even though they advocated child care, reproductive rights, equal employment opportunities, and other issues that resembled feminists' demands. But by the early 1970s, some African American activists began to identify as "black feminists," a label that carried fewer negative associations and whose meaning they could shape. Embracing a philosophy rooted in both women's and African American liberation struggles, black feminists generally rejected integration into the larger feminist movement. Instead, they articulated a position that analyzed the interconnections of race and sex oppression and remained tied to racial liberation struggles.

Black Power

In its broadest definition, Black Power emphasized self-determination and self-definition by African Americans in every area of life, from personal identity to politics, culture, and economics. Any number of black activists had been expressing these ideas,[5] but in the middle of the 1960s, the concept emerged at the center of the freedom movement after Stokely Carmichael, SNCC's onetime leader and Howard University graduate, used the term *Black Power* to assert racial pride, unity, and empowerment. After 1966, many Americans came to associate Black Power with the Black Panther Party for Self Defense, probably the most prominent and provocative black liberation organization of the era. Members openly carried guns—legal in California—and displayed military-style discipline to demonstrate their insistence on the right of self-defense. As local chapters formed across the country, the party won the support of many who appreciated the Panthers' contributions to their communities. Portrayed as dangerous insurgents, however, the party's activities also garnered sensationalist media coverage and interference from law enforcement. Repressive pressures fostered dissent within party chapters and instigated confrontations between Panthers and the police. Such provocations hampered the party's activities but also increased the group's standing within black and radical communities.[6]

Such sensationalist media images, however, obscured the complexity of demands for Black Power.[7] Rejecting, in various combinations, integration, nonviolence, and assimilation into existing social and political structures, male and female activists called for racial solidarity, control over their own communities and organizations, and an end to police intrusion. In the late 1960s, SNCC and CORE promoted racial separatism as a political strategy, and many prominent members of SNCC began to ideologically link the struggle for racial liberation in America to anticolonial movements in Africa and other parts of the world. The Black Panther Party advocated a class revolution that encompassed a race struggle and prioritized coalition politics as a means to foment this revolution. Other Black Power proponents tried to forge a new culture through scholarship, rituals, and programs that reaffirmed positive aspects of black community and reconsidered white dominance.[8]

Envisioning new social and political relations forced black liberationists to turn to the issue of gender and gender roles. In fact, gender roles became lightning-rod issues in part because of simultaneous occurrences; namely, the growth of the women's liberation movement and the response to Daniel Patrick Moynihan's report, *The Negro Family: The Case for National Action.* Moynihan's report illuminated the alleged social problems that derived from women's familial authority and implied that African American progress lay in promoting male leadership. Although Moynihan was concerned with individual families, black activists applied his analysis to the larger, metaphorical family of the black community, with some arguing that race oppression would be eliminated through initiatives that elevated black men to their rightful places at the head of families and communities. Dr. Frances Welsing's speech at Howard picked up this theme, as did antipoverty initiatives, such as those described in chapter 1, that prioritized job training and placement for men.[9]

Washington's Julius Hobson expressed his thoughts about these issues after he left CORE in 1965 to start the Washington Association of Community Teams (ACT), known on its letterhead as "The Organization of Militants." Declaring family stability and community solidarity as long-range aspirations, ACT's platform encouraged the "cultivation of respect for the dignity of the black man" and exhorted black women "to build our men for leadership in the community and the home."[10] At a time when Hobson and many other black Washingtonians knew how effectively racist laws, hostile police, and even well-meaning white progressives encroached on their freedom, many concluded that community could only be built through emphasizing African Americans' shared struggles rather than by focusing on the ways class and sex differences threatened racial solidarity.

Other activists joined Frances Welsing in targeting feminism as a force that would block liberation initiatives. Reginald Booker, who had belonged to D.C.'s CORE chapter, criticized feminism for promoting individual women's ambitions and preventing black unity. Booker alleged that the women's liberation movement was irrelevant to African Americans because it represented "a phenomena among white middle class women who want to do what they want to do." Booker acknowledged that black women suffered from "the economic lynching of the black male," but he also accused them of being manipulated by white men in order to keep black men subservient. "In a lot of instances," Booker explained, "there are black women who make more money than their husbands because of the fact that the white man sees it feasible . . . [to] use the black woman as a buffer against the black male." Eldridge Cleaver of the Black Panther Party similarly argued that black women allied with white men in a war against black men, although, he claimed, women frequently did so unknowingly. Such imagined alliances simply ignored African American women's victimization at the hands of white men. So did Booker's statements diminish black women's accomplishments, attributing African American women's success to white men's desire to foster competition between black men and women. Depicting African American women as tools of white supremacy, Booker and Cleaver revealed their distrust of black women and suggested that women's progress might undermine black liberation.[11]

Female activists, such as those who spoke at Howard, also jumped into this debate about sex roles and racial liberation. Unlike Reginald Booker and Eldridge Cleaver, black women frequently acknowledged that women confronted distinct forms of oppression but many avoided arguing that women should pursue their own interests. Inez Smith Reid of the Black Women's Community Development Foundation (BWCDF), supported women's initiatives to strengthen African American communities. The BWCDF funded programs to assist female juvenile delinquents and women offenders as well as economic development projects that targeted women as their constituents. Reid insisted, however, that the organization never worked "exclusively for women" because black women's work traditionally extended to the entire community. "Blacks haven't been afforded the luxury of helping one portion of the community," Reid claimed, because "the overall need has always been so great."[12] In contrast, Gwen Patton, who was immersed in antiwar and antipoverty organizing in the black community, resisted demands that women take a back seat to men. Like her coworker at Pride, Inc., Mary Treadwell, Patton believed that African American liberation required cooperation between the sexes. She reminded her sisters in a 1970 article, "We must try to realize that we are building a whole and complete army. We have yet to know about a Revolution that was waged by men only. In fact, we have yet to know about rebellions when only the men threw bricks at the cops. We are talking about a People's Army which includes men, women, and children who are fanatics about their freedom."[13]

To Make a Black University

As the 1960s progressed, the ideas of students at Howard University were transformed by local and national movements for black liberation, women's liberation, and students' rights. By the middle of the decade, the efforts begun by NAG to reform the University blossomed into a mass movement to eliminate campus practices that promoted students' acculturation into a homogeneous middle class while suppressing collective action. Despite widespread civil rights activism off campus, Howard administrators had continued to reinforce conservative social mores by emphasizing propriety over politics and, according to student activist Tony Gittens, treating students like children. When Paula Giddings arrived on campus in 1965, she found with disappointment that Howard was generally untouched by the political ferment sweeping the country. Giddings also was appalled by the excessive attention that male students paid to women's appearance. After Adrienne Manns enrolled at Howard in 1964, she disappointedly discovered that few courses focused on African American literature, history, or music. Rather than keeping up with the times and trying to build racial solidarity that could be the basis for addressing problems that troubled black society, Manns concluded that the university supported the status quo by educating the elite for their own success.[14]

By the fall of 1966, however, the black liberation movement intruded on campus life, igniting a fire that transformed Howard's culture and the ideas of many students. When Stokely Carmichael spoke on campus in 1966, two years after his graduation, more than 1,500 students cheered his call for a "revival of blackness." To thunderous applause, Carmichael insisted that "White America cannot condemn herself so we have done it. We condemn her." He warned the students of the need to join the revolution: "you are black brothers and sisters and you better come home. . . . If you don't come on home, the gate is going to be closed."[15] Moved by Carmichael and other Black Power proponents, students on campus between 1966 and 1970 rushed to support the black liberation movement by uniting in a race-conscious movement to remake Howard.

Increasing activism on campus in these years stimulated dialogue regarding the role of educated women and men in black liberation struggles. The campaign to choose the homecoming queen in the fall of 1966 symbolically marked the start of the Howard student movement. Typically, fraternities picked the candidates, supporting the women who visually—by way of skin color, clothing, and overall image—represented mainstream ideals of beauty. But in 1966, a group of students backed Robin Gregory because her experience as an activist, her academic standing, and her hair represented Black Power and racial pride. Gregory had worked with D.C. SNCC in 1964, serving as a liaison between the Washington office and field staff in Mississippi. Through this work she met female civil rights workers who wore their hair naturally and inspired her to do the same. Gregory treated her candidacy as an opportunity to raise political issues, expressing her impatience with the campus's politically conservative and sexist environment. To the surprise of many, and to the consternation of the university's administration, Gregory won the position. In a sign that students connected her candidacy with Black Power, when Gregory was coronated in the fall of 1966, people spontaneously celebrated by marching out of the ceremony, through campus, and into the surrounding neighborhoods chanting "Umgawa, Black Power." Gregory embodied the new generation of African American campus activists and her appearance reflected students' commitment to developing racially specific forms of leadership. Ewart Brown, who became president of the student assembly the following spring, declared that natural hair sent a message about the transformation under way in black America.[16] To student Paula Giddings, Gregory's campaign exemplified the new movement "not just in terms of politics but in terms of what women should be doing as well."[17] The event was emblematic in other ways too, foreshadowing the popularity that black nationalism would reach, the importance of cultural demonstrations of "blackness," and the position of women in that movement.

The emerging emphasis on Black Power combined with student frustration over university policies led to frequent disruptions during the subsequent years. By one count, more than 115 separate incidents of student unrest occurred between December 1966 and June 1969. These incidents typically took place at administrative buildings or in the Women's Quadrangle, the area adjacent to the women's dormitories.[18] Robin Gregory especially nettled the administration by playing a leading role in protests rather than settling into a more traditional role for the university's most prominent woman student. She helped coordinate a protest, for example, during a 1967 visit to campus by Lewis B. Hershey, head of the Selective Service agency. As the United States increased its military presence in Vietnam, Hershey's visit and Howard's ROTC requirement, mandatory for all male students, seemed to show the school's complicity with a federal mission that risked black men's lives for a questionable cause. Gregory and other students hung Hershey's likeness in effigy and disrupted his speech by chanting "America is the black man's battleground." The university tried to expel Gregory and other activists accused of orchestrating the demonstration and announced new policies limiting future protests, but students responded by boycotting classes and insisting that no disciplinary action be taken in retaliation for political activities.[19]

The chant that "America is the black man's battleground" resonated among a student population that both feared the effect of the Vietnam conflict on black communities and supported black men's fight against racism within the United States. These priorities reverberated in the language students used to protest university policy. Metaphorically associating militance with manliness, students attacked institutions that allegedly prevented the development of strong male leaders. Student leader Tony Gittens claimed that the college "emasculated" black men, continuing a process begun by their mothers. According to Gittens, university personnel thwarted students' independence by dictating what to wear, how to decorate their rooms, and even when to bathe. Holding both the university and mothers responsible for the "weakened" condition of black male students, Gittens's charge associated women—and those who acted like women—with supporting the political and social status quo. Male political leadership, in contrast, would seek to transform the status quo and promote men's self-determination over their education.[20]

Gittens's analysis of families and universities echoed ideas advanced in Moynihan's report, *The Negro Family: The Case for National Action.* Extending Moynihan's matriarchy thesis beyond the role of women per se, Gittens argued that "Negro" institutions deprived male students of their manhood. He thus linked "Negroes" and women together as collaborators in an effort to subordinate black men and resist the rise of militant—and male—revolutionaries. Other African American activists similarly associated "Negro" with outdated aspirations for assimilation into white society and acceptance of middle-class values. In the case of Howard, students argued that the university's dependence on federal funding made it a "Negro" institution, whereas a "black" school would function autonomously. H. Rap Brown, a SNCC leader and Washington resident, distinguished the terms in his 1969 autobiography. According to Brown, "negro america . . . is a mirror of the big white world and does the white world's job inside the Black community. Negro america becomes the official policeman for white america." In contrast, "blackness" rebelled against white and "Negro" mores. "The biggest difference between being known as a Black man or a negro is that if you're Black, then you do everything you can to fight white folks. If you're negro, you do everything you can to appease them," Brown explained.[21] Howard professor Nathan Hare expressed similar sentiments: the Black Power movement on campuses aimed to "overthrow . . . the Negro college with white innards and to raise in its place a militant black university which will counteract the whitewashing black students now receive in 'Negro' and white institutions."[22]

Influenced by Black Power ideology, the sentiments of their male peers, and, no doubt, their own sense of obligation, women played a distinct role in the escalating protests at Howard. Although Gittens associated women with political conservatism, on campus, women students engaged in protest activities alongside, and separate from, their male counterparts. One day in February 1968, more than 100 women protested after campus police allegedly mistreated students involved in a disturbance at the Women's Quadrangle. Several months later, residents of a women's dorm boycotted against high prices at a campus eatery.[23] These incidents demonstrated women's political agency and skill as organizers, traits nurtured by the communities they established within their dormitories. Without the leadership or participation of men, women students took action on their own behalf.

But when women and men joined together in protests, the philosophy that associated male leadership with political militancy and dominance surfaced to shape the roles that students played. Affirmations of manhood sometimes reinforced women's sexual objectification by stressing their availability to Howard men. In early 1968, protests centered on the Women's Quadrangle, where students attempted to destroy a fence the university erected to restrict them from congregating in the area. Students objected to the fence as a barrier that prevented men's access to women's living space. And on one day, several male students reportedly ran through the Women's Quadrangle in their underwear to indicate their support for Black Power. These protests subtly demonstrated cultural expectations that women were supposed to be sexually available to men, a conviction reinforced by the simultaneous lack of collective outrage about the sexual harassment women students endured.[24]

Such patterns were evident in the spring of 1968, when more than 1,000 students took over the administration building for what became a four-day siege.[25] In the absence of the regular staff, students took responsibility for running the switchboard, cleaning the administration building, and drumming up donations from local restaurants. Five students were selected to meet with administration officials and trustees to discuss students' grievances and negotiate an end to the sit-in. This group included Adrienne Manns, who, as editor-in-chief of the student newspaper, the *Hilltop,* occupied a prominent role on campus. To Tony Gittens, another student representative, Manns and other women were well suited to negotiate with the administration and trustees because they were bright, articulate, and assertive. Although women possessed these admirable qualities, Gittens detected that women deferred to men's inclination to take visible leadership roles. Implying that women felt impatience with men's grandstanding, Gittens remembered that women preferred to "not be in front of the camera and to get along with the work that needed to be done." Manns concurred that men generally were "up front" in political activities on campus, including the takeover, although, unlike Gittens, she did not attribute such behavior to women's preferences for behind-the-scenes work.[26]

The gender patterns described by Gittens and Manns spread beyond the student leadership to the masses taking part in the takeover. Despite participating in equal numbers, women's and men's involvement differed, with men becoming public speakers and offering physical protection while women followed instructions and mobilized support from individuals and small groups. Marilyn Robinson, a senior, was told by one of the student leaders to manage the university switchboard, informing callers that they had reached "the new Howard University."[27] Other women spread word of the revolt within the student body. According to two journalists for the *Hilltop,* throughout the takeover, "squadrons of black sisters canvassed every building on the main campus urging bodily support of the demonstration by talking to individual students and making verbal announcements to classes or written announcements on the blackboards." As women mobilized students, men pronounced their collective demands. "Most of the young men gathered on the front steps of the 'A' Building with loudspeakers in hand. They sang songs of indignation about the conditions at Howard," the *Hilltop* reported. In case university employees or the police attempted to turn the students out of the administration building, "a special corps of Black brothers were prepared to protect their 'home' and sisters" by surrounding the building, while "the sisters were instructed to proceed in an orderly way to the second and third floors and remain seated."[28]

In the aftermath of the takeover, students won concessions from the university that expanded opportunities for student governance and ended policies that had restricted political activism. The administration gradually lifted curfews that confined women students to their dormitories during particular hours and allowed men in women's residences. In 1970, the university opened its first mixed-sex dormitory. The curriculum expanded to offer new courses in African American history, music, literature, and black studies, and a greater community orientation emerged. As some of the barriers between the university and the community lifted, representatives of activist groups came more freely onto campus and students were encouraged to get involved in political projects, although some students and off-campus activists continued to push the university to do more to become relevant to the needs of the masses of the country's black citizens.[29] By 1972, black nationalism pervaded campus politics, according to a survey that found nearly two-thirds of Howard's freshmen characterized themselves as political "radicals" or "liberals." Giving meaning to these labels, such students indicated they supported educational reforms that would continue to decrease the administration's influence over campus life, while concurrently boosting their own role in setting policies. Those surveyed also criticized the federal government for failing to do enough to ensure black equality and women's autonomy in the areas of education, employment, and family planning.[30]

Regulations and political attitudes changed; however, women's role on campus generally did not. One student remembered that "women were less than welcome" in many campus activities, recalling that activists "wanted the bodies [participation of women] but they didn't want to hear what you had to say." Continuing the pattern seen with Robin Gregory's selection as homecoming queen, students measured women's value to black liberation in terms of their bodies, using physical traits to convey militancy and to reject white standards of beauty. Some students observed that even when they proved their political commitment to racial liberation by taking part in protests, their colleagues pressured them to change their appearance, especially rejecting straightened hair as proof of their blackness.[31] Michele Wallace, who attended Howard for one semester in 1969, chafed at the overt sexism. She observed that "the 'new Blackness' was fast becoming the new slavery for sisters." Having recently begun to identify herself as a black feminist, Wallace soon left the university, "a place designed to acquaint you with the shortcomings of black female status if ever there was one. Between the fraternities and the Black Power antics, misogyny ran amok on a daily basis down there," Wallace later wrote. When Loretta Ross arrived in the fall of 1970, her political consciousness was awakened after she was introduced to two important books, Alex Haley's *Autobiography of Malcolm X* and Toni Cade's anthology, *The Black Woman*. But although the practice of passing such literature among students helped build racial consciousness and community, Ross encountered pervasive sexism that threatened women's opportunities to participate as full and equal members of campus life.[32]

Unlike Wallace and Ross, other women celebrated the distinction between women's and men's roles and embraced distinct gender norms as a foundation for black unity and community improvement. In 1970, a group of more than 200 female students started an organization, WOMB, to work with young children in the city. Their name was not an acronym but a word chosen to connote the kind of "fertility and nurturing that is necessary" for black family and community growth. According to Roselyn Smith, one of the group's founders, WOMB accepted the mission to educate "the black woman politically and spiritually to aid in the liberation of all black people." Their main project, "Operation Zygote," ran recreational and educational programs for black children. Smith indicated that black women could play an important role in liberating the race through "trying to build up the family system which has been torn down. And it is our hope that by working with our men, we can liberate them." Harkening back to Moynihan's claim that black women succeeded at men's expense, WOMB women committed themselves to "removing ourselves from a position of perpetual dominance to stand beside our men; inspiring new potentials and talents as individuals."[33]

By 1970, a burgeoning feminist movement gave WOMB an ideological foil to contrast with its own vision. WOMB's representatives generally viewed women's liberation and black community growth as incompatible because individualism and racism pervaded feminists' demands. Feminism's "preoccupation with Free sex, birth control," and gay rights, WOMB claimed, would work against black activists' efforts to strengthen families.[34] Responding to the D.C. Women's Liberation Movement and NOW's call for women to join the August 26th Strike Day, a WOMB member told the press, "The white Women's Liberation Movement wants to segregate the woman from her man, while WOMB wants to develop the unity of the black man and woman." Further explicating their position, WOMB members argued that feminism was both irrelevant and in contradiction to black liberation. According to the group, the feminist movement "negates everything WOMB stands for. The white woman seeks to liberate herself by not doing things such as washing dishes and taking care of her family. WOMB recognizes these things as means of unifying the family and liberating black people."[35]

Student Association Secretary Pamely Preston expressed similar views when she told a *Washington Post* reporter that women's liberation held little significance for African Americans. "As far as I'm concerned," she said, "the women's liberation movement is trite, trivial, and simple. It's just another white political fad." Preston deemed white feminists' issues frivolous in comparison to the serious concerns of African Americans. "Black people have some of the same problems that they had when they were first brought to this country. That's what we've got to deal with." She conceded that negative stereotypes harmed black women, including depictions of African American females as "loud, obstinate, domineering, emasculating and generally immoral." But she did not believe the damage caused by such caricatures warranted adding women's liberation to the black agenda.[36]

Black Panther Party

Formed in California in 1966, the Black Panther Party for Self Defense (BPP) spread across the country, establishing chapters in major cities and producing some of the most prominent radical activists of the day: Huey Newton, Eldridge and Kathleen Cleaver, Bobby Seale, and Angela Davis all claimed allegiance to the group at one time.[37] The party attempted to merge a black nationalist ideology with a commitment to socialism. Party members initially concentrated on organizing society's dispossessed—members of the black working class, street people, prisoners, and the poor—without whom the BPP considered revolution impossible. The Panthers' approach, however, appealed to a much broader constituency of activists who mobilized at the local level to battle abuses of state power and coordinated projects to strengthen black neighborhoods and build racial solidarity.[38]

In D.C., a BPP chapter formed in the summer of 1970 and operated through 1973, albeit with frequent changes in membership, location, and programs. The chapter struggled to recruit members and sustain its programs, buffeted by internal dissension exacerbated by federal law enforcement surveillance and interference. Police frequently arrested D.C. members for doing no more than distributing literature. Although members typically were acquitted of the charges against them, the arrests disrupted the chapter's programs by tying up money for bail and holding people in jail.[39] Police raids forced the chapter to relocate its offices and programs several times between 1969 and 1972, generally moving into spaces in the northwest section of the city not far from Pride, Inc., and the D.C. Women's Liberation Movement. Infiltration by the FBI makes any figures problematic, but the D.C. chapter claimed more than 100 members at its inception, falling to forty by 1973.[40]

Local party activists tried to satisfy Washington residents' demands for protection from abuse and for better housing, transportation, and jobs. Like WOMB, the Panthers emphasized that black Americans were engaged "in a long struggle and our wealth and reserves are manifested in our children." Racial liberation would come from making the next generation strong in mind and body, an effort that required meeting the daily needs of city residents and creating programs to politically educate young people.[41] Concentrating on the city's poor, the BPP attempted to make up for deficiencies in antipoverty programs that they believed intentionally operated to suppress black militancy. Malik Edwards, who joined the chapter in 1970, suspected that the government intentionally pumped money into the poverty agencies in order to turn people away from more militant groups. "Nobody was going to follow the Panthers if they could go down to the poverty program and get a check," Edwards reflected.[42] Like all party chapters, the D.C. Panthers provided free breakfasts to children, an effort hampered by police raids, which depleted the funds available to run the program.[43] After-school programs delivered pan-Africanist education and recreation, while Hard Knocks University at H and 3rd Streets, NE, offered classes to adults as an alternative to expensive, exclusive, and politically moderate colleges in the area. All programs emphasized the growth of political consciousness. "First the revolution must take place inside one's own mind," chapter members wrote to the *Black Panther.* "For revolutionaries, that which advances the struggle for self-determination and national salvation should be considered moral and anything that holds back the struggle should be immoral," the authors argued.[44]

In addition to the breakfast program, Washington's BPP chapter distributed free clothing and food and arranged free transportation to banks for elderly residents who needed to cash or deposit welfare and Social Security checks. Twice a month, the BPP arranged buses to Lorton Reformatory, taking family and friends to the remote Virginia penal facility run by the D.C. Department of Correction. By providing free travel to visit the prison, the D.C. party helped incarcerated men stay connected to their loved ones and, the Panthers' believed, thereby helped prisoners maintain a sense of autonomy despite the oppressiveness of jail. The People's Free Health Service operated a clinic in a southeast D.C. church basement, where Howard University medical students volunteered their time to provide limited medical treatment to "anybody who needs the care and doesn't have the money." Health service workers also went throughout the city, testing people for hypertension and sickle cell anemia, a blood disorder that almost exclusively affects African Americans.[45]

These survival programs consumed most of party members' and volunteers' time and attention, and distinguished the BPP's work from that of SNCC or welfare rights activists, who primarily used direct action protests to try to influence public policy and pressure public officials to respond to residents' demands. Catherine Showell, a nurse who served as the People's Free Health Clinic's health coordinator, reassured *Washington Post* readers that the project's purpose was community survival, not destruction. "We aren't going to shoot anybody," Showell asserted, acknowledging the group's reputation. "This is a survival program to bring quality medical care to the people. Soon a lot of the city's hospitals are going to close their doors to the indigent. We are going to help those people. . . . Illness doesn't have a color bar. Why should we?"[46]

From its inception, the BPP encouraged women's involvement, calling on them to struggle alongside men for liberation. By some estimates, they composed two-thirds of the national organization's members. Women headed chapters in New York, New Haven, and Boston; Elaine Brown of Oakland eventually headed the national party. On the local level, women often ran survival programs and many served as officer-of-the-day, in charge of daily operations. Arrests and police apprehensions disrupted party hierarchy, blurring the lines between those designated to leadership roles on the chapter level and those who were not appointed to formal leadership. As a result, rank-and-file women's contributions and commitment to the party generally were seen as equal in value to men's.[47]

Unlike Black Power activists at Howard, the Panthers condemned women's exploitation and tried to implement guidelines to govern men's treatment of their female counterparts. Drawing its ideas about revolutions from the examples of Cuba, Vietnam, Russia, and China, the Panthers understood that women could join revolutionary armies and classless societies could emerge from attempts to create communal lifestyles. Despite the Panthers' philosophical commitment to gender equality, the stubbornness of sexism required persistent attention. Early on, the party's minister of education, Eldridge Cleaver, warned that sexist behavior contradicted the group's political goals. "We have to recognize our women as our equals," he insisted in a 1969 article, committing the party to fighting sexism because "revolutionary standards of principles demand that we go to great lengths to see that disciplinary action is taken on all levels against those who manifest male chauvinism." A directive issued by the Panther leadership soon after, "8 Points of Attention," ordered members to "not take liberties with women." In Washington, the local chapter publicly supported campaigns on behalf of women's issues, viewing these as an extension of their own efforts. In 1970, a chapter representative joined members of sixteen other D.C. groups in issuing a press release supporting a welfare rights campaign to win supplemental furniture grants. That same summer, Black Panthers attended the August 26th Women's Strike for Equality, the same event that WOMB shunned, selling their newspapers and supporting the cause. Thus, rather than advancing racial liberation based on a gender hierarchy that promoted men's leadership, the Panthers advocated gender equality as a way to advance a political and social revolution.[48]

Despite the party's protestations against male chauvinism and in favor of women's liberation, women nonetheless experienced restraints on their activities. Nkenge Toure was recruited to the party as a Baltimore high school student. Assigned to work in the District's chapter in 1971, Toure performed many jobs: she sold the Panther newspaper, helped run the breakfast program and the prison program, served as officer-of-the-day, and coordinated outreach for the People's Free Health Service. After most chapter members moved to California in 1972 when the party consolidated its activities, Toure stayed behind to coordinate the People's Free Health Clinic.[49] Despite her pivotal role in the D.C. chapter, Toure realized that something less than full gender equality shaped her private relations within the BPP community. Panther members lived communally in order to facilitate their political work and replace traditional families with structures that would prefigure revolutionary ways of living. Within these groups, Washington party members still adhered to a sexual division of labor, however. In the house where Toure lived, women "wound up doing the cooking, extending sexual favors, and feeling taken advantage of." In addition to caring for men, women looked out for party members' children, an assignment that perpetuated the association of women with domesticity. Men could date, or "deal with" women from outside the party, but women were expected to reserve their personal attentions for party members. Thus, not only were women expected to shoulder domestic responsibilities in addition to their other jobs, but they also experienced more constraints than men.[50]

Whether such rules were intended as proprietary or protective, they shaped women's relationship to the party. But rather than causing women to flee the party in objection to double standards, many downplayed the impact of male chauvinism relative to the camaraderie and feelings of belonging that party membership nurtured. Toure belonged to the party for several years and married another member. Osa Massen, who became a community worker in 1970, considered the party a family that welcomed her into its folds. The self-described troubled teen watched out for members' children, sold the *Black Panther* newspaper, and staffed an information table outside the party's office. Through her participation, Massen grew self-confident and politically conscious, and she appreciated the opportunity to make a meaningful contribution to her community. Assuming roles as little sister and wife within the family created by the local chapter, Massen and Toure gained security and seized opportunities to grow in confidence and skill. In contrast, Adrienne Manns resisted joining the chapter. Despite her affinity with aspects of the Panther's politics, her dislike for the group's gangster image kept Manns from seriously considering working with the group.[51]

In 1970, the Panthers acted to explicitly articulate the elimination of women's oppression as a revolutionary demand when it organized the Revolutionary People's Constitutional Convention (RPCC). Washington BPP member Gerald Wood announced in the *Black Panther* that the RPCC would gather activists in Philadelphia during Labor Day weekend in order to inscribe their visions into a new Constitution for the United States. Open to all revolutionary activists, the convention demonstrated the BPP's support for a movement to unite oppressed peoples, regardless of race, sex, sexual orientation, or economic status. By coordinating the gathering, the BPP could assert its place at the vanguard of this revolutionary movement.[52]

The BPP's planned convention coincided with a mounting concern for sexism and a call for women to play a more prominent role in party activities. In August, a month before the convention, Huey Newton, supreme commander and a party founder, published an article in the *Black Panther* newspaper encouraging Panthers to recognize gays and women as oppressed groups and to welcome members of these liberation movements as allies.[53] A few months later, *Quicksilver Times,* one of Washington's underground newspapers, printed an extended interview with two anonymous Panther women about women's role within the party and the party's reaction to the women's liberation movement. The women declared their commitment to ending male chauvinism in the BPP and exhorted their sisters to take on greater responsibility within the party. The party viewed sexism as bourgeois behavior, they explained. "In a proletarian revolution," the women told *Quicksilver Times,* "the emancipation of women is primary. We realize that the success of the revolution depends upon the women." Therefore, black men had to realize that their "manhood is not dependent upon the subordination of black women, but rather . . . manhood is, in fact, dependent on [the] strength he also gets from a revolutionary relationship. A relationship is more fruitful when, in fact, the woman is the other half and not the weaker half." Hinting that women's position in the party had been a topic of concern, the anonymous women asserted that a transformation of women's role in the BPP was under way: "Sisters have been writing more articles, they're attending more to the political aspects of the Party: they're speaking out in public more and we've even done outreach work in the community."[54]

The vast ideological differences that challenged coalition politics were on display when 6,000 representatives from women's liberation, gay liberation, New Left, and black groups assembled in Philadelphia to draft a new constitution. Huey Newton delivered an address that championed fellowship among all oppressed people and stressed that unity would emerge from the shared struggle to attain human dignity.[55] But Newton's call for solidarity reaffirmed the party's recognition of the differences that distinguished conference participants. Convention organizers had delegates break into identity-based groups. Separate workshops, led by Panther members, gave gay men, women, workers, artists, street people, political prisoners, and the elderly an opportunity to develop platforms to present to the larger body. Delegates produced documents calling for neighborhood control of police, schools, the courts, and the means of production. A women's workshop affirmed "the right of all women to be free," a goal that could be attained through the creation of communal households and the elimination of patriarchal families; the guarantee of equal employment and adequate incomes; the end of sexist education and sexually exploitative media; and women's training in self-defense and weaponry. Women also needed free and safe contraception, delegates declared, and to be rid of forced sterilization and coercive birth control programs meant to prohibit poor people and women of color from controlling their fertility.[56]

Despite the comprehensive statement issued by the RPCC delegates regarding women's right to self-determination, the convention seemed to generate conflict rather than an interracial alliance in support of women's liberation. Disagreement related primarily to the distinct ways that white feminists, such as those in the DCWLM, and women in the Black Panthers chose to pursue women's liberation. Whereas the DCWLM and other radical feminists advocated most of the proposals forwarded by the RPCC women's workshop, they resisted language and activities that seemed to make women's liberation secondary to other causes. DCWLM members, along with radical white feminists from New York, felt slighted when Huey Newton's speech failed to mention feminism and gay liberation but declared that "we will have our manhood even if we have to level the earth." A female Panther led the women's workshop, but according to some white feminists, the presence of male guards lining the walls made the atmosphere inhospitable.[57] These acts led some feminists to question the party's commitment to gender equality. For their part, the Panther organizers criticized feminists for trying to control the gathering. Some party members questioned the depth of white activists' commitment to working on an equal basis with black activists. According to one male BPP representative, the party leadership was consumed with "trying to deal with the demands of several different radical white factions, while Women's Liberation [was] trying to run everything."[58]

The Panthers held a follow-up convention in Washington two months later, intending to introduce the new Constitution and establish the new "government of the people."[59] But a flood of organizational and ideological obstacles stalled the process and exacerbated tensions among activists. Negotiations to hold the convention at Howard University broke down when the school imposed a large fee for the use of their facilities. The BPP attributed Howard's unreasonableness to the general lack of support it enjoyed on a campus where students strongly opposed interracial alliances. But other local activists pitched in to help with local arrangements. Washington's Gay Liberation Front and the D.C. Women's Liberation Movement collected food and organized transportation. Local churches provided space for registration and for an opening rally, and a local college made rooms available for women convention participants to hold discussions separate from the larger gathering.[60]

An estimated 2,500 to 7,000 activists attended the November convention, a number much smaller than the 25,000 the Panthers anticipated, but still a sizeable gathering for a Thanksgiving weekend. Because of organizational problems, however, none of the planned constitutional sessions actually convened. And, in a repeat of Philadelphia, dissension mired the attempt to generate a sense of unity among proponents of a revolution. Instead, participants representing diverse constituencies attempted to use the gathering to promote their own agendas.[61]

Radical feminists tried to use the conference to build solidarity among women. Disillusioned after Philadelphia, they vowed to continue a relationship with the Panthers and not turn against a group already facing severe repression at the hands of the government. Throughout the fall, DCWLM members planned for the RPCC by discussing sexism, racism, and their participation in the larger revolutionary movement. Consequently, the D.C. feminists had anticipated that the November RPCC would foster a productive exchange of ideas leading to deeper awareness of oppression. As they remarked in an article encouraging other feminists to come to Washington, "Through our contacts and experiences with third world liberation struggles we become more conscious of our racism and privilege." Revealing their own assumptions about other activists, however, they argued that other women would benefit from learning from feminists. "We intend," they wrote, "that third world contact with revolutionary women will enable them to become more conscious of sexism."[62]

Ultimately, more than 500 women, mainly white radical feminists and revolutionary activists, congregated during the RPCC to discuss women's relation to the black and Left movements. Over several days, they considered how they could organize a revolutionary movement focused on racism, imperialism, the Vietnam War, child care and the socialization of children, lesbianism, work, aging, media, culture, and health care.[63] Washington feminists placed great significance on gathering with other women to discuss sex-based issues, but most black women avoided these sessions. At the same time, attitudes expressed by Panthers' irked radical feminists. In a keynote address, Huey Newton consistently used "man" and "manhood" to describe human beings and human dignity. When members of the audience interrupted his speech in protest, Newton asserted his support for women's equality and conceded that his language reflected his "bourgeois tendencies." He acknowledged that women previously had been forced into an inferior role in the BPP but described a transformation in the BPP that women initiated. "As we adapted our political understanding," Newton claimed, "we saw that the resources that we had in the Party were not being used." Newton went on to credit women party members with convincing the group that "women are the most oppressed of the oppressed."[64]

Despite Newton's concessions, few bonds were forged between black and white women activists. White feminists emerged from the weekend disappointed by the BPP's response to women's liberation, disturbed at the difficulty in unifying female activists, and dismayed at prospects for working within the larger radical movement. Their commitment to organizing separately from men became stronger, leading some to form a lesbian feminist collective shortly after. At least one black woman at the RPCC meetings in Washington challenged white feminists not to withdraw from Third World struggles as a result of their dissatisfaction with the Panthers. She pointed out that white women "tend to view the Panthers as the only group of third world revolutionaries" and, moreover, noted "the tendency is to feel at opposite poles from the whole third world liberation struggle" when in disagreement with the Panthers.[65]

For black activists who viewed their white counterparts as incapable of sharing power, the November conference reinforced frustration at white co-optation and control. Prior to the gathering, Pearl Stewart, the Howard University *Hilltop* editor, used her position at the paper to criticize both the Panthers and their white allies. Raising the specter that the black movement was being exploited by outsiders, and implying that representatives of other movements were weak or lazy, Stewart argued, "I don't believe that black people should . . . align themselves with the Gay Liberation Front or the Women's Liberation Front. I think if these people feel . . . that their rights have been overlooked and that they need to . . . make their grievances known that they should do this on their own front and not use Bobby Seale as a hero."[66] After the RPCC, an anonymous editorial in the Howard *Hilltop* expressed particular anxiety about gay men's presence at the convention. Rather than anger at white dependence on black radicals, this editorial writer stressed that interracial alliances put African American activists under the control of white activists with dubious agendas. By working with white activists at the RPCC, the BPP allowed itself to be controlled by the agenda of "white boys . . . white fags and rejects," who opposed the nationalist sentiments heard on Howard's campus. The university's students, by contrast had "learned that there is no point in trying to help a nigger who's got a whitey on his back. . . . It's not rational for Black people in 1970 to be still following the dictates of white radicals, or even to be dealing with them at all." Instead, the editorial argued, "Black people must come together, with or without the Panthers, but definitely without whites, for our own survival and liberation. We have no more time to waste, trying to accommodate Blacks who have more interest in gay whites than in their own oppressed people."[67]

White activists, too, took a pessimistic stance toward the RPCC. Reporters for *Quicksilver Times,* a Washington underground paper, found little positive to say. "By nearly any standard," the paper concluded, "the bleak weekend of the Revolutionary People's Constitutional Convention caused more problems than it solved." Outlining the difficulties, the reporter continued, "In terms of the original objective—the writing and ratification of a constitution—it failed. In terms of promoting a strong sense of black-white revolutionary cohesion, most people left Washington, D.C. depressed, frustrated and complaining. In terms of strengthening black internal solidarity, it widened the split between the Black Panther Party and black nationalists."[68]

In many ways, the lessons of the RPCC were similar to those of earlier alliances that the DCWLM had joined. The attempt to form coalitions brought black liberation, gay liberation, and women's liberation groups into contact in new ways. But even among those who shared common goals, political priorities and strategies came into conflict; direct interaction at the RPCC exacerbated, rather than smoothed, these differences. Black students at Howard who refused to join with activists whose motives they distrusted found no reassurances to correct their earlier impressions. Likewise, feminists left the RPCC with confirmation of their belief that they should organize separately from men and African American women. Some lesbian feminists in Washington became convinced that they could form a revolutionary vanguard, replacing the Panthers as the constituency most able to foment a movement for sex, class, and racial liberation. The RPCC forced the D.C. Panthers, too, to reassess their commitment to interracial organizing and to eventually conclude that interracial alliances left the party in a "twilight zone," unable either to boost their support in the city's black neighborhoods or to make headway building an antiracist revolution with white activists.[69] The conventions, then, appeared to be an instance when familiarity bred contempt. Attempting to find common ground gave activists something concrete to criticize, accentuating differences and disagreement and leading to retrenchment rather than expanded alliances.

Black Liberation and Feminism

In the fall of 1974, when hundreds assembled for the Howard University symposium on the position of African American women in racial liberation struggles, a much smaller group of women from the Washington chapter of the National Black Feminist Organization (NBFO) began to gather for consciousness raising. Members met in similar groups in eight chapters across the country. Disinclined to expect either white women or black men to address their race and sex-specific concerns, the fifteen Washington members of the NBFO gathered for discussion and to undertake projects to eradicate the particular forms of oppression they experienced. As Jo Benoit, one of the founders in D.C., put it, "We can't expect anyone to organize around the specific oppressions that black women experience: not white women, because they don't experience racism; not black men, because they don't encounter sexism."[70] Along with participants in NBFO chapters elsewhere, Washington members stressed the importance of building unity among African American women, nurtured through consciousness raising and political activities.

Emerging at the intersection of movements for women's liberation and racial liberation, the NBFO demonstrated black Washingtonians' changing perspectives on feminism. At Howard University, women's roles as mothers, wives, and helpmates had been treated as a point of strength by WOMB and as a sign of racial progress by those swayed by Moynihan's thesis. By 1974, however, the particular role that women played in community development and in political movements became an issue for open debate on campus and elsewhere.[71] As participants at the RPCC had done, many African American women showed a willingness to embrace issues that formed the core of white feminists' demands—day care, ERA, and equal opportunities in work, schooling, and politics. Mary Treadwell and numerous welfare rights activists joined campaigns to fight for reproductive rights, mostly avoiding pronouncing themselves feminists but nonetheless showing a willingness to enter interracial women's coalitions to press for specific demands. Moreover, women's experiences in the Black Panther Party and black nationalist political organizations had alerted many that the struggle for liberation required fighting male chauvinism within the African American movement. Thus, by the time the NBFO chapter formed in Washington, many black women had found ways to publicly express agreement for particular women's issues while eschewing feminism per se.[72]

The formation of the NBFO presented another path, demonstrating for some black women the value of claiming feminism as their own. With their unapologetic embrace of feminism and their recognition of the links between racial and sexual oppression, NBFO's Washington chapter represented a groundbreaking, albeit short-lived, effort to bring feminist analysis and practices to address the distinct concerns of black women in the District. Washington chapter members primarily came from the middle class, but they tried to act on issues that would improve the lives of African American women of all backgrounds. In addition to discussing the concerns of professional women, NBFO pledged to take up unemployment, job training, household workers, and welfare. Other concerns focused on black women's self-image, child rearing and day care, the ERA, forced sterilization and the need for abortion, and the oppression experienced by black lesbians. With minimal direction from the national level, local chapters developed activities to further the cause. In one of their first activities, D.C. NBFO members went to Capitol Hill to register their opposition to the amendment that proposed to ban Medicaid funding for abortions. For two weeks, chapter members lobbied at the Senate to protest a change that they believed would have dire consequences for their less-affluent sisters. The chapter also coordinated protests against a television show that depicted black women in a degrading manner. At the invitation of the Washington Area Women's Center, set up to replace the D.C. Women's Liberation Office after it closed, NBFO members worked on establishing a feminist credit union, trying to help women secure economic independence. But the chapter did not move its offices into the city's Women's Center as many other feminist organizations had done.[73]

With its distinct identity and refusal to relocate to the Women's Center, the NBFO stood separate from the city's predominantly white feminist organizations. But NBFO members still chose to associate with the broader women's movement in both ideological and practical ways. Carolyn Handy, one of the local chapter's founders, stated that many members already identified themselves as feminists and wanted to send a message that feminism and blackness were compatible. "It's time that minority women stand up and say, 'Listen it's our movement, too, and we're supportive of our white sisters, and if you have any questions about our commitment, here we are,'" Handy declared. At the same time, Handy emphasized that NBFO did not intend to siphon women away from other feminist organizations but would try to build connections and improve communication between feminists from different backgrounds.[74]

For their part, white women's liberationists in Washington seemed unsettled by the terms on which the NBFO formed. Articles in *off our backs* that detailed the founding of the group recorded reporters' discomfort with African American women's insistence on a racially separate feminist organization. Conceding that white feminists had failed to acknowledge their racism and ignored the role of race and economic privilege in shaping their agendas, the *off our backs* reporters nonetheless conveyed their unhappiness at African American women's decision to organize apart from white women. Despite their disgruntlement, they took from NBFO's formation awareness that white feminists would need to admit, and conquer, their racism before effective communication and coalitions could occur.[75]

Washington's NBFO chapter folded by the end of 1974 after less than a year of activity. With only a handful of members, the group's ambitions undoubtedly exceeded their ability to coordinate projects and events that could have a big impact. Still, the chapter's formation presented new possibilities for local feminists to reformulate their movement. Feminism, along with black liberation campaigns, presented a language and a vision of a new society that could be adapted and tailored to reflect the perspectives of members of the NBFO. Calling on white feminists to broaden their understanding of oppression and their agendas, the NBFO simultaneously contested the claim that feminism was solely a white woman's movement. Rather than sidestepping or denying women's oppression, the NBFO helped expand the parameters of feminism and establish the legitimacy of a movement that linked racial liberation and women's freedom. By so doing, the NBFO helped pave the way for other African American women—Howard University students, welfare rights activists, and others—to see black feminism as a label they might proudly wear. Along with the attempts at coalition building exhibited by the Black Panther Party, the NBFO was one sign of the continued overlap between movements that shared a conviction about the need to liberate women by opening opportunities for full participation in the country's economic, political, and cultural life.

The NBFO represented, too, factionalization within the feminist movement, as groups of women used the broad banner of women's liberation to promote demands particular to specific constituencies. This trait was not new, as the 1970 Strike Day and reproductive rights coalitions had earlier demonstrated. The tendency toward factions worried some, such as *off our backs* reporters who seemingly mourned a loss of unity, and perhaps control, that had never existed. For others, however, including members of the NBFO and the lesbian feminist separatists discussed in the next chapter, the splintering of the feminist movement expanded their opportunities to define women's liberation on their own terms and with their own views at the center.

6

Lesbian Feminism and Separatism

Less than six months after the Revolutionary People's Constitutional Convention assembled in Philadelphia, a small group of white women founded the Furies. The D.C. lesbian collective emerged out of its members' sense of estrangement from other feminists and their determination to mobilize women for a revolution. To those activists beginning to identify as lesbians, the DCWLM and other liberation groups seemed to deal with lesbianism in disparaging ways. Furthermore, many of the issues tackled by black liberation and radical feminism—reproductive rights, child rearing, and relationships with men—seemed critical for women's liberation broadly but of less significance to lesbians. Despite their seemingly marginal position within the broad revolutionary movement, lesbians also represented a potential model for the independent, liberated woman that feminists imagined.[1]

The Furies grew in the context of these multiple pressures, and the group helped to facilitate new forms of feminist organizing in Washington. In contrast to many of the women's organizations examined elsewhere in this book, the Furies did not attack laws and policies that disadvantaged women, nor did they intend to attract masses of women. Impatient with the results of political and statutory reform, and inspired by other revolutionary organizations, particularly the Black Panther Party and the Weathermen, the Furies advocated more radical means to overthrow male supremacy and transform the world. Rather than pushing for inclusion in political organizations and a society that expressed hostility toward their presence, the Furies sought to turn separatism into political advantage. Pushed to the social, economic, and political margins in the United States and within radical movements, lesbian feminists paradoxically gained the advantages of insight into the workings of patriarchy and capitalism, and their anger could fuel a revolution. Thus, lesbian feminists—especially the Furies themselves—could lead a revolution by virtue of their position in society.

The Furies set two main objectives for their group. Their collective would function as a place where they could immediately act upon their political beliefs and, at the same time, strategize ways to eradicate women's oppression. The projects the collective undertook were meant to stimulate their own thinking and produce tools for disseminating their ideas to other women. The Furies' primary vehicle for spreading their ideas, and the group's most lasting achievement, was their newspaper, *The Furies.* Produced from January 1972 to June 1973, the publication outlived the actual collective, functioning as a means "to develop ideology, to give more room for difficult issues to be fought out and over the years to pull together an ideological community that could then be welded into a party or some form of operating political caucus. The purpose of the Furies," the group argued, "was none other than the creation of an intellectual leadership within the women's movement."[2]

The Furies collective exhibited a deep conviction and commitment to women's liberation, but they also possessed significant shortcomings. In particular, the Furies' decision to work through a small, separatist collective where they promoted a narrow set of prescribed behaviors that they considered revolutionary led to burnout and myopia. This hampered the group's achievements and made it impossible to achieve their long-term goal of leading a women's liberation movement. The import they granted to their ideas promoted new thinking about the link between the personal and the political, but sparked criticism and opened the Furies to charges of elitism. Thus, the Furies' ultimate goal of mobilizing feminists was undercut by the effort to conform action to theory. Nonetheless, the Furies offer an instructive example of the way that feminism was driven forward by energies and experiments that also limited the movement's influence and undermined its impact.[3]

Lesbianism and Feminism: Theoretical Connections

Prior to the formation of the Furies in 1971, gay and lesbian activists in Washington participated in numerous initiatives that gradually eliminated discriminatory laws and encouraged social interaction. Gathering in bars, restaurants, and private homes, gays and lesbians developed a sense of community and shared identity. The solidarity that developed through such social interaction not only often reflected racial and sex segregation, but also became a foundation for political organizations that formed in the 1950s. Notably, a local chapter of the Mattachine Society—a national organization founded in California in 1951—fought to overturn the city's antisodomy statutes and prevent the dismissal of gay federal employees. At the height of the Cold War, when gay men and women were considered threats to national security, members of the Mattachine Society of Washington picketed in front of the White House, protesting the federal government's practice of discrimination. A few women joined these campaigns, but Mattachine's efforts primarily drew in men.[4]

Throughout the 1960s, gay men and women in SDS and other New Left and civil rights organizations complained of invisibility and oppression.[5] By the end of the decade, however, the scope of gay politics and culture expanded from its earlier focus on personal relationships and job discrimination to promote acceptance of gays' and lesbians' presence in radical movements and in society at large. In June 1969, a police raid on a gay bar in New York City erupted into violence when the patrons resisted arrest. The so-called Stonewall Riots heralded a mood of resistance that catalyzed a movement to forthrightly fight discrimination and demand legitimacy. After Stonewall, the growing movement centered on claims that homosexuality represented a source of pride, not shame, which challenged derogatory stereotypes. The slogan "Gay Is Good," a derivation of "Black Is Beautiful," encapsulated this new approach. The cross-fertilization of ideas demonstrated by these slogans enraged Pearl Stewart, editor of Howard University's newspaper, and others who condemned gay activists for stealing ideas from, but not advocating for, the black liberation movement. But the ideas of gay liberation caught fire in Washington, where new political groups formed, including a chapter of the Gay Liberation Front (GLF) that began in 1970 and the Gay Activists Alliance (GAA), established the following year.

As District residents won expanded electoral power with the creation of popularly elected municipal positions, gay activists sought to influence city government and grassroots politics. Frank Kameny, an openly gay man and founder of the Mattachine Society of Washington, ran in 1971 for the newly created position of nonvoting delegate to the U.S. House of Representatives. Kameny was never considered a serious contender for the representative position, but his campaign spurred gay and lesbian activists to prove the electoral power that their community could wield. Along with supporting Kameny, members of the GLF and the GAA asserted a gay presence in the larger radical movement, raising their banners at antiwar demonstrations and

Black Panther Party rallies. A sense of lesbian community emerged through an open house hosted by Lilli Vincenz, a member of the Mattachine Society and the GAA, a social event held every week from 1971 to 1979. Uniting the larger community, the *Gay Blade* (later the *Washington Blade*), a publication begun in 1969, provided news and announced upcoming events to readers who shared a sexual identity and some political interests.[6]

Bars, political organizations, the lesbian open house, and the newspaper facilitated social connections and group identity, but gay activists did not necessarily hold a common political orientation nor did their organizations incorporate many women or African Americans. GLF's membership was overwhelming white and male, a composition that discomfited members who nonetheless did little to reach out to women. In contrast, the organization did attempt to recruit African American members, organizing pickets against bars that practiced racial discrimination and relocating meetings from a predominantly white neighborhood into a church in a mostly African American area. African American gays and lesbians, however, confronted barriers that made it difficult to join political organizations; for example, native Washingtonians feared coming out and being publicly associated with gay organizations while in close proximity to their families. Mistrust of gay liberation organizations, expressed, for example, by the editor of the Howard University newspaper in her critique of the Panther's RPCC, demonstrated the kind of antigay sentiment that kept the gay rights movement in Washington predominantly white until the late 1970s.[7]

Throughout the 1960s, members of women's liberation and gay liberation groups maintained little consistent contact. The August 1970 Women's Strike day, discussed in chapter 3, was an exception. NOW, the main coordinator of that day's events, had become renowned for the antigay comments of its first president, Betty Friedan, who accused lesbians of forming a "lavender menace" that threatened the women's movement. The Washington NOW chapter operated independently from Friedan, but nonetheless shared the taint of her accusation and became a target for activists advocating a reconsideration of the relationship of lesbianism to feminism. Joan Biren and Sharon Deevey, the DCWLM representatives on the Strike Day planning committee, insisted on inviting Joan Carmodey, an African American lesbian and GLF member, to speak at the event. In her speech, Carmodey stressed that gay and African American women belonged in the women's movement. Carmodey asserted that "being a lesbian and being black just add to the list of oppressions I as a woman of America feel." Although she avoided mention of the role women played within the gay liberation movement or of African Americans within the feminist movement, Carmodey asserted that lesbianism offered a path to liberation, "allow[ing] us to reject all the dehumanizing masculine and feminine roles this society forces on people, and . . . build[ing] a new way of relating to each other as equal sisters."[8]

In contrast to activists who constructed a group identity as white gay men, lesbian feminists like Carmodey and the Furies sought to create an alternative identity, merging sexual orientation, gender identity, and a radical political philosophy. The twelve women who formed the Furies collective in the spring of 1971, all white and under thirty, brought extensive experience working for civil rights, against the war, and within women's liberation groups. Many previously belonged to the DCWLM, including Charlotte Bunch and Sharon Deevey, and made up part of the informal leadership of the local women's movement, positions that stirred animosities within the supposedly nonhierarchical movement. Other members—Rita Mae Brown, Nancy Myron, and Jennifer Woodul—had joined feminist and gay rights groups in New York before moving to the District.[9] Before coming out as lesbian, several members—including Deevey and Bunch—had been married. For these participants, the experience of living without husbands or male partners enhanced their understanding of the connections between women's economic status and family structure. In contrast, for women like Biren who had identified as lesbian prior to their involvement in the women's movement, lesbian feminism provided a way to overcome internalized shame and affirmatively embrace an identity demeaned by the dominant society.[10]

In the years leading up to the formation of the Furies, the collective's future members retained their commitment to ending racial discrimination and the larger radical movement, even as they concentrated on women's emancipation. Like the Black Panther Party and the Weathermen (later known as the Weather Underground), which had formed in the splintering of SDS the previous year, the Furies believed that an imminent global revolution would explode from the embers flamed by small radical groups, a conclusion supported by Franz Fanon, Mao, Che Guevara, Regis Debray, and others whose writings discussed revolutionary movements around the world. They also drew inspiration from traveling to Vietnam, Cuba, and other places where anticolonial or independence movements seemed to demonstrate the urgency of fighting against America's political and economic imperialism. Two members had recently moved from Chicago, where they had worked to support the defense of the Chicago Seven, men whose arrests for inciting violence during the 1968 Democratic National Convention made them examples of government repression. One of them, Tasha Peterson, was the daughter of Dave Dellinger, a noted pacificist who had stood trial.[11]

Closer to home, their interactions with black liberation activists influenced the Furies' perception that lesbians should lead the larger revolutionary movement. Joan Biren and Sharon Deevey attended the Revolutionary People's Constitutional Convention (RPCC) organized by the Black Panther Party in September 1970. At the convention, Biren and Deevey participated in a workshop to discuss the experiences of lesbians and to draw up a plank of demands to be incorporated into the new constitution. Even though some women's liberationists and lesbian activists felt dismayed by their treatment at the convention, Deevey and Biren reveled in the opportunity to meet other lesbian feminists and to connect to a larger lesbian movement. Helaine Harris, Susan Hathaway, and Ginny Berson all helped to organize the follow-up convention later held in the District. At both RPCC gatherings, future members of the Furies attended because they supported the Panthers' call to consolidate connections between revolutionary movements, but came away convinced that lesbians must separate from groups with other agendas. In particular, many lesbian feminists interpreted the Black Panther Party's rhetoric and actions as signs of the intractable nature of men's resistance to women's liberation and indications that feminists would only meet derision and hostility when working with mixed-sex groups.[12]

The formation of the Furies mirrored the impulses toward communal living that radical activists around the U.S. had begun to express by establishing separatist groups and collectives where they could intensify their political commitments. As a member of one commune in Berkeley, California, observed, collectives fulfilled activists' need "for close-knit communication and mutual support" that was missing from the larger movement. Collectives also presented opportunities to experiment by developing new forms of relationships and domesticity, including the rejection of monogamy, exploration of same-sex intimacy, and shared child raising. But even when women took a lead role in designating communal rules, collectives did not always offer them support and freedom: some women reported that living in mixed-sex communes exploited their sexual vulnerability, while lesbians sometimes experienced hostility or invisibility.[13] Washington feminists had gone a step further, creating women's collectives where members could find solace from the sexism of the male left and inspiration that would nurture collective change.[14] A women's anti-imperialist collective had formed in 1970, affiliated with the DCWLM. Because men's chauvinism drained them as individuals, the collective's members called on feminists to create communes where women could build closer, more trusting relationships with each other, thereby furthering their personal growth and arming for political struggles. Members of the anti-imperialist commune recognized that future women's collectives might include lesbian relationships, but they expressed uncertainty about whether "lesbian sexuality is the ultimate liberation from men." Whether or not lesbianism represented the pinnacle of women's liberation, members of this commune nonetheless conceded that true sexual liberation constituted an essential part of the process of becoming liberated people.[15]

Within months, however, some DCWLM members began to argue for the importance of lesbianism as a form of women's liberation. Rita Mae Brown was one such proponent. Brown had recently moved to Washington from New York where she very publicly had resigned from the city's chapter of NOW because of the organization's uneasiness about lesbians' involvement. She subsequently participated in several radical feminist groups in Manhattan, including Radicalesbians, the authors of a provocative essay, "Woman-Identified Woman." That essay argued that "[U]ntil women see in each other the possibility of a primary commitment which includes sexual love, they will be denying themselves the love and value they readily accord to men, thus affirming their second-class status."[16] In a March 1971 article in *off our backs,* written after Radicalesbians had disbanded and Brown had moved to the District, she extended this idea further, proposing that a movement for women's liberation could be centered on women's love for each other.[17] Brown's magnetic personality and powerful ideas attracted others to support this lesbian feminist position. At the same time, support for lesbian feminist separatism crescendoed in response to the hostility that many women reported when they came out as lesbians within the DCWLM and radical movement.[18]

After months of struggling to open discussions about the role of lesbians in the women's movement, the women split from the DCWLM and *off our backs* to set up their collective.[19] At least initially, the Furies proposed that separatism from men and heterosexual women was imperative only because other groups failed to take lesbianism seriously. In this regard, straight women, as much as men, perpetuated women's oppression. As Rita Mae Brown insisted, "Lesbians must get out of the straight women's movement and form their own movement in order to be taken seriously, to stop straight women from oppressing us, and to force straight women to deal with their own Lesbianism. Lesbians cannot develop a common politics with women who do not accept Lesbianism as a political issue."[20]

In some ways, the Furies' perspective echoed that of black nationalists who, looking through the lens of race, viewed themselves as leaders in the struggle against white supremacy and imperialism. They also mirrored the claims of the Weathermen that a small group could foment a revolution and serve as an example for other activists to follow. According to the Furies, male supremacy enforced heterosexuality, compelling women's submission and dividing people by class, race, and nationality. Women benefited from their relationships with men, enjoying financial resources and protections that extended from fathers and male partners. Moreover, the respect and social acceptance that women gained through their relationships with men motivated them to maintain the status quo.

In contrast, lesbian feminism represented the means to end such oppression; through it, women renounced the privileges of heterosexuality, challenged all forms of supremacy, and rejected cultural imperatives that socialized women to shape their lives around relationships with men. Charlotte Bunch asserted that a lesbian rejected "the male definitions of how she should feel, act, look and live. To be a lesbian is to love oneself, woman, in a culture that denigrates and despises women."[21] Thus, Bunch and the Furies concluded, lesbians were uniquely qualified to lead the movement to end capitalism, racism, and imperialism. As Rita Mae Brown wrote in a 1972 essay, once a woman embraced lesbian feminism and became strengthened through uniting with other women, her view of the world would change. "Once you feel your strength you cannot bear the thought of anyone else being beaten down," Brown argued. "All other oppressions constructed by men become horrible to you, if they aren't already. Class and race, those later-day diseases, have sprung from sexism itself. No oppression is tolerable. All must be destroyed. Once you have come out you can no longer fall back on race and class privilege, if you have any." Lesbianism thereby transformed women's class status by decreasing their investment in maintaining capitalism and racism and turning them into revolutionaries, although, admittedly, "becoming a lesbian does not make you instantly pure, perpetually happy and devotedly revolutionary."[22] But by distinguishing lesbian feminists from "anyone else"—those who might experience racism—Brown's statement implied that only white women with class privilege would identify as lesbian feminists. This definition, coupled with the group's insistence that sexism formed the basis for all forms of oppression, provided a rationale for the Furies to abandon outreach to diverse groups of women, thereby reinforcing the message of the RPCC and gay liberation organizations that lesbian feminists' interests stood apart from those of other activists.

For the Furies, as for other activists, the feminist adage "the personal is political" contained an equally influential counter-notion, "the political is personal." This secondary meaning translated into a set of prescribed beliefs about how women should demonstrate their commitment to women's liberation. The Furies argued that women's liberation would only come from a renunciation of worldviews that devalued women and reinforced female dependence on men. More specifically, the Furies viewed lesbianism as a political imperative. Ginny Berson explained, "Lesbianism is not a matter of sexual preference, but rather one of political choice which every woman must make if she is to become woman-identified and thereby end male supremacy. Lesbians, as outcasts from every culture but their own[,] have the most to gain by ending race, class, and national supremacy within their own ranks." Their experiences of oppression, therefore, required that "Lesbians must become feminists and fight against woman oppression, just as feminists must become Lesbians if they hope to end male supremacy."[23]

Although the Furies emphasized the political aspects of lesbian identity, they did not deny sexual desire. Collective members joined in romantic relationships with each other and with women outside the group, and relationships among women in the collective played an important role in the group's composition. At least six of the women were partnered with others in the original collective; as the initial core disintegrated, new relationships accounted for the entry of some different women into the living spaces and into the newspaper. But their analyses primarily stressed the political implications of lesbianism, and the group largely ignored the impact of their own relationships in communicating about the collective. Indeed, writings by the Furies revealed ambivalence regarding sexual pleasure as a determining factor in lesbian feminist identity. Any woman could be lesbian; conversely, they contended, a failure to feel sexually attracted to women indicated an acceptance of the male worldview and the traditional social roles it fostered. This ideology disavowed the role of physical and emotional attraction, instead favoring intellectual and political grounds in determining intimate relationships. Although this idea validated lesbianism, it taught women to not trust their sexual feelings. In so doing, the Furies contradicted feminists' view that liberated women would find sexual satisfaction and empowerment by exploring their own sexuality.[24]

Not surprisingly, such ideas provoked conflict and disagreement within Washington's feminist movement. Some activists considered the Furies' separatist proclamations unnecessarily strident and particularly difficult for those who were mothers. Alice Wolfson experienced discomfort with the collective's insistence that male children prevented women's liberation and that only women who gave away their sons could become women-identified women. Others considered the Furies too antimale in tone and too focused on conformity to a single ideology. Fran Chapman of *off our backs,* for example, objected to the Furies' requirement that sexual preferences should be subsumed to politics. "If it is true, and I suspect it may be, that lesbianism generates energy, assertiveness, and strength," Chapman charged, "to demand that women 'become' lesbians so that they may be more useful to the women's movement seems only slightly less inhuman that demanding that 'mentally ill' people submit to behaviorist manipulation so they can more quickly become useful members of society."[25] Finally, other lesbian feminists rejected separatism and continued to work to promote lesbians' issues in NOW and other less militant organizations. In 1971, such women helped push through national NOW a resolution affirming that "a woman's right to her own person includes the right to define and express her own sexuality and to choose her own lifestyle" and recognizing that the oppression of lesbians constituted a "legitimate concern of feminism." Although these statements did not result in any immediate action within the District's NOW chapter, the resolutions represented an important step toward increasing the acceptance and visibility of lesbian feminists within groups that prioritized the reformist approach that the Furies had rejected.[26]

Putting Theory into Practice

In their effort to shape the direction of feminism, the Furies faced three major challenges. First, although they sought to ultimately build a mass movement, the Furies established practices that inadvertently worked against this goal. Second, the analysis and actions the Furies advocated through their projects both mobilized and excluded other women. In the end, their programs yielded mixed results, in part because of the strong reactions their analysis inspired, and in part because of the manner in which the Furies delivered their message. Finally, interpersonal dynamics, essential to personal and political transformation, made it difficult to carry out their ideas for social change.

Within the collective, members wrestled with the problem of how to build a mass movement, their central motivation. They practiced karate, read Trotsky and Greek myths, studied the Chinese and Russian revolutions, and researched prominent figures from women's history. According to Ginny Berson, these activities evidenced the group's obsession with history, but also demonstrated "the serious role we believed we were taking on. We were going to create a revolution like nothing anyone had seen before. We had to know how other revolutionaries did it—to emulate what we could, and to avoid what we should."[27] Building on their studies of the past, they drafted a five-year plan to organize women in other cities, assigning the Furies a leading role in developing ideas and strategies for taking power and assembling a functioning political party. By conceptualizing actions to take place in the next five years, the group hoped to ensure women's liberation fifty years in the future. Bunch, who authored the plan, imagined that by the year 2021, "women will have taken power in many regions in the U.S., [and] are governing and beginning to create a new feminist society." This new society entailed a long-term view of lesbian feminist separatism: "[W]e have built alliances in which we are the dominant power, with some minority groups and with a few male groups (especially gay males). We have minimal, but not warring, relations with some other U.S. regions where minority groups have taken power and where the women are advancing rapidly but not yet in total control." The former United States had become "a Federation of Feminist States," she continued, governed by a lesbian-feminist party.[28]

The proposed Federation of Feminist States, like the Furies collective, was based on the premise of limited, but not necessarily antagonistic, interaction between lesbian feminists and other radicals. But the Furies' proposal depreciated the agendas and approaches of these other activists. The notion that lesbian feminists would hold social and political control no doubt would have incensed activists, such as those who attended the RPCC, who already criticized feminists for trying to dominate the radical movement. Nor would women then working with Women's National Abortion Action Coalition (WONAAC) for repeal of abortion laws have agreed with the Furies' repudiation of reformist approaches. Furthermore, the Furies' idealistic plan contrasted with the practical efforts of other gay liberation activists to exert influence by pressuring political candidates to work against discrimination. At the same time the Furies formed, for example, D.C.'s Gay Activists Alliance (GAA) was organizing meetings to lobby local officials and political candidates on behalf of antidiscrimination measures. These efforts led the school board, then headed by Marion Barry, to adopt a fair employment resolution covering all school employees and, in 1973, the city passed Title 34 of the D.C. Human Rights Law, granting gays and lesbians legal protection against discrimination in private or municipal employment, housing, and public accommodations.[29]

Thus, in many ways the Furies' ideas were out of step with the larger movements with which they overlapped. Rather than a cause for concern, the collective interpreted their departure from the ideas and agendas of other groups as a sign of their leadership and a demonstration of the crucial role they could play in building a mass movement. Their small group could constitute a temporary structure from which lesbian feminists could formulate an agenda for future outreach and large-scale mobilization. Ginny Berson, writing on behalf of the collective, explained that the path to women's liberation would have to come from attempts to organize a mass movement "because the institutions of sexism, the governmental, economic, and social structures which uphold male supremacy and capitalism and racism are not local, but national and even worldwide." Furthermore, although women and lesbians might feel empowered within small groups, they did not force society to redistribute power. Therefore, Berson claimed, feminists needed to organize a national political party "which can build a power base and which can therefore threaten the power of the oppressor."[30]

Although the Furies perceived that feminists had failed to think about their movement in appropriately broad, and long-term, ways, they expected that the collective's activities would rectify this earlier shortcoming.[31] *The Furies* newspaper, for instance, presented a forum for the presentation of political ideas. Workshops to teach skills and theory to local women constituted other primary ventures. Each initiative drew on the Furies' ongoing analysis, forced clarification of their politics, and pushed them to work out internal differences. The presentation of their ideas outside the collective, however, was fraught with conflict. Their insistence that lesbian feminism—personified by their own group—represented the revolutionary vanguard failed to appeal to many women activists and stirred controversy. In addition, vanguardism became institutionalized in projects that left little opportunity for the development of others' leadership and instead perpetuated divisions between the movement's "thinkers" and "doers." The resistance their ideas generated in others, compounded by dissension within the collective, ultimately limited the Furies' ability to mobilize women as they intended.

At first, the Furies emphasized the political education of local women as the main venue for interaction outside the collective. They organized seminars and workshops to inspire, educate, and mobilize diverse groups of D.C. women, including African American and Hispanic residents of their neighborhood, welfare rights activists, women's liberationists, and lesbians they met at the city's gay bars. The workshops taught mechanical skills, such as electrical wiring, and survival skills, such as self-defense. Taking advantage of their own time for study, the Furies considered their effort an example of how "women with economic privilege . . . should organize to meet the survival needs of women without economic privilege." Eventually, the group hoped to establish a center equipped with exercise rooms, carpentry workshops, a darkroom, and a sewing room. By teaching skills and fostering women's empowerment, the center would nurture feminist leadership among the women who used it. Thus, like community schools established by the Black Panther Party, the Furies' educational programs could facilitate long-term goals and meet short-term needs related to a feminist movement.[32]

The skills workshops, however, exposed the gaps between the Furies' ideas and their execution. The collective targeted a broad audience for the workshops, posting advertisements at local women's bars, in newspapers such as *Quicksilver Times* and *off our backs,* at the free health clinic, the food co-op, the women's center, welfare rights offices, the black nationalist New Thing Art and Architecture Center, and in self-service laundries in the Adams Morgan neighborhood. But the workshops and skills center stumbled because the collective was ill-prepared to offer such classes. Biren recalled that before she could teach an electrical wiring workshop, she first borrowed books from the local library in order to learn the skill herself. Despite their lack of qualifications, the Furies believed in the importance of such educational opportunities. Biren explained that the workshops represented "middle-class white feminists trying to do something that theoretically made sense. We thought of ourselves as organizers, that meant we should be organizing somebody else. So we thought that meant we have to offer something that's useful. . . . The problem was, we didn't know how to teach these skills, because we didn't have them."[33]

Other forms of outreach that drew on the group's analytical strengths, although controversial, were more sustained and successful than the skills workshops. Members of the Furies coordinated political discussion groups, held poetry readings, arranged film screenings at a lesbian bar, and directed a theory workshop. In March 1972, according to Washington's *Gay Blade,* the Furies held two events at the Community Bookshop: a poetry reading by Rita Mae Brown and a lesbians-only workshop led by members at the Furies. Unlike the skills workshops, these sessions targeted a narrower audience and, in contrast to programs directed to "women without economic privilege" that concentrated on women's "survival" independent from men, the theoretical presentations emphasized the unification of women around a program of shared analysis. And whereas the collective posted signs throughout Adams Morgan and other racially and economically diverse neighborhoods to publicize the skills workshops, they announced the film showings and seminars in the city's gay, women's, and alternative newspapers, venues less likely to reach the general public.[34]

In any case, educational workshops and skills seminars played a secondary role to the Furies' major project, writing and publishing. Like the *off our backs* collective, the Furies recognized that controlling a media outlet could further their attempts to mobilize supporters, challenge mainstream ideas, and bring about a revolution. The Furies first assumed organizational and editorial responsibility for publishing a special issue of *Motive,* a magazine published by the United Methodist Church. For this project, the collective solicited articles from around the country and involved lesbians in all aspects of production, including typesetting and writing. After *Motive,* the group initiated *The Furies,* the independent paper written and published by the collective. Their publications became the main venue for spreading their ideas and providing direction to the feminist movement.

In a January 1972 statement in the paper expounding on the need for such leadership, the Furies charged that feminists, in trying to sever their connections to the male New Left, had neglected the importance of theory. The consequent lack of clear thinking impeded feminism. "For too long," they contended, "women in the Movement have fallen prey to the very male propaganda they seek to refute. They have rejected thought, building an ideology, and all intellectual activity, as the realm of men, and tried to build a politics based only on feelings—the area traditionally left to women." But although women's feelings were relevant to their liberation, a mass feminist movement would require a solid theoretical foundation.[35] Drawing on ideas about lesbian feminism developed within the collective, *The Furies* would help lesbian feminists "decide where to go and what our priorities are. Groups will get together and stay together because of a firm political commitment and common strategy will transcend traps like overemphasis on personal relationships and will eliminate political indecision."[36]

The Furies' determination to guide feminism brought them into conflict with other women activists, especially those who viewed theory, hierarchy, and leadership with suspicion. Women's liberationists in Washington, as elsewhere, mistrusted any motivations that enticed women to assume leadership roles in their movement. Members of the DCWLM had earlier warned, "There is the danger that one becomes a leader for strongly ego-oriented needs. There is a problem when a leader inclines toward a vested interest in leadership per se and the prestige it confers." In part to deter the development of leaders, radical feminists in the DCWLM and *off our backs,* for example, rotated tasks like leading meetings and running an office. Radical feminists also disputed the notion of ownership of ideas by not signing articles in women's publications. The DCWLM discovered that these ideals were difficult to practice; nonetheless, many radical feminists remained convinced they could create an egalitarian and inclusive movement.[37] In contrast, the Furies argued that the feminist movement's disdain for leaders created confusion, turned women against each other, and distracted from the more important goal of liberating women. Addressing this issue in an article in *The Furies,* Rita Mae Brown urged feminists to distinguish between "leaders" and "stars." According to Brown, movement "stars" were those individuals selected as token figureheads by the "white, rich, male media establishments." But true "leaders" rose from the movement's ranks by virtue of hard work and ability to foster initiative in others. Rather than criticism, these leaders deserved recognition for their experience and insight. The Furies intended to become leaders in this sense of the word.[38]

Comfortable with the role they delegated to themselves, the Furies initially managed every aspect of their paper, including writing, typing, printing, and distribution. Once the collective shrank in size, the paper began to solicit written and photographic contributions from other women. In some ways, their control was pragmatic; few printers and distributors would help put out a lesbian publication, so collective members had to learn typesetting (by taking classes at local trade schools), while others maintained the subscription lists and coordinated mailings. By investing in learning skills and trades, the collective demonstrated the long-term political importance of publishing.[39]

At the same time, the group's control of content signaled that they reserved theory as the domain of a small coterie of women—those who produced the paper—and conceived their readers as "students" rather than collaborators in movement building. As a result, alternative views received minimal coverage in their publications. The first issue of the paper contained reports from lesbian groups in Philadelphia, Denver, Boston, Seattle, and several California cities, and called for readers to send news, but subsequent issues did not include updates. Even when they included descriptions of activities around the country, the group prefaced reports with editorials offering political critiques. In the view of the Furies, the movement needed lesbian groups to concentrate on political issues and develop ideology, pointing the way to future directions.[40]

The Furies claimed to understand the theoretical importance of lesbianism to feminism, but they faltered in figuring out how to move from their ideas to effective actions. The notion that all women should be lesbians required the Furies to reject traditional family structures and experiment with new models of living that might transform the larger society. Believing that "revolution begins at home," the collective became a kind of laboratory where each member tried to overcome patterns of behavior that reflected both her class status and her internalized hatred of women.[41] Such personal changes would form the foundation of a larger political struggle, they insisted, and would break down patriarchy by making politics, not family, the reason people lived together. Seeking to put these ideas into action, the twelve Furies and their three children occupied group houses where they shared money, clothing, bedrooms, automobiles, and responsibility for child care. To focus their intellect and build physical strength for the upcoming revolution, they studied karate, history, and political theory. Every aspect of collective living became subject to interrogation: through frequent and lengthy meetings, often lasting late into the night, the group discussed their lives, reaching for theoretical insights that could guide their long-range strategies.[42]

The impact of class on women's lives became one issue of constant discussion and consternation. Theoretically, they considered class oppression a derivative of male supremacy that would disappear with the end of sexism. In the meantime, however, differences based on class privilege precipitated conflict within the group. Many radical activists of the period had attempted to repudiate class privilege through communal living and through changing their dress and appearance. The bib overalls, flannel shirts, and T-shirts favored by SNCC and SDS members as a way to establish a connection with working-class communities, for example, were taken up by many feminists as symbols of their departure from mainstream class and gender conventions. But the Furies considered such efforts at downward mobility merely "a middle class romanticization of poverty" that denied the realities of what those in want actually experienced.[43] Instead, they sought more substantive or lasting means to address the problems that class differences posed to the radical movement.

Members understood that occupational status affected economic and political opportunity. Some held jobs where they could directly challenge patriarchy and capitalism, as in the salaried positions Rita Mae Brown and Charlotte Bunch held at the IPS. But most women in the collective worked at low-income service jobs, received public assistance, or were students. To compensate for the differential earning potential and types of jobs held by members, the Furies devised a percentage-based system for pooling their wages, taking into account the amount each earned and the benefits each derived from past "heterosexual privilege." The formulas intended to relieve working-class women from "straight jobs" and to redirect middle-class women's education and skills toward the benefit of the collective. Thus, people who had completed college and consequently enjoyed the prospect of professional jobs were expected to find remunerative positions that could help support others in the collective.[44]

Although the group's redistribution of resources could be seen as penalizing the more privileged members, the approach typified the Furies' attempt to minimize the negative impact of middle-class women's behavior on feminist activity. In discussion sessions and then published articles, the group identified so-called middle-class behaviors, such as the expression of guilt and denial, that allegedly were used to control working-class activists. The socialization of middle-class women, they implied, supported patriarchy and capitalism to a greater extent than that of working-class women. Although former members now believe the group romanticized the radicalism of working-class women and stereotyped middle-class women as complaining and self-indulgent, at the time the collective thought that their critique of class privilege would help create a broader women's movement.[45]

Criticism of middle-class women's emotional manipulation directly connected to the Furies' critique of consciousness raising, one of the feminist movement's primary techniques for personal and social transformation. By the time the Furies formed in 1971, more than two dozen consciousness-raising groups were affiliated with the DCWLM and another nine were coordinated through the National Capital Area Chapter of NOW.[46] Furies' members agreed that consciousness raising could instigate both individual and collective change. But they also feared that the technique risked reinforcing the status quo, allowing emotions alone to guide political action rather than theory or history. Emotions evolved from experiences that were limited by class and race, the Furies theorized, and feelings could be "used to excuse inaction and inability to change." Also, because patriarchal culture trained women to make relationships of primary importance in their lives, they relied on emotions as a means to sway each other. Therefore, the group concluded, if feminists wanted to make revolutionary change, discussion of personal experiences and feelings needed to accompany the simultaneous study of political theory and the history of social movements and women's condition throughout the world.[47]

Despite the group's insistence that feminists should minimize the significance of personal relationships and emotions in their lives, these forces ultimately contributed to the collective's dissolution. Rather than separatism offering relief from conflict, women in the Furies experienced tremendous stress as a result of their distance from family and friends. Aware that the FBI was monitoring their activities, the Furies also feared that the collective would be attacked in a manner similar to the violent force that had broken up chapters of the Black Panther Party and other groups vying to lead the revolution. Although this threat proved unjustified, it nonetheless heightened members' suspicions of each other and of outsiders, thereby increasing the tensions they experienced. Furthermore, the collective was challenged to implement their ideas within the context of their passionate and sometimes antagonistic relationships.[48] At times the collective itself caused emotional distress, particularly when members criticized each others' behavior. In the view of participants, the middle-class women whose actions were deemed objectionable or manipulative should change their behavior for the good of the collective and the movement. But such ideas sometimes revealed contradictory impulses. Biren's doctoral study of sociology at Oxford University, for example, should have enabled her to make important contributions to the collective's ideology and become a movement "leader" in the Furies' definition of that term. Instead, collective members accused Biren of using her elite education to verbally take advantage of others and demanded that she find other ways to communicate. Not only was such criticism personally destructive, but in stifling Biren, the Furies appeared to clash with their stated views regarding the importance of developing both theory and leadership. Effectively silenced within the group, but willing to change her behavior for the sake of women's liberation, Biren turned to photography, the form of expression for which she eventually became best known in the movement.[49] In another example of the internal conflict the Furies' ideas caused, the group sent away the three small children who lived with them, arguing that child care diverted too much attention from other political activities. Several Furies remember this painful decision as the beginning of the collective's demise.[50]

Perhaps the communal processes they developed strained members' patience the most. Because they sought to closely analyze all aspects of their group dynamics, they subjected every decision to scrutiny and extensive discussion. As Biren remembered, "We would spend months figuring out how to divide the money. We knew we had to put it all in—all the cars, all the money, all the clothes, everything was pooled. That we knew. It was how it got divided out that was the problem. Could we have individual toothbrushes? . . . Everything was up for grabs. Nothing was assumed about anything and it was just exhausting to figure it all out." Although this process presented the possibility of fresh understandings of social dynamics and power, it also exemplified the Furies' conundrum: even when they sought to diminish the centrality of personal relationships and emotions in their lives, the work of maintaining their household, studying and writing, earning money, guarding against FBI infiltration, and coordinating projects drained the women's energy, intensified their feelings about each other, and ultimately made it difficult to accomplish their larger goals. Under such circumstances, the group frequently reverted to behavior that was inconsistent with their ideas.[51] Rita Mae Brown reflected that the Furies "began to create within ourselves the dynamic of a fascist state," wherein authoritarianism led to distrust, divisiveness, and, ultimately, the destruction of the group. As a confused struggle over the Furies' priorities ensued, the group expelled Joan Biren and Sharon Deevey. Biren and Deevey, who had remained lovers and who had fought to keep children in the collective, were accused of wielding too much power and showing insufficient commitment to the group's political aims. Several months later, the group ejected Brown, who had orchestrated the earlier expulsion and who the remaining members now considered too dominant. Shortly after, the collective disbanded, although a core group of members continued to put out *The Furies* for another year. In retrospect, some members of the Furies now think the expulsions were motivated by personal antagonism rather than by political justifications. Believing that attention to personal relationships should accede to political analyses did not ensure that such a practice could be followed.[52]

Legacy of Lesbian Feminism

As the preceding discussion demonstrates, much of the Furies' theory did not translate into viable action. Still, the group played a pivotal role in bringing attention to lesbians' presence in the women's movement and legitimizing lesbian feminism as a political issue. Their notion that sexual identity was socially constructed rather than biologically determined and their understanding of the ways that enforced heterosexuality served male supremacy came to constitute central arguments of feminists. Finally, by taking pride in their identities as lesbians and political women, their theory and action provided a powerful but problematic model for future activists. Feminist groups in places as different as Durham, North Carolina, and Dayton, Ohio, subsequently credited the Furies with helping them understand lesbianism as a political issue.[53] Moreover, after they left their collective, former members devised new means to spread feminist theory and culture throughout the city and into mainstream America. In doing so, they built an infrastructure that supported the feminist movement and substantively broadened both the movement's ideological foundations and the diversity of its adherents.

After the collective broke up, former members began projects that would further women's liberation but could incorporate diverse views and paths for achieving that end with more success. The journal *Quest,* founded in 1974 by a group that included Rita Mae Brown and Charlotte Bunch, was one such effort. *Quest* combined ideas and action in ways that *The Furies* had not and encompassed a broad vision of women's liberation that included activists with a range of organizational and movement affiliations. Between 1974 and 1982, *Quest* regularly published interviews with activists involved in women's health care, antiapartheid, environmentalism, and the battered women's movements. Other Washington women involved with the production of *Quest* participated in the movement against sexual violence, set up local feminist radio shows and a cable television channel, and initiated the Washington Area Women's Center. Both activists and academic scholars, including white women and women of color, aided in the production of the journal. This publication thereby extended *The Furies'* intended effort to "promote a continuing, active search for ideologies and strategies that will bring about the most comprehensive change by the most effective methods," as *Quest* stated in its introductory issue. But it also moved away from the Furies' claims to represent a revolutionary vanguard to a more expansive consideration of alternative perspectives on social change.[54]

Other former members of the Furies also took up ventures in publishing and media as their primary method of political action. Joan Biren published compilations of her photographs and established Moonforce Media to produce and distribute feminist films. Lee Schwing, Helaine Harris, Jennifer Woodul, and Ginny Berson started a women's recording company, Olivia Records, the first women's record producer in the United States. Charlotte Bunch and Rita Mae Brown each published collections of their theoretical essays. Subsequently, Bunch and Brown developed their intellectual work in other areas, with Bunch concentrating on global feminism from a university setting and Brown writing fiction. Coletta Reid worked with the Diana Press in Baltimore, where she helped produce *Quest* and two anthologies of articles from *The Furies.*[55]

These later endeavors took feminist activism in new directions. In their work after the collective collapsed, former members continued to advocate the revolutionary potential of lesbian feminism, but they all emphasized outreach rather than isolation. The publications, films, and music that former members produced and distributed through Olivia Records, Moonforce Media, and *Quest* helped build connections among women and inspire continued struggle. The new enterprises also reflected a growing cultural movement within the gay and feminist communities, spurring the creation of businesses, media, and events developed by and for gays and lesbians. In Washington in 1973, shortly after the Furies broke up, Lammas bookstore opened, selling books written by and for women and providing a space for social gatherings and performances. By creating a sense of community and disseminating the movement's ideas, these endeavors brought new women into the movement, especially those not involved in the earlier ideological struggles. Moreover, such projects and organizations neither presumed nor explicitly tried to enforce similarity among women. In fact, they intentionally attempted to facilitate consideration of diverse perspectives and experiences, rejecting the earlier emphasis on conformity to a narrow political imperative—that all women must become lesbians—as impractical and unappealing to women of differing racial, economic, parental, or sexual identities. Instead, through the production and dissemination of music, journals, photography, and film, the group's members sought to build a foundation for a common women's culture.[56]

The Furies thus affected the Washington women's movement in complex ways. Turned off by the Furies' exclusivity, some feminists developed activities and groups explicitly intended to transcend race, class, and sexual differences. These initiatives included those started by former members of the Furies and others created by feminists who established spaces for those women alienated by the ideological dissension within the local movement. The Washington Feminists was one such group. Established by women affiliated with George Washington University, the group coalesced during the summer of 1971 at the same time that the DCWLM suffered through the departure of the women who formed the Furies. The Metropolitan Abortion Alliance disbanded during this same period. Bev Fisher helped found the Washington Feminists because she wanted to avoid the ideological struggles experienced in the DCWLM and to bring new women to the movement. Although the Washington Feminists included many lesbians, members nonetheless continued to envision the possibility of a broader women's movement.[57]

Washington Feminists was instrumental in creating a multipurpose women's center to replace the old DCWLM office. Bringing women's activities together under one roof, the women's center linked numerous feminist projects, including a counseling collective, the Women's Legal Defense Fund, the National Capital Area Chapter of NOW, a school to teach skills such as basic auto mechanics, and a rape crisis hotline.[58] The location of groups and projects like these in a single space—a large building near Dupont Circle—encouraged women's use of the resources and services they offered. The close proximity of these projects and the center's publication of a monthly newsletter informed supporters of activities under way and explained how these projects contributed to the women's movement. Lesbians held prominent positions in these new initiatives, a signal that because of the Furies, lesbian activists no longer needed to legitimate their participation in feminism or to establish the relevance of lesbianism to feminism. By 1973, articles expressing a lesbian feminist political view appeared in the newsletter of the local NOW chapter and an action group focused on lesbianism and sexuality formed under NOW's auspices. In 1975, a slate of openly lesbian women ran for seats on the chapter's board. Although some members feared their election would disrupt the chapter, the women won their seats.[59] However, an attempt to form a separate lesbian office within the new women's center failed to materialize, either because lesbians continued to show reluctance to affiliate with heterosexual or liberal feminists or because they perceived no need to meet separately. Certainly, separatism remained a personal preference for some women, but the claims that lesbianism constituted an overall solution to women's oppression became muted as more lesbians felt comfortable exposing their existence within groups that also contained heterosexual women. Such claims also fell off in the face of strong critiques issued by women of color, pointing out how separatism required lesbians to perceive sex, rather than race or class, as the most salient aspect of one's identity.[60]

For despite the Furies' insistence that revolutionary lesbianism offered a path to eliminate racial oppression, and in spite of efforts by the Washington Feminists and the Women's Center affiliates to create inclusive projects, lesbian feminism remained a white women's movement in Washington. Women who struggled daily against the injustices and indignities of racial and class oppression must have found the Furies' arguments laughable, if not reprehensible, even if they benefited from the increased visibility and legitimacy that the Furies helped usher in. For African American women, political arguments that subsumed racial oppression to sexism supplied evidence of white feminists' racism and ignorance regarding race. In contrast to white feminists' emphasis on solidarity based in shared sexual or gender identity, African American women maintained strong ties to black liberation efforts and to black gay men. Michelle Parkerson, who moved to Washington in the mid-1970s, indicated that racism in the larger society made racial solidarity seem more pressing—and more possible—than gender separatism within the black gay community. This view was supported by Valerie Papaya Mann, who came out in Washington in the mid-1970s, joining a circle of African American lesbians who resisted gender separatism as a form of unwelcome isolation.[61]

In addition, as gay liberation organizations grew in visibility and assertiveness, the backlash against them became more heated. Attending to the predominantly white composition of the city's gay rights groups, African American activists cast that movement as threatening to black liberation. In 1972, for example, the *Gay Blade* reported that some Black Muslims had begun circulating petitions asking D.C. residents to press the school board to rescind a fair employment resolution that covered gay employees.[62] Even African American organizations, such as the Black Panther Party, that had supported gay liberation tended to perceive that movement as external to African American communities.

Such criticisms of the gay movement, combined with a commitment to racial liberation, reinforced African American gays' attention to their racial identity and created an impetus to merge demands for racial and sexual freedom. Although African American gay men and lesbians differed in many ways, including their access to resources needed to create social spaces, racial solidarity created a sufficient foundation for political organizing. In 1978, the D.C. Coalition of Black Gays began, allegedly the first black gay organization in the country. Established partially to take legal action against bars that refused to admit African American men, the coalition expanded to address racism within the gay movement and other community concerns. Two years later, Sapphire Sapphos formed, a group of lesbian women of color, as did a gay student organization at Howard University. The creation of these organizations demonstrated African American lesbians' sense of their distinct needs and interests, although those concerns often overlapped with those of African American men or white feminists. Members of Sapphire Sapphos, for example, met regularly for social occasions, joined marches against sexual violence, and volunteered at a battered women's shelter. According to one member, the organization consistently looked "for ways to network with both the white women's community and the Gay male community. . . . You can't do that when you're all by yourselves."[63]

As the feminist movement grew to incorporate more small groups and single-issue organizations—the larger transformation that the Furies represented—the movement grew more welcoming to diverse populations of women. Gradually, lesbians and other women of color joined what had been white women's organizations, getting involved in some of the new projects that affiliated with the women's center and bringing different understandings of women's oppression. Firmly opposed to separatism from men and unwilling to minimize the significance of racism, feminists of color introduced ideas and vitality that changed the shape of the women's movement.

7

Coalition Building against Sexual Violence

When Nkenge Toure joined the staff of the Washington, D.C., Rape Crisis Center (RCC) in 1975, she was driven by both political and personal motivations. In the Baltimore public housing complex where she grew up, Toure knew about the sexual abuse her neighbors endured and she experienced this firsthand when she was raped while still in high school. As a student, she responded to this event by directing her anger and depression toward politics. From 1970–74, Toure worked on various Black Panther Party (BPP) projects in the District, where she met and married her husband. Together, they ran the party's health clinic until inadequate finances forced them to abandon the effort. In its place, they began a politically oriented bookstore that opened its doors to meetings of community women who wanted to act in response to a series of rapes in the area. As a result of Toure's role in organizing women to prevent more assaults, she made contact with the RCC and began to volunteer there.[1]

In 1972, feminists affiliated with the Washington Area Women's Center had started the RCC to address the short-term needs of rape victims and to prevent sexual violence through education and action. With its many programs, the RCC filled an essential gap in the services available to the District's women. Until a shelter for battered women opened in 1976, the RCC operated the sole crisis service for women victims of physical and sexual violence. Beginning as a volunteer, Toure soon moved onto the paid staff where she served as an administrator, hotline coordinator, and community educator. Throughout her six-year tenure at the RCC, Toure played an important role in initiating programs geared toward the city's black residents.

Despite—or because of—Toure's involvement with the RCC, she remained critical of the feminist movement's shortcomings when it came to addressing the particular concerns of the city's black majority and a growing Hispanic population. After having devoted years toward racial liberation efforts, Toure found it difficult to work alongside white women who downplayed the centrality of race and racism to women of color. She persevered, however, committed to transforming the RCC into an institution that could effectively serve "her sisters," their families, and the larger community.[2]

As Toure's personal history and political activity illustrate, feminism, in the specific form of the antiviolence movement, affected the directions pursued by black liberation activists; at the same time, such activists shaped the strategies used to promote women's issues. In these ways, the movement against sexual violence that flowered in D.C. in the 1970s emerged at the intersection of black liberation and feminism and necessitated changes in the ways that activists thought about, and acted against, racial and sexual oppression. By the mid-1970s, the separatist impulse that directed the Furies collective and the activities of some Howard students had begun to lose its power as an ideological framework. At the same time, new groups and facilities such as the RCC that took a single-issue approach to ending women's oppression attracted activists who otherwise avoided identifying as feminists. Antiviolence initiatives combined theory and action more effectively than most previous efforts because participants' commitment to serving their sisters mandated flexibility and attentiveness to diverse views and experiences. For women of color, affiliation with—and eventually leadership of—antiviolence initiatives provided opportunities to shape daily operations, outreach activities, and programmatic agendas. By influencing these organizations from within, women of color could simultaneously challenge their racial communities' antagonistic views of feminism and refashion feminist responses to those communities' needs.

Within the RCC and the larger movement against sexual violence, black and white activists built on distinct histories and resources. For more than a century, black female activists and authors had tried to expose how sexual violence was used to regulate and contain the labor, reproduction, and dignity of black women and men. Aware of an intertwined past of rape and lynching, black women saw violence as a community concern and an expression of political power. Black women and men both became victims of sexual violence, linked through a social and legal system that failed to protect women from rape and men from accusations of criminal sexual behavior that justified mutilation, murder, and disfranchisement.[3] By contrast, white radical feminists looked to a more recent history of activism to win women's liberation, viewing antiviolence programs, such as the RCC and other institutions that could directly serve women in the aftermath of sexually violent attacks, as a means to fight sex oppression. Patriarchy and male supremacy would weaken, feminists argued, when women fought back against society's assumptions about the causes of sexual violence.

In order to promote interracial cooperation, which Washington activists eventually considered essential to effectively mobilize against rape and sexual violence, women had to confront the damaging racial stereotypes that suffused the criminal justice system and disadvantaged African Americans economically, politically, and socially. In the District, as elsewhere in the country, African American men and women were accused of, and victimized by, sexual assault at rates incommensurably high given their proportion of the population.[4] Attempts to address this reality were complicated by white feminists' control of the agendas of the fledgling institutions they founded to prevent violence and care for women victims. As a multifaceted movement to protect women from assault by strangers, husbands, fathers, and partners evolved, black and white activists in the District struggled side by side and sometimes against each other to develop analyses and institutions that would meet their goals.

The effort to interpret and eliminate the causes of sexual violence occurred within the context of Washington feminists' inability to realize their goal of uniting all women in a collective struggle and their subsequent reassessment of the strategic benefits of black and female separatism. A shift in organizational structures accompanied this move away from separatism; feminists' willingness to develop more conventionally run institutions, relying on paid staff and supported by governmental and private funding agencies, unexpectedly made it possible, and imperative, to integrate African American, low-income, and heterosexual women into formerly white and mainly lesbian groups. African American women occupied a dual stance in these initiatives, simultaneously supporting feminists' missions but also challenging previously accepted ideas, a position that expanded the borders of the women's movement.

Institution Building

Throughout the 1960s and 1970s, many Washington women personally experienced the devastating impact of sexual violence within their families and communities. Forcible rapes, a crime tracked by the FBI, occurred most often in urban areas and among black women, making D.C.'s population particularly vulnerable. Indeed, during these two decades, the numbers of forcible rape recorded in the Washington metropolitan area consistently exceeded those registered in many other cities. Although such statistics are unreliable, based as they are only on reported incidents and excluding husbands' assaults on their wives, they nonetheless indicate the widespread nature of the problem[5] (see table 7.1). Even before a distinct movement against sexual violence developed, District women had protested specific incidents of violence and the community's failure to muster a serious response, but they had not framed such attacks as particular to women. In 1966, for example, Etta Horn and other activists in southeast Washington had gathered at a police precinct to express their outrage at the murder of a resident of the Barry Farms housing projects. The victim, a mother of six young children, was shot during an argument with the father of one of her children. Compounding the tragedy of the woman's death, Barry Farms inhabitants insisted that police could have prevented the assault had they not ignored calls about the fight. To the protesters, this lack of intervention typified police officers' neglect of the poor neighborhood.[6]

The women's liberation groups that emerged at the decade's end soon took up sexual violence as a political matter. By highlighting the social nature of private lives, radical feminists made sexual violence an issue for discussion in consciousness-raising groups. In order to lessen the fear and shame about sexual violence that restricted women's lives, the DCWLM urged women to learn martial arts and other forms of self-defense. Self-defense classes, such as those organized by the DCWLM and the Furies, might arm women for self-

Table 7.1. Rates of Reported Forcible Rapes*

Year	U.S. Rate (per 100,000 inhabitants)	D.C. Metro Area	District of Columbia
1968	15.5	21 (N = 579)	
1972	22.3	42 (N = 1,234)	
1975	26.3	41.4 (N = 1,255)	N = 520**
1979	34.5	45.3 (N=1,364)	N = 489

*Reported rapes printed included in 1969, 1973, 1975, and 1980 publications of Federal Bureau of Investigation, *Uniform Crime Reports for the United States* (Washington, D.C.: Government Printing Office).

**Figures for the city of Washington, D.C., were not available separately for prior years.

protection, but they also stressed an individual approach to the problem of abuse and implied that women were responsible for preventing violence.

Washington women's understanding of sexual violence was affected, however, by a January 1971 speak-out on rape coordinated by the New York Radical Feminists (NYRF). Using a method that had worked to mobilize women against restrictive abortion laws, the NYRF forum—and a follow-up conference two months later—gave women an opportunity to talk openly about their experiences of sexual violence. Susan Brownmiller, who attended the NYRF event and later wrote an important book about rape, recalled, "The bold idea of summoning women to gather in public to talk about rape, as authorities, to put an unashamed face on a crime that was shrouded in rumors and whispers, or smarmy jokes, had never been attempted before, anywhere."[7] These initial events helped lay a theoretical foundation for analyzing rape that shaped the work of activists across the country. A manifesto produced by the NYRF outlined the principles that would remain fundamental to many feminists' interpretations of rape throughout the decade. First, they stated that "the violent rapist and the boyfriend/husband are one," implicating all men as potential rapists and beneficiaries of sexual terrorism. Furthermore, the NYRF concluded that "the act of rape is the logical expression of the essential relationship now existing between men and women. It is a matter to be dealt with in feminist terms for female liberation." In other words, rape represented only one form of men's power over women; activists needed to transform intimate heterosexual relationships in order to liberate women from male domination. Finally, by labeling rape a political crime, feminists stressed that power, not desire, lay at the foundation of sexual violence.[8]

The ideas percolating among New York feminists were carried to Washington where, in early 1972, members of the George Washington University Women's Liberation group organized a conference on rape.[9] Several months later, a small group of young white women—mostly rape survivors who were already active in women's liberation projects—founded the RCC and affiliated with the Washington Area Women's Center (WAWC).[10] The WAWC and the RCC both epitomized Washington feminists' emphasis on creating resources to meet the "real daily needs of women."[11] One of the first of its kind in the nation, the RCC put Washington feminists on the cutting edge of a national grassroots movement to advocate on behalf of female victims. Feminist-run centers in New York, Detroit, and Berkeley, California, soon followed. By 1976, approximately 400 autonomous feminist-run rape crisis centers existed in the United States. Within a year, between twenty and forty volunteers, recruited through the newsletter of the WAWC, staffed the D.C.

center. Like the earlier DCWLM, the center initially operated collectively, working by consensus and eliminating managerial hierarchy within the institution by giving the all-volunteer staff a say over policy and an opportunity to work in all the various jobs within the facility. Volunteers received training, but compassion and commitment, rather than education or professional experience, were the traits desired in staffers.[12]

Right away, the group settled on telephone counseling as their main function and required every member of the RCC to staff the crisis phones, initially located in one member's home. Within a year, the center was handling several hundred calls each month from women who had been recently raped and those still recovering from past attacks.[13] When answering the phones, RCC counselors emphasized practical issues: access to free medical care and legal assistance, the importance of self-defense, safety, and general preventive measures. Rather than encouraging callers to report assaults to the police or take legal action against their attackers, RCC staff offered information so that callers could decide a plan of action appropriate to them. Despite their sympathy for callers, RCC members believed that by adopting a "tough, unemotional line" in phone counseling, they offered "a strong antidote to the feelings of guilt, shame, powerlessness, ostracism, [and] paranoia that conspire to overwhelm the rape victim."[14] The RCC supplemented its counseling work with educational initiatives to teach women about their rights and train them in preventive techniques and to organize men and women to stop sexual abuse.

Through these projects, the RCC introduced specific ways of thinking about violence against women. Whereas the protestors who gathered in southeast Washington in 1966 emphasized women's vulnerability to assault as a consequence of their poverty and inadequate police protection, the RCC defined rape as "an institutionalized act of power, aggression and terror performed by men against women." Therefore, sexual violence intimately related to women's right to control their own bodies. The RCC recognized, too, how deeply rape reflected popular stereotypes about women's and men's sexuality. In particular, they observed, the general public greatly exaggerated the frequency of rapes between black men and white women and, accepting myths of black women's promiscuity, downplayed the extent to which African American women became victims. Finally, feminists understood the degree to which fear of sexual violence affected women's lives, and, conversely, the power they could gain through interpreting attacks not as isolated incidents that women provoked but as one manifestation of social control over women's lives.[15] Thus, hotline calls and victims' discussion groups could present opportunities for political organizing. As one RCC spokesperson told a *Washington Post* reporter, "Rape can, or ought to be, a politicizing experience—the disadvantages of being so defenseless are suddenly made much clearer. It can force reconsideration of basic assumptions."[16]

As the previous statement suggests, RCC organizers viewed their work on sexual violence within the context of a women's liberation movement. Thus, although the RCC's methods and outlook differed from the broader attack on male supremacy earlier favored by the Furies, the NBFO, and the DCWLM, women affiliated with the center took advantage of opportunities to spread their influence and ally with other feminists. In 1974, for example, a spokeswoman from the RCC was a featured speaker at a conference on health and sexuality organized by the local NOW chapter. Melding the personal and the political, the RCC speaker described her own assault and presented evidence about the frequency of rape in the United States, a sobering contrast to other panelists who related humorous stories to emphasize why women needed to take charge of their sexual and physical health. Although the RCC described rape as an expression of male power, the participation of the center's representative at a conference on health and sexuality stressed the importance of understanding sexual violence within the context of a range of issues related to women's ability to control their bodies.[17]

That same year, RCC representatives joined the D.C. Women's Political Education Coalition (WPEC), a group organized by the D.C. Commission on the Status of Women. Their colleagues on the coalition came from conservative and liberal women's organizations who sought to raise support for various public policies. WPEC members wrote a position paper detailing shortcomings in the District's rape laws and inadequacies in government-sponsored programs to prevent rape. WPEC recommended that the city institute new procedures to record rape statistics, expand the legal definition of rape to include other violent sex crimes, start prevention programs for high school students, fund community-based groups already helping rape victims, enact a victim compensation bill to cover medical expenses of abused women, and increase the number and sensitivity of personnel dealing with rape cases. The WPEC advised the government to fund the Rape Crisis Center and to take advantage of RCC expertise to provide seminars for D.C. government personnel.[18]

The RCC's involvement in the WPEC demonstrates radical feminists' recognition of the benefits of working with government agencies, including police and the city council. This cooperative approach was also evident in RCC activists' participation on commissions and boards set up by government offices, their testimony at public hearings, and their willingness to accept public money for programs. In 1973, a RCC member worked on the D.C. city council's public safety task force, evaluating laws and bureaucratic procedures for handling rape cases. Such cooperation was no doubt a response to an escalation in the numbers of rapes reported within the District and citizens' growing dissatisfaction with the conditions necessary to get convictions under local laws. Between 1968 and 1972, the numbers of rapes reported annually in the city grew from 187 to 617. The number of arrests also increased, from 101 in 1968 to 439 four years later, but fewer than half the rapes reported to police led to prosecution of the rapist and, of those, less than 50 percent of the accused were actually convicted. The increased numbers of reported rapes probably indicated feminists' success in eliminating obstacles to reporting such violations rather than a worsening problem.[19] Still, police and hospital procedures remained cumbersome, stifling those who wanted to report crimes, humiliating women who already had suffered the demeaning experience of assault, and doing little to ensure that rapists would be caught and tried. One highly publicized case demonstrated why the conviction rate remained low and how the city's laws were ineffective in putting offenders behind bars. In 1972, a jury acquitted a man who had confessed to raping two George Washington University students. Legal technicalities had excluded the alleged rapist's confession, and jurors ruled that the victims lacked sufficient evidence of bodily injury to prove they had resisted their attacker to the extent required by law.[20] The case, according to a *Washington Post* reporter, revealed the "excruciating dilemma" a rape victim faced: if a woman resisted an attempted rape, she risked retaliation from an enraged attacker, but if she acquiesced, she "substantially reduces the chances that her assailant will ever be convicted."[21]

Responding to such incidents, the city council's public safety task force recommended "drastic" changes in the way municipal agencies handled rape cases. As a whole, the suggestions reflected both a desire to protect women from nonconsensual sex and an affirmation of their right to sexual activity. A task force proposal to reduce sentences for rapists was meant to yield a higher degree of convictions. Suggesting that the city lower the age of consent from sixteen years to twelve years, the task force hoped to exclude consensual sex between teenagers from the definition of rape. Finally, the inclusion of sodomy and rape between individuals of the same sex was intended to recognize the possibility of same-sex rape and affirm the right to consensual gay sex. Through these proposals, the task force attempted to bring evidence and sentencing regulations in line with those for other violent crimes.

The task force put their proposals before the public, convening hearings at which community members could weigh in on the issues. RCC representatives exhorted the city to develop criminal justice processes that recognized women's unique experiences. Their statement stressed that rape constituted "an act of violence and terror by men against women supported by a legal system with low prosecution and conviction rates. Rape is not a sexual act; it is rather an act of power that utilizes sex as a mode to humiliate and demean the victim."[22] They recommended, for example, that the city's laws more clearly distinguish between "consent" and "submission" when determining coercion.[23] The RCC also made less abstract suggestions, such as increasing the number of women who handled rape cases at hospitals and police stations and proposing that RCC members play a formal role in establishing police procedures and training hospital personnel to deal efficiently and compassionately with assault survivors.[24]

Representatives of other District groups challenged the proposals of the task force and the RCC. Whereas the RCC essentially ignored the discriminatory nature of the courts, other women questioned the expediency of legal reforms given the ways that race and class stereotypes corrupted the criminal justice system.[25] Mary Treadwell, then executive director of Pride, Inc., and former member of SNCC and WONAAC, linked racial oppression with gender oppression in her opposition to the proposed changes. Raising the issue of the historical ties between race and rape, Treadwell reminded the task force that although most rapes occurred between individuals of the same race, crimes in which black men allegedly raped white women disproportionately resulted in capital punishment sentences. She also tied sexual violence to the country's past by pointing out that "a quick comparison of skin coloring among Black Americans will prove that at some point during slavery or beyond, some white man probably *raped* one of their black female ancestors who identified her very survival with submission to the slavemaster. The very definition of the term *slave* as 'one completely under the domination of a specified person or influence' could be contemporized to define today's rape victim, be she black or white."[26] Given this history, Treadwell objected to white feminists' consideration of sexual violence as solely an issue of sex oppression and their willingness to settle for legal reform rather than revolutionary change. Because the task force's report displayed "current teachings of the women's movement rather than sound legal principles," she questioned its credibility and expressed skepticism about the process undertaken by the city council to reform rape laws and procedures. The current hearings were unlikely to "spur a centuries-old white male dominated power structure into changing attitudes and laws," Treadwell averred. Instead, the task force should consider ways to create a society oriented toward preventing rape by remedying atrocities committed by the white American government—poor education, unemployment, bad health care, and substandard housing—that forced black men "to discharge anger best through the sadistic sexual act of rape."[27]

Into the Mainstream

As the inclusion of RCC members on the WPEC and D.C. city council public safety task force demonstrated, within several years of the center's founding, the feminist antirape movement had moved from the margins to the mainstream. Mary Treadwell's statement that officials' approaches to public safety were shaped by the "current teachings of the women's movement," although meant as a criticism, indicated that, in her mind, the ideas promoted by the RCC had spread beyond a small band of activists to alter public consciousness about rape as a social concern. Within the context of the time, "joining the mainstream" by shifting popular views of rape represented a victory, not a repudiation of radicalism.[28] In contrast to abortion and welfare rights advocates, who sought, with limited success, to reshape extant policies and to enter ongoing conversations among lawmakers and policy setters, radical feminists who worked against rape and sexual violence largely started from scratch. Beginning by working separately from criminal justice or public health structures, radical feminists created their own institutions, grounded in feminist principles, to confront sexual violence. The city's legal and criminal justice system then struggled to keep up with emerging understandings of the causes of sexual violence and to address inadequacies in the procedures set up to support victims and prosecute offenders.

By the middle of the 1970s, feminists' analysis of the politics of private life spread to incorporate other forms of sexual violence—rape, wife battering, incest, pornography—extending the range of services and resources available to women. Establishing shelters, crisis centers and hotlines, and publications, more activists came to the antiviolence movement and, through it, exerted a greater influence over public views and government policies. In 1974, white feminists founded the Feminist Alliance Against Rape (FAAR) to publish information about the antirape movement. Membership in FAAR overlapped with the RCC, but their agendas differed. Whereas the RCC primarily served local women through emergency services and public education, FAAR concentrated on disseminating feminist theory and information about women's efforts to eliminate rape to activists working throughout the United States.

Several years later, FAAR joined with two other groups to produce *Aegis,* a publication with a broader focus on sexual violence, including battered women.[29] In 1976 the Task Force on Abused Women was started by women who were affiliated with the Women's Legal Defense Fund (WLDF) and the WAWC. The Task Force on Abused Women pushed for legal reforms and developed programs to inform and educate the public about the widespread problem of battered women and to aid those who had been abused. Members of the task force soon focused on establishing shelters to offer counseling, emergency housing, and assistance for battered women and their children. In August 1976, these efforts led to the opening of the House of Ruth shelter for abused women; another center for abused women, My Sister's Place, followed in 1979.[30]

The FAAR, RCC, the Task Force on Abused Women, and the two shelters combined direct service to needy women, legislative and procedural reforms, feminist networking, and public education. Their efforts to highlight sexual violence received favorable responses in the media and from the city government and women's organizations. The D.C. Department of Human Resources funded the RCC to coordinate educational programs, including the publication of a pamphlet, "Rape: A Reference for Women in D.C.," and rape prevention workshops for public school students. My Sister's Place also received public funds to support its operations. The Task Force on Abused Women led seminars for D.C. superior court judges and police to familiarize them with the problems abused women faced in prosecuting their assailants, and the group drafted model legislation to protect battered wives. And, as a symbolic act but one that indicated how far the plight of abused women had entered the political mainstream, in 1978 the D.C. city council proclaimed an April "Anti-Rape Week" and encouraged District citizens to support events organized by the Rape Crisis Center.

Although emboldened by their programs' successes, feminists nonetheless struggled to control their agenda and ideology as the antiviolence movement broadened. One challenge came from local governmental and social service agencies that offered possible funding sources for feminist projects and possibly provided partners for outreach. Most antiviolence initiatives in Washington preferred private sources of support, particularly women's volunteer labor and money donated by activists to keep the projects afloat. The RCC, however, accepted municipal money to create new programs and resources, a move that brought limited financial security but threatened to undermine its independence and shift its agenda. According to RCC staff, government agents monitored their public speeches and collected personal data about all the center's volunteers. In addition, city money typically could be spent only for public education programs, despite the crying need to fund direct service to victims.[31] The RCC's experience was typical; money available on a national level generally excluded allocations for staff salaries or daily operational costs. Across the country in California, state funds financed the creation of two rape crisis programs based in African American communities in Los Angeles. Intended to serve a largely ignored population, these centers nonetheless demonstrated the continued influence of funding agencies in determining the programs and priorities of antiviolence programs. Furthermore, as sexual violence programs took on greater public accountability, they often lost much of their feminist edge. In Dayton, Ohio, for example, a county project for victims of all crimes, including rape, ignored feminists' input about educational programs and services and even refused to hire feminists.[32] As these examples demonstrate, the recognition of the prevalence of rape and of the connections between sexual violence and women's struggles to control their own bodies did not necessarily translate into programs that upheld women's right to self-determination. Organizations' financial dependence on public agencies exacerbated this problem, making it difficult to speak negatively about government bureaucracies without fear of economic retaliation.

Despite these drawbacks, RCC staff recognized potential benefits to accepting public money and interacting with public servants. Whereas earlier reproductive rights and welfare rights advocates had interacted with local and federal government officials in a manner that was generally confrontational, sexual violence workers viewed contact and mutual assistance with public officials as one of their main tactics. By participating on the public safety task force and training police and other personnel who interacted with rape victims, RCC staff attempted to influence the stereotypes and expectations of city employees who distributed money to community programs. Likewise, the Task Force on Abused Women held seminars for police and judges, and thereby tried to directly influence those whose actions they sought to change. Through their cooperation, antiviolence workers signaled that local government and municipal agencies were bodies open to change, not immovable structures. In a reversal from earlier activism, the RCC's feminists accepted that reformist initiatives could benefit the women's movement and positively change women's lives.

Valle Jones, a founding member of the Task Force on Abused Women, recalled that the D.C. government generally appreciated their work. Police officers especially benefited from assistance in handling domestic violence cases. Yet local police sometimes disagreed with the RCC's tactics and questioned the group's effectiveness. In 1975, members of the police department's sex squad complained to a *Washington Post* reporter that the RCC received virtually no calls from black women. Detectives also objected that the RCC refused to advise women to report rapes to the police, a criticism that the RCC countered by pointing to the suspicion that black and poor women felt for law enforcement. But the tension between the police department and the RCC did not undermine the collaborative relationship. Although the D.C. government could exercise some control over the RCC's programs, the indispensable role that the RCC played as the only group offering support for the victims of sexual violence surely strengthened their hand.[33]

Nevertheless, criticism of the RCC's success in making services available to all Washington women carried weight, raising doubts about the center's legitimacy to receive public funds and the validity of feminists' claims to speak on behalf of all women. In this light, RCC recognized the importance of adding salaried employees as a means to diversify the organization's staff and programs. Since its founding, the RCC had expressed its commitment to bringing black and working-class women into the collective. For years, however, the group failed in this endeavor, partly because the RCC recruited volunteers through announcements in the WAWC newsletter and venues that yielded women already in contact with the city's feminist organizations. The staff's homogeneity reinforced the perception that the RCC was a facility for middle-class white women, and the demographics of the center's clientele mirrored that of the women who ran it.[34] But in order to reach out to a wider population, the RCC conceded that it had to institute structural and pragmatic changes, such as directing resources into staff salaries. By offering paid employment, the RCC allowed women to become involved on the basis of their commitment to the work rather than their financial resources.[35] Therefore, employing staff who reflected the city's population represented a means to forge gender unity around the issue of rape and became necessary for the RCC's credibility as a project truly serving the public. Reflecting these possibilities, in 1975 the RCC hired Michelle Hudson to coordinate education projects and Nkenge Toure to serve as general administrator, the first African American woman to direct any rape crisis center in the United States.[36]

Rape, Racism, and Reality

For the RCC, the appointments of Hudson and Toure did more than simply make African American women more visible. Under their leadership, the facility embarked on new directions that altered the RCC's relationship to the larger community and connected the sexual violence movement to demands for racial liberation and economic justice. Other antiviolence projects in D.C. were similarly transformed, as was the web of movements that intersected with the campaign against sexual violence.

At the time that Hudson and Toure became part of the RCC staff, the relationship between feminism and the black liberation movement remained generally antagonistic. Through the mid-1970s, many black radicals continued to believe that organizing specifically around women's issues, including rape and wife battering, counteracted the urgent need to shore up racial solidarity as a defense against other forms of violence and repression. To many in African American communities, feminism represented a form of repression, not liberation, by seeming to promote white women's demands at the expense of people of color. Nathan Hare, who had supported the earlier student movement at Howard University, made this point clearly when he argued in a 1978 article that society's current attention to a "rape scare" masked "an opportunistic appeal to press coverage and sympathy for the feminist movement." Hare admitted that rape was a problem in the black community, but belittled the impact of the antirape movement by pointing out that "the black woman is getting raped while the white woman is doing the screaming." Rather than ending sexual violence, he concluded, feminists' work reinforced the common stereotype of black male rapists, insulting African American men and furthering a racist agenda. Similarly, scholar-activist Angela Davis criticized feminist studies of rape that perpetuated the myth that black men were the most frequent sexual offenders.[37] These ideas also resonated within Washington. An RCC organizer who worked in D.C.'s Spanish-speaking neighborhoods, for example, reported that residents considered feminism irrelevant to their needs and antagonistic to family life, an institution that they considered central to cultural survival. Women who participated in black nationalist organizations related, too, that feminism was considered an unwelcome intrusion despite the pervasiveness of sexual abuse within that movement.[38]

Still, Nkenge Toure and Loretta Ross, who succeeded her as the RCC's director, as well as other women of color who joined antiviolence projects in these years, balanced their suspicion of feminism with a sense of urgency to address problems that severely affected women in their communities. Linked through their shared participation in several black nationalist and community-based political organizations, Toure and Ross also shared the experience of being survivors of rape. Having endured sexual violence, they understood on a personal level the devastating impact that violence wreaked on women's lives. In addition, as members of black nationalist groups and the Citywide Housing Coalition, an organization that tried to raise public awareness of the negative impact of gentrification and urban development on Washington's poor, black residents, Toure and Ross observed racism and sexism at work. Through participating in programs that brought together representatives of black liberation groups from around the world, Ross and Toure came to understand the pervasiveness of men's use of violence to oppress women, a consciousness that made Ross question, "How can you mount a revolution when your army is at war with itself?"[39] Toure similarly came to believe that rape hurt racial liberation efforts because violence diminished black women's contributions to their communities. In a more pragmatic sense, Michelle Hudson, the first black woman on the RCC's staff, considered her presence important to counter both the racism and sexism that pervaded the criminal justice system and the racism of white feminists. All of these women perceived their vital importance as bridges between feminism and black liberation movements as well as intermediaries who could create more effective connections between the predominantly white antiviolence projects and the city's majority black population.[40]

The sense of necessity to address violence against women of color increased throughout the 1970s when several high-profile incidents called attention to the vulnerability of women of color to sexual attack and challenged the notion that the antiviolence crusade promoted white women's interests only. The most notorious case involved Joan Little,[41] an African American woman incarcerated in North Carolina. Little made headlines in 1974 when she escaped from prison after murdering a white jailer who attempted to rape her. The state put out a dead-or-alive warrant that incited a massive search for Little and generated national sympathy for her case. Across the country, legions of activists, including many who previously had dedicated little attention to the specific issue of sexual violence, raised funds for Little's legal defense and to ensure that she received fair treatment during her incarceration and trial. The NOW and the NBFO, for example, joined in protests at the courthouse where Little was tried, and representatives of the Southern Christian Leadership Conference, the organization founded by Martin Luther King Jr., spoke on Little's behalf.[42]

Later, attention focused on the cases of Dessie Woods, Yvonne Wanrow, and Inez Garcia, who, like Little, fought against sexual violence. Dessie Woods, a black woman, was convicted of murder for killing her white would-be rapist. Similarly, Yvonne Wanrow, a Colville Indian, was convicted by an all-white jury for murdering a known child molester in self-defense after he broke into a neighbor's house. Inez Garcia, a Hispanic farmworker, murdered a man she claimed had raped her. Initially convicted of second-degree murder, Garcia's verdict was overturned on appeal and following a concerted campaign to generate sympathy for her cause. To those who gathered money and moral support for the defense of these women, their cases reverberated with the significance of demonstrating the intersecting nature of racial, sexual, and economic oppression. To some, these women symbolized the rape victim who fought back, a figure of strength and resistance. As the epitome of a liberated woman, strong in body and confidence, each defendant transcended race and class to become a unifying figure. But to others, the fate of these women reinforced the lack of justice afforded to low-income women of color within the United States. As members of society who least benefited from race, sex, or class privilege, poor women of color epitomized women's vulnerability, not their strength. Others believed these cases exemplified the "unequal power between women and men that encourages rape" and women's struggles to retain control over their bodies.[43]

The national campaigns and local events staged on behalf of Little, Woods, Garcia, and Wanrow increased public awareness of sexual violence and the possibility of self-defense and symbolically put women of color at the center of the antiviolence movement. By demonstrating the impact of racism, sexism, and poverty, these cases also helped establish a sense of solidarity among women of color that would become a foundation for a Third World feminist movement.[44] Loretta Ross, later an executive director at the RCC, recalled that in these cases, women of color legally established all women's right to take action against their rapists. Musician and performer Bernice Johnson Reagon was so moved by Joan Little's courage and plight that she wrote a song for her ensemble, Sweet Honey in the Rock. To Reagon, Little represented a powerful reminder of women's strength, rapists' vulnerability, and prisoners' humanity. Sweet Honey premiered the song in 1976 in Washington during a concert on behalf of political freedom in Central and South America. Sweet Honey also appeared at benefits to support Little's legal defense and "Joan Little" became the group's first song played on the radio. Through its performances, Sweet Honey exposed audiences to Little's story and contributed to the campaigns to defend her. At the same time, including "Joan Little" on a concert program that also featured songs on topics such as political violence in Latin America tied sexual abuse to these other issues, connected Little's cause to a global human rights movement, and reinforced the notion that women of color worldwide shared related burdens and struggles.[45]

The vulnerability and resistance exemplified by Little, Woods, Wanrow, and Garcia also pushed the District's antiviolence movement to take stock of its limits. In Washington, the RCC, the FAAR, and My Sister's Place—all founded by white feminists and all based in the city's northwest section—responded by trying to expand and diversify in membership and outreach. A small number of African American activists, many connected to each other through their shared membership in other political organizations, were ready to get involved in the fight against sexual violence, but their participation required FAAR, RCC, and My Sister's Place to change both their internal practices and their programs. Women involved in Washington organizations during this period recalled different strategies and the reactions they evoked in participants. My Sister's Place had been started by a group of close friends who were white, college-educated, young, and mostly lesbian feminists. The group retained its homogeneity, unwittingly alienating many women who sought their services or who might consider volunteering their time. Having an organization focused on wife abuse that was run by women who had never been married and, moreover, by many who did not have intimate sexual relationships with men automatically distanced the staff from the abused women they served. The staff tried to respond openly whenever residents of the shelter raised the issue of the lesbian presence at the facility, but the barriers remained until more heterosexual women joined the center.[46]

In addition, some of My Sister's Place's practices turned off new collective members. Initially, the volunteers and staff met on Friday nights, an arrangement that did not interfere with the founders' family or social lives because they were already friends who opted to spend nonwork time together. But this practice excluded women who preferred to spend evenings with husbands and children, did not work a conventional five-day workweek, or chose not to socialize with the group members. My Sister's Place volunteers gradually realized that this practice reinforced homogeneity and accepted that they had to adjust how they operated in order to diversify. By accepting the necessity of change, My Sister's Place could hire and retain black women staff members, including Michelle Hudson, who had previously worked at the RCC. Fund-raising demanded outreach too, and required that the staff establish new connections, such as encouraging members of the Junior League to contribute money and volunteer at the facility. In order to raise funds outside the radical feminist community, staff at My Sister's Place also had to assume a more professional approach to their work, changing their personal appearances and adopting more formal administrative procedures.[47] Thus, a subtle process of institutionalization transpired that distanced organizational practices from their more intimate forms, subsequently bringing more women on board as volunteers and expanding the clientele.

Diana Onley Campbell was one of the first black women to join My Sister's Place and later became the first woman of color to work with FAAR. A D.C. native who had joined civil rights protests as a high school student, Campbell found the sexism of black nationalists galling when she attended Howard University in the early 1970s.[48] Later, as a member of FAAR, Campbell challenged group practices that she considered responsible for perpetuating the collective's class and race homogeneity, such as the expectations that collective members would pay expenses out of their own pockets and that they would devote their nights and weekends to working on the publication. Most tellingly, Campbell sensed her white colleagues' discomfort at discussing racial issues once women of color joined the collective.[49]

In addition to changing the internal practices of antiviolence groups, women of color spearheaded projects geared toward previously neglected populations. The RCC translated their publications into Spanish and established support groups for abused Latinas, thereby establishing a feminist foundation within Washington's Hispanic neighborhoods. My Sister's Place hired bilingual staff who could communicate with members of Spanish-speaking families who sought emergency assistance.[50] Other RCC projects focused on working with men to prevent sexual violence. A series of workshops the RCC conducted with men confined at the Lorton Detention Center in 1975 and 1976 resulted in "Prisoners Against Rape," a group that included confessed rapists, who analyzed the ways that incarcerated men used rape to establish and enforce hierarchies within prison. The RCC also offered instruction and support to Black Men Against Rape, a group formed to diminish the frequency of rape in certain areas of the city, particularly in the southeast section, by patrolling neighborhoods and taking measures to raise public awareness.[51]

These new initiatives demonstrated a different framework for understanding how to prevent sexual violence and address its impact. For one, the RCC projects indicated the center's willingness to treat men, even sexual offenders, as allies rather than enemies and to treat sexual violence as an issue that could not be separated from other community concerns or understood apart from racism and poverty. To Toure, the RCC's mission needed to incorporate both short-term measures, such as community education and self-defense classes, that could prevent rape, and longer-term initiatives to eliminate "this society as it presently stands, with its promotion of racism, classism, sexism, capitalism, and imperialism."[52] Loretta Ross, recruited by Toure as a volunteer in 1978 and named executive director the next year, concentrated on expanding the center's programs to address poverty, racism, police brutality, and homelessness, factors that often increased women's vulnerability to sexual violence.[53] Both Ross and Toure appreciated the political commitments that led the founders and board of the RCC to transform the center, but sensed resistance when they implemented initiatives that took the center in directions that tested white feminists' core assumptions about rape and sexual violence. In 1979, for example, Ross organized a forum on women's roles in the black nationalist movement that included activists from the Black Panther Party, the Nation of Islam, the National Black United Front, and the African People's Socialist Party who publicly discussed the restraints they experienced within the movement. The center's board members, however, required Ross to justify how this panel related to the movement against rape. Similarly, the center's work with male criminal offenders generated objections from white feminists who considered it a diversion from organizing women.[54]

Although some feminists associated with Washington's antiviolence against women movement criticized the new directions, others responded positively and joined women of color in arguing about the need to broaden the movement's approaches. In a 1978 article, Deb Friedman of FAAR and the RCC urged feminists in the antiviolence movement to recognize gender, race, and class as interlocking systems of oppression, with sexual violence as a mechanism that reinforced them all. Looking at the past, Friedman argued that "the particular experience of black people in this country inextricably links racism with the act of rape. The discriminatory prosecution of black men for the crime of rape and the gross lack of sanctions against the rape of black women (by white men particularly) constitutes the reality through which black men and women view rape." Given this history, Friedman called on antirape organizers to connect struggles against sexism and racism by concretely demonstrating ways they would address the concerns of different populations and by "noticeably and vocally" opposing efforts "to make men from oppressed groups, e.g., black men, appear more responsible for rape than white middle-class men." Finally, Friedman insisted that feminists needed to recognize the social conditions and ideologies that made black women particularly vulnerable to rape. These included "racist structures that force more black women to live in insecure housing, work late-night jobs, and use inadequate public transportation," Friedman argued. At the same time, "racist myths that say that black women are more active sexually and therefore invite rape," perpetuated "racist ideologies that value the well-being of black women even less than that of white women."[55]

The disagreements within the antiviolence movement over the best ways to understand and combat sexual assault also translated into conflict over specific actions, including an April 1978 slate of events called Stop Rape Week. A coalition of women's organizations, spearheaded by the Task Force on Abused Women, the RCC, and the newly formed D.C. Area Feminist Alliance (DCAFA),[56] coordinated a series of programs to drum up support for their ongoing work, reach out to the city's black and Hispanic populations, and highlight the problem of violence. Activities occurred at scattered locations throughout the city, many at venues within the black community. One panel, convened on the Howard University campus, focused on "Women Who Fought Back"; another evening session addressed the topic of "Latin Women and Rape." Capping the week's activities, a citywide march snaked through the Adams Morgan neighborhood down to DuPont Circle, where hundreds rallied and listened to a lineup of speakers and performers who proclaimed women's rights to reclaim the streets and to resist violence. At the rally, Nkenge Toure, Valle Jones, and Betty Diaz represented the RCC; Nan Hunter spoke for the DCAFA; and Linda Leeks of the Dessie Woods Defense Committee and the African People's Socialist Party addressed the crowd. They stirred the 800 men, women, and children in the audience by proclaiming women's right to express their anger, cheering the event as an expression of female unity, and exhorting women to reclaim the streets. Buses, arranged by organizers, carried people to and from the location of the march and rally, bringing residents from neighborhoods in southeast D.C. and other parts of the District.[57]

The logistics of the march and rally demonstrated the organizers' commitment to drawing participants from across the city's neighborhoods and distinct communities. So did the statement of principles that the coalition of organizers composed and that nearly seventy organizations endorsed. The principles they articulated stressed women's right to control and protect their bodies and to lead the fight against violence. They also called for others to support women in their struggle, demanding that the community at large—including men—offer assistance and work through neighborhood, religious, and work-related groups to prevent violence against women. In addition, they called for free medical treatment and compensation for victims of sexual assault and legal reforms to facilitate rape prosecutions and expand women's right to self-defense; they also requested that the city council set up shelters for battered women and children, improve a municipal center that provided emergency assistance to battered women, and provide regular funding for the RCC.[58] Beyond these specific demands, the march's statement of principles laid out long-term transformations that were needed to end violence against women. The "ultimate answer," according to the principles adopted by the march organizers, "lies in changing the basic power relationships between men and women in this society. . . . We have to create new values and systems that are based on equality, respect, and self-determination for all people, and to fight to eliminate values and systems that are based on beliefs of supremacy of one group of people over another and on hatred and degradation of people and exploitation."[59]

But as feminists had done in past cooperative efforts, the coalition of women activists who planned this event for months struggled to find consensus. One particularly contentious issue concerned the appropriateness of seeking endorsements from mixed-sex groups. The march coordinators agreed to ask for the support of mixed groups, believing such a step would help broaden the constituency of the antiviolence movement by testing the perception that feminists were attacking men. Loretta Ross and Nkenge Toure both belonged to the Citywide Housing Coalition, a group fighting the displacement of the city's poor residents as a result of new residential and commercial development. By gaining the backing of this group, the march organizers politically linked sexual violence to other issues that reflected the concerns of the city's African American population. Conversely, working separately from men would have alienated the RCC and other antiviolence groups from the larger community and would have excluded from participation women who worked for political change within mixed-sex groups.[60] But other women objected that such outreach would dilute the push for women's liberation that was the antiviolence movement's ultimate goal. Members of the Washington Area Women's Center, for example, withdrew from the march, upset by the contradiction they perceived between men's participation and the underlying principle that all men were potential rapists.[61]

On the night of the Stop Violence march, the organizers clashed again regarding men's participation. RCC affiliates invited members of Rap, a mixed-sex group of recovering substance addicts, to march at the very front of the parade. Such a stance, they believed, would ensure a strong black presence at the event. But the RCC's actions alarmed other marchers who viewed men's prominence at the front of the march as a sign that women needed male protection. Eventually, the proponents of a mixed march prevailed and Rap occupied the front of the parade, an indication of the increasing influence of women of color in the movement and a reflection of organizers' willingness to risk alienating some feminists for the goal of creating a multiracial march. Although the week's events caused some women, including representatives of the Women's Center, to drop out, other participants considered the community action against violence an important and positive development for the city's women's movement.[62]

Demonstrating the impact of African American activists on the antiviolence against women movement, the Stop Violence Week events signaled the transitions that followed this change in personnel and participants' mixed reactions to the shifting tactics and ideas that guided the Washington movement. The week's activities also revealed the consequences of coalitions, highlighting the ideological splits and differing political priorities embraced by women who agreed on the broad goal of ending sexual violence. Even when some activists moved to broaden feminism's base and to introduce interpretations and programs that demonstrated a greater understanding of the interconnections of sexism, racism, and economic oppression, other women perceived this broadening as a violation of feminism. By expanding feminism's ideas and approaches into areas that recognized the intertwining nature of racism and sexism, activists took the movement in new directions and away from mobilizing within single-sex and racially homogeneous groups. But this transformation also threatened to distract from the goal of women's liberation. By exposing differences among women activists and demonstrating the compromises required for the movement's growth, the Stop Violence protest harkened back to some of the earlier arguments that had divided the DCWLM and confronted the coalitions that formed in the late 1960s to fight for reproductive rights and the ERA. With African American women's presence solidly established at the center of the antiviolence movement by the late 1970s, however, the response to disagreements regarding the intersecting nature of race, sex, and women's liberation differed from previous disputes that had caused feminists to emphasize gender separatism and accept, albeit unhappily, the predominantly white composition of their movement. Instead, black and white activists in the RCC, My Sister's Place, the DCAFA, and other groups strengthened their resolve to fight racial homogeneity and to expand feminism's borders, even at the cost of losing the support of feminists who advocated separatism from men.

The successes of the antiviolence movement suggest that the adoption of a single-issue focus, such as improving the treatment received by rape victims and establishing crisis housing for women escaping abusive relationships, helped to bridge the different ideologies and identities that women activists brought to their work. Likewise, a more formal organizational structure that emphasized action over theory facilitated the involvement of a more diverse constituency of women, a development that shifted the analytical foundations on which such organizations based their work. These changes helped create an infrastructure of services and built a movement that extended over time. The vigilance, persistence, and trust required to maintain a dialogue about the interplay of sexism, racism, elitism, and homophobia paid off in a multiracial coalition to fight violence against women that in both ideology and services expanded to make the experience of women of color central to feminist work. By welcoming the participation and leadership of African American women, the antiviolence movement played a critical role in transforming how feminism was practiced and conceived within Washington, D.C.

Conclusion

In 1980, D.C. activists organized two events that reflected changes in the city's feminist movement as well as the persistence of tensions that had beset the movement during the past decade. In May, the D.C. Area Feminist Alliance (DCAFA) organized a conference, "Combating Racism in the Women's Movement." Since its formation three years earlier, the DCAFA had joined approximately two dozen feminist organizations to struggle together against sexism. By forming a coalition, the DCAFA intended to enhance the effectiveness of the individual groups involved in the fight for women's liberation. Furthermore, as an alliance, the DCAFA foregrounded activists' commitment to finding agreement despite differences that continued to define the separate approaches, emphases, and ideas of feminist groups.[1]

The relationship of African American women to organized feminism was one central concern that continued to occupy feminists' attention and divide activists from each other. Ten years after the August 26th Women's Strike for Equality, Washington feminists still struggled to define the real and theoretical connections between racism and sexism and to balance the desire for gender solidarity with recognition of women's differences. The 1980 DCAFA conference targeted local white women who wanted to confront the impact of racism on the feminist movement, thereby defining racism as a women's issue and a form of oppression inextricably linked to sexism.[2] Calling for feminists to examine the personal, institutional, and structural manifestations of racism, conference organizers hoped to bring together activists who were willing to acknowledge "white racism as our problem" and view racism as a critical, not tangential, component of women's liberation. "Dealing with racism is essential to the survival of the women's movement," conference organizers proclaimed, admitting that the movement's future depended on its ability to continue to expand beyond the small and racially homogeneous groups that characterized the second wave's first decade. "Not only has racism divided women and thus weakened us, it divides feminists from other people consciously fighting oppression with whom we can potentially ally." In addition to helping feminists make strategic connections, DCAFA representatives argued that confronting racism would help women "better understand our own oppression as women by understanding the connections, similarities, and differences between racism and sexism."[3]

Two months later, the RCC convened the First National Third World Women's Conference on Violence. More than one hundred women and men from around the United States gathered at the Washington rape crisis facility to discuss the impact of feminism and violence on their communities and to assess the usefulness of the resources, strategies, and analyses developed by the antiviolence movement. With time and space away from white feminists, people of color could contemplate their role in the antiviolence against women movement, build networks to support their work, and specifically address the violence that disproportionately affected men and women in their communities. In recognition of the importance of the gathering, white women associated with the RCC provided logistical support, offering child care, transportation, and other resources essential to pull off the conference.[4]

According to Nkenge Toure, one of the event's planners, attendees focused on these concerns: "How are we affected by violence against women? How is it interpreted in our communities? What are its causes? What is our relationship to the experiences of others outside our immediate communities who are working on this issue?"[5] Conference participants answered these questions by affirming that effective sexual violence prevention needed to extend beyond efforts undertaken by white feminists. Instead, effective campaigns against violence had to "reflect third world culture and customs . . . politics and aspirations . . . and perceive the direction in which third world women want their lives to take in terms of family, lifestyle and relations with men." At the same time, women needed to amass support within their racial and ethnic communities for the struggle against violence and for self-defense. This demand placed African American women at the symbolic and pragmatic intersection of campaigns for race and sexual liberation. This position contrasted with the roles they perceived they occupied within these movements; within antiviolence against women groups, for example, women of color concluded that a glass ceiling constrained the staff positions they held within rape crisis centers and battered women's shelters. Conference participants concluded, "Third World women, on the threshold of the 1980s, are in a pivotal position to forge the links between the white women's movement and our own Third World communities."[6] Struggles for prominence between black and Latina women at the conference also demonstrated to participants that they could not gloss over differences among the many ethnic groups included under the category "Third World." In the end, delegates agreed, according to Toure, that "the greatest points of unity seemed to be an understanding of the vastness of our task as third world women to develop ideology, direction, programs and community support toward the elimination of violence against Third World women."[7]

Both conferences, Combating Racism in the Women's Movement and the First National Third World Women's Conference on Violence, represented milestones within Washington. The establishment of a formal national network of Third World women active in the antiviolence movement marked a crucial step in making black, Latina, and Native American women equal partners with white feminists in the movement to stop sexual violence and ensure that their communities received the services they need. Coming together at the conference, Third World women battled to establish their place as participants, allies, and critics of organized feminism. Simultaneously, white feminists in Washington were taking steps to transform their movement so it could expand and survive. By organizing a conference specifically to challenge white activists' prejudice, and by supporting women of color's demand to claim separate time and space at the Third World Women's Conference, Washington's white radical feminists expressed their commitment to pushing their movement to both recognize and act on the basis of the differences that shaped women's experiences.

By showing the continued evolution of Washington's radical feminist movement, these forums represented on a micro level the challenges and changes experienced by the city's women's movement. Working separately in groups focused on specific issues or in groups defined by the political ideology or racial or sexual identity of their members, Washington's radical women tackled a constellation of concerns by mustering their distinct, but sometimes overlapping, ideas, tactics, constituencies, and resources. From the mid-1960s through the end of the next decade, members of the Rape Crisis Center, Washington Area Women's Center, D.C. Commission on the Status of Women, D.C. Area Feminist Alliance, National Welfare Rights Organization, and Pride, Inc., along with representatives of national organizations based in the District, repeatedly came together to develop programs and tactics that fitted their particular context; choosing, for example, protest tactics that targeted federal agencies and thereby maximized their visibility on a local and national level. By voicing their disparate views and perspectives on women's roles and issues, women activists together fashioned a broader movement of concerned citizens working to analyze sex roles in society, improve women's condition, and define women's opportunities on their own terms.

The close-up examination of women's activism in Washington in the 1960s and 1970s undertaken in this book shows that definitions of the movements themselves—civil rights, antipoverty, welfare rights, radical feminism, black power, lesbian feminism, and antiviolence—followed often unpredictable paths. The ideas, strategies, and agendas devised by activists to address one specific issue at times converged and diverged with other local campaigns within a particular social, political, and economic context. Simultaneously, individual personalities and the reactions of antagonistic and supportive forces guided grassroots efforts. The view of 1960s and 1970s social movements at a city level, therefore, prompts a redefinition of the forces that guide and govern political campaigns: theory, generated by activists within local groups and influenced by literature and ideas disseminated nationally and internationally, developed hand in hand with practice, both responding to local conditions and revealing pragmatic and visionary designs. Both analysis and tactics evolved and changed in the process of implementation, especially when different constituencies met and tried to work through differences and disagreements.

This study of women's grassroots activism in 1960s and 1970s Washington, D.C., thus yields several implications for the understanding of social movements. First, a case study of activism in one city reveals the complexity and fluidity of political campaigns and the extent to which such campaigns, and the activists involved in them, resist easy categorization. Nkenge Toure, Charlotte Bunch, Mary Treadwell, and Etta Horn exemplify women whose contributions to Washington's social change movements extended beyond the boundaries of single organizations. Seeing the connectedness of struggles for sexual, racial, and economic liberation, such women involved themselves in multiple campaigns and organizations. By virtue of the many activities to which they devoted their time and energy, these activists created ideological and practical bridges that linked the era's movements.

Second, women's grassroots activities in the District complicate ideas about identity politics. Because efforts to solve problems, more than rigid adherence to theory, drove much activity within Washington, women activists created coalitions and alliances even as they participated in identity-based movements. Alliances depended on activists' willingness to form partnerships with individuals and groups outside their own circles and on their ability to construct shared agendas and goals that superseded differences in identity, theory, and tactics. Proponents of Black Power modeled racial separatism in a variety of ways, mostly promoting black leadership and solidarity without completely pulling back from interracial alliances. Even the most vehement advocates of separatism, the Furies, who argued in favor of separatism not only from men but also from women activists who allied with men, nonetheless arranged skills workshops and other outreach activities that connected them to activists who did not share their ideology. The existence of such cooperative activity indicates that identity politics did not necessarily or exclusively foster separatism but, rather, that activists sometimes advocated separatism even as they practiced it in a fluid manner. This duality accomplished results at the ground level at the same time that it created tensions that activists struggled to resolve.

In Washington, the issues around which women initiated campaigns and organizations that most effectively encompassed racial, economic, and sexual differences—such as the move to reform local abortion policies or to address sexual violence—tended to focus on specific, concrete problems and solutions. Furthermore, such campaigns incorporated participants in a way that allowed for diverse opinions about the causes of women's condition yet defined a series of specific goals on which activists could agree. In contrast, collective efforts that prioritized the production of theory over mass organizing or rigidly adhered to separatist ideas, like the Furies, found movement building difficult and inclusivity impossible to sustain. To the extent that women succeeded in building campaigns that connected diverse activists and groups, they found the experience enlightening and informative. Although collaboration yielded concrete outcomes, such as the introduction of legislation, the incorporation of women in decision-making bodies, or the creation of policies, it also affected participants and campaigns in unanticipated ways.

Third, this examination demonstrates radical feminism's fluidity and ability to encompass dissent. Significantly, as political campaigns and groups converged, they changed course. Ironically, however, as demonstrated by the cooperatively staged abortion reform campaign, the Women's Strike Day march and rally, the Revolutionary People's Constitutional Convention, and the Stop Rape Week, coalitions often served as points at which activists clarified their ideologies and identities, defined on the basis of the differences that distinguished them from their partners in alliances rather than on the basis of common ground. The learning process activists underwent and the frustrations they experienced when engaged in such collaborative endeavors punctuated differences as well as highlighted commonalities. Rather than heralding coalitions as points of unity and sisterhood, we must recognize the tendency to demarcate oppositional identities and political positions that can arise in their wake. This accentuation of differences discouraged activists who viewed gender solidarity as key to women's liberation, but they also nurtured fruitful anger and analysis in response to the perceived failures of coalitions. Furthermore, at the same time that women activists traveled complicated paths and influenced each other's understanding of self and collective identity, the smaller groups and larger movements to which they belonged grew along trajectories that were simultaneously interconnected and relational as well as oppositional and separate. Thus, campaigns for sexual, racial, and economic liberation in the 1960s and 1970s must be examined for their influence on each other as well as for being autonomous movements in their own right.

This study of women's political activism in Washington, D.C., then, tells the story of how women addressed questions of commonality and difference and thought about the forces that divided and united them. In the process, women emerged as powerful actors in their community and as profound influences on the major social movements of the period. By revealing the tensions, travails, and triumphs of radical women activists, a multilayered and complex picture of second-wave feminism emerges. On the local level, radical feminism emerged as part of a reciprocal process, albeit a generally unintentional one. Through constant overlap and interaction, campaigns for radical feminism, black liberation, and economic justice exchanged ideas and people, in the process fostering both internal tensions and intermovement conflict that sometimes resulted in setbacks and sometimes led to productive new directions. Within self-defined feminist groups, activists debated the nature of women's oppression and struggled to balance their desire for gender solidarity with the realities of the differences that separated women. African American women's participation in welfare rights and black liberation groups nurtured not only their political skills but also an awareness of the impact of gender oppression that gradually influenced movements for economic justice, racial liberation, and feminism. Eventually, these divergent streams of activism merged, transforming the movement against sexual violence and yielding distinct black and Third World feminist movements. Separate but interconnected, these branches of feminism provided a foundation for further women's movements that extended into the 1980s and beyond.

Notes

Introduction

1. Claudia Levy and Alex Ward, "Women Rally to Publicize Grievances," *Washington Post,* 27 August 1970, A1, A7; Haynes Johnson, "'Equal Rights Now,' Exhort Women Protesters," *Washington Post,* 27 August 1970, A1, A6; "2 Rallies Planned By Women in D.C.," *Washington Post,* 26 August 1970, A10.

2. "Toward a Mass Feminist Movement," resolution passed at the 1971 national convention of the Socialist Workers Party, reprinted in Jenness, *Feminism and Socialism*, 148.

3. "It's NOW for a FEW Bold Ladies," *Washington Daily News,* 27 August 1970, 1, 5; "Men View Biggest Lady's Day of All," *Washington Daily News,* 27 August 1970, 5; Myra MacPherson, "Battle of the Sexes Becomes a Word War," *Washington Post,* 27 August 1970, C1, C4; Lillian Wiggins, "'I'll Fight Not with Men, but with the System,'" *Washington Afro-American,* 29 August 1970, 1, 18.

4. Gluck, "Whose Feminism, Whose History?" in Naples, *Community Activism and Feminist Politics*; Thompson, "Multiracial Feminism."

5. Studies of black feminism include White, *Too Heavy a Load*; Roth, *Separate Roads to Feminism*; Baxandall, "Re-Visioning the Women's Liberation Movement's Narrative"; Springer, *Living for the Revolution*; Nadasen, *Welfare Warriors*; and Guy-Sheftall, *Words of Fire.* Case studies include Polatnick, "Diversity in Women's Liberation Ideology"; Nelson, *Women of Color and the Reproductive Rights Movement*; Ross, "African American Women and Abortion," in Solinger, *Abortion Wars.*

6. Stephanie Gilmore brilliantly challenges the "liberal" and "radical" feminist labels in "Rethinking the Liberal/Radical Divide: The National Organization for Women in Columbus, Memphis, and San Francisco, 1966–1982," Ph.D. diss., Ohio State University, 2005. See also Barakso, *Governing NOW.*

7. Overviews include Davis, *Moving the Mountain*; Rosen, *World Split Open*; Brownmiller, *In Our Time*; Evans, *Personal Politics*; and Echols, *Daring to Be Bad*. For a discussion of second-wave feminism and the New Left, see Kesselman, "Women's Liberation and the Left in New Haven."

8. Springer, *Living for the Revolution*; Roth, *Separate Roads to Feminism*; Nelson, *Women of Color and the Reproductive Rights Movement*.

9. In a study of black nationalism, E. Frances White similarly argues that protest movements are challenged by both mainstream views and alternate discourses raised from within and outside the movement; White, "Africa on My Mind," 80.

10. Meyer and Whittier, "Social Movement Spillover."

11. Other scholars have attempted to broaden the definition of feminist theory. See King, *Theory in Its Feminist Travels*, 1–54; Collins, *Black Feminist Thought*.

12. In several case studies, scholars demonstrate that feminism must be understood at the local level in the context of distinct political, social, and economic forces that shaped priorities and resources. See Ezekiel, *Feminism in the Heartland*; Freeman, "From the Lesbian Nation to the Cincinnati Lesbian Community"; Enke, "Smuggling Sex through the Gates"; Gilmore, "Dynamics of Second-Wave Feminist Activism."

13. Nicholas von Hoffman, "Feminine Revolution-within-the-Revolution," *Washington Post* (n.d., circa January 1969), Women, 1968–1969 Article File, D.C. Community Archives, Washingtoniana Division, Martin Luther King Jr. Public Library, Washington, D.C.

14. Gilmore, "Dynamics of Second-Wave Feminist Activism."

15. Fraser founded the D.C. chapter of the Women's Equity Action League. Fraser, "Insiders and Outsiders," in Tinker, *Women in Washington*, 122.

Chapter 1: Mobilizing for Political and Economic Rights

1. Jaffe and Sherwood, *Dream City*, 48–49; M. Margaret Green, "A Soft-Spoken, No-Nonsense Activist," *Washington Star*, 7 November 1971, F-3.

2. Green, "Soft-Spoken, No-Nonsense Activist"; Halberstam, *Children*.

3. Paul W. Valentine, "Peace Movement Held Racist," *Washington Post*, 17 June 1972, A1, A10.

4. Mary Treadwell, "Black Women," *WONAAC Newsletter*, 21 October 1971, 7.

5. Jaffe and Sherwood, *Dream City*, 101; Sally Quinn, "Marion Barry Marries," *Washington Post*, 27 May 1972, B3. In 1983, Treadwell was convicted of defrauding the federal government of money allocated to Pride to manage a public housing project. She served about eighteen months in jail. Later she worked for the D.C. city government and was elected to the Advisory Neighborhood Commission. In the late 1990s, she was again accused of theft for taking funds from the Advisory Neighborhood Commission that she chaired. Found guilty of these charges, she served several months in jail in 1998. Lillian Wiggins, "Treadwell Has Paid Her Debt to Society," *Washington Informer*, 8 July 1987, 10; Yolanda Woodlee, "Judge Sentences Treadwell to Four Months in Prison," *Washington Post*, 31 January 1998, B4.

6. Studies of the black freedom movement in midwestern and northern states include Theoharis and Woodard, *Freedom North*; Woodard, *A Nation within a Nation*; Meier and Rudwick, *CORE*; Lang, "Between Civil Rights and Black Power."

7. "Survey Recommends End to Segregation"; National Committee on Segregation in the Nation's Capital, *Segregation in Washington*; Halberstam, *Children*, 540–44; Dudziak, *Cold War Civil Rights*.

8. This case, *Bolling v. Sharpe*, was heard on appeal by the Supreme Court as part of the *Brown v. Board of Education* suit. See Kluger, *Simple Justice*; *Washington History* 16 (Fall/Winter 2004–5).

9. Accounts by participants in the 1940s and 1950s desegregation campaigns include Caplan, *Farther Along*; Murray, *Autobiography of a Black Activist*. The records of the Coordinating Committee are in Reel 14, *Papers of Mary Church Terrell* (Washington, D.C.: Library of Congress, 1977).

10. Meier and Rudwick, *CORE*, 50–54.

11. For the history of SNCC, see Carson, *In Struggle*; Ransby, *Ella Baker*, 239–329; Greenberg, *Circle of Trust*.

12. Carson, *In Struggle*, 103–4; Kopkind, "Future of 'Black Power,'" 16. Participants' descriptions of NAG's activities come from Carmichael with Thelwell, *Ready for Revolution*; Brown, *Die Nigger Die!*, 59, 66–69; Smith, "I Learned to Feel Black," in Barbour, *Black Power Revolt*, 207–18; Sellers with Terrell, *River of No Return*, 57–66; and biographies listed on the Veterans of the Civil Rights Movement Web site, http://crmvet.org.

13. Interviews with Paula Giddings, Adrienne Manns Israel, Anthony Gittens, and Robin Gregory, conducted by Blackside, Inc., for *Eyes on the Prize II*, Washington University Libraries, Film and Media Archive, Henry Hampton Collection.

14. Carmichael with Thelwell, *Ready for Revolution*, 136–62. The fight against curfews continued into the late 1960s and is discussed in chapter 5.

15. During a wave of protests on Howard's campus in 1968, many activities centered on the women's dormitories and involved large groups of women. For reflections on curfews as an asset when it came to political organizing, see Due and Due Stevens, *Freedom in the Family*, 44.

16. Carson, *In Struggle*, 72; Carmichael with Thelwell, *Ready for Revolution*, 161, 265–67; Cobb, "Black Power."

17. Carson, *In Struggle*, 103–4.

18. Ransby, *Ella Baker*, 348–50; Greenberg, *Circle of Trust*, 152–76; Carson, *In Struggle*, 215–43. Although many accounts have stressed the interracial nature of SNCC before 1965, Howard Zinn's 1964 history of SNCC reminds readers that the role of white activists always generated discussion within the organization. Zinn, *SNCC*, ch. 9. For more on the shift to cities, see Mike Thelwell, "Toward Black Liberation," quoted in Greenberg, *Circle of Trust*, 154; Carmichael with Thelwell, *Ready for Revolution*, 477–78; Stoper, *Student Nonviolent Coordinating Committee*, 35–37; Carson, *In Struggle*, 231.

19. Greenberg, *Circle of Trust,* 127–51; Evans, *Personal Politics.*

20. Marion Barry to SNCC Executive Committee and Staff, 14 March 1966, Reel 61, *Student Nonviolent Coordinating Committee Papers, 1959–1972* (Sanford, N.C.: Microfilming Corporation of America, 1980).

21. D.C. SNCC's Steering Committee Memo, 8 August 1966, Reel 61, *SNCC Papers.*

22. Richard Corrigan, "SNCC Claims 90 Per Cent Success with Its Benning Road Bus Boycott," *Washington Post,* 25 January 1966, A1; "Bond in District, Praises Boycott," *Washington Afro-American,* 29 January 1966, 1; "SNCC Speaks Out," *Washington Afro-American,* 2 February 1966, 4; Smith, *Captive Capital,* 239–42; Dorothy Burlage, interview by author, 21 February 1995; Burlage, "Truths of the Heart," in Curry et al., *Deep in Our Hearts,* 123.

23. "Store Boycott Planned by New Rights Group Supporting Home Rule," *Washington Post,* 22 February 1966, C1.

24. D.C. Mobilization Committee Minutes, Reel 58, *SNCC Papers.*

25. "Julius Hobson: A Goad for Change," *Washington Post,* 2 July 1972, B1, B8; Booker, "Washington's Civil Rights Maverick."

26. CORE Correspondence, D.C. Community Archives, Collection 1, Series 2, Box 1, Julius W. Hobson Papers, MLK Library. Unemployment figures compiled by the Equal Employment Opportunity Commission and announced by Ben D. Segal, director of the EEOC Office of Liaison, during a speech to the D.C. Chamber of Commerce. "Segal Says Community Progress Needs True Racial Cooperation," *Washington Afro-American,* 29 January 1966, 8.

27. Ad Hoc Sub Committee for an Effective Washington CORE Chapter to James Farmer, 8 May 1964, Reel 20, *Congress On Racial Equality Papers, 1941–1968* (Sanford, N.C.: Microfilming Corporation of America, 1982); Meier and Rudwick, *CORE,* 197–98, 286–92.

28. Booker, "Washington's Civil Rights Maverick," 141–42; Meier and Rudwick, *CORE,* 185–88, 227, 241; Smith, *Captive Capital,* 257–58; Dudziak, *Cold War Civil Rights,* 167–69.

29. Information about participants in the D.C. SNCC chapter was gleaned from chapter files, Reels 58 and 61, *SNCC Papers,* and from the listings at the Veterans of the Civil Rights Movement Web site, www.crmvet.org. For CORE, see "Washington CORE—Active Voting List," 24 March 1964, Reel 20, *CORE Papers.* Charles Payne argues that SNCC's structure and philosophy made it open to women in a way that older civil rights organizations were not. Payne, *I've Got the Light of Freedom,* 268. See also Ransby, *Ella Baker,* 310–11.

30. "Proposed Constitution of Washington CORE, Majority Draft, March, 1964," Reel 20, *CORE Papers*; Meier and Rudwick, *CORE,* ch. 10.

31. Five women and four men brought charges to the national Steering Committee seeking Hobson's ouster, but no women joined the seven men who presented evidence in his support. "Minutes of the May 22, 1964 Steering Committee Meeting," Reel 20,

CORE Papers; Julius W. Hobson, interview by Katherine Shannon, 3 July 1967, RJB 4/322, transcript, Civil Rights Documentation Project, Moorland-Spingarn Research Center, Howard University.

32. Naomi Eftis to James Farmer, 19 October 1964, and "Report of Community Organization Committee to Washington CORE," 13 October 1964, Reel 20, *CORE Papers*; "Freedom School Opens with 60 in Attendance," *Washington Afro-American,* 17 October 1964, 7.

33. James D. Williams, "The Committee," *Washington Afro-American,* 16 April 1966, 1–2.

34. "New CORE Leader to Seek 'Black Power' in District," *Washington Afro-American,* 9 July 1966, 1; "Washington CORE Officers, December 11, 1964," Reel 20, *CORE Papers*; FBI Memo on D.C. Core, 30 November 1966, FBI Files.

35. Evans, *Personal Politics,* 108.

36. Tina Smith, interview by author, 17 May 1994; Sharlene Kranz, interview by author, 23 August 2004; D.C. Steering Committee Memo, 8 August 1966, Reel 61, *SNCC Papers*; Gregory interview, Hampton Collection.

37. "No Faint Heart," *Washington Afro-American,* 7 May 1966, 4.

38. Kranz interview; Sharlene Kranz biography at Veterans of the Civil Rights Movement Web site, www.crmvet.org/vet/kranz.htm (10 June 2003).

39. Sexual relationships between black men and white women in SNCC have received extensive attention from historians and former participants. The impact of these relationships among Washington, D.C., staff and volunteers is hard to discern from available primary sources, although Marion Barry's infidelities were well known. Schultz, *Going South,* 118–19.

40. Mary Stratford, "No Changes Forecast in Local SNCC Setup," *Washington Afro-American,* 21 May 1966, 1–2; Betty Garman interview in Stoper, *Student Nonviolent Coordinating Committee,* 285–303; Betty Garman, interview by author, 17 April 1994; Betty Garman to Marion Barry, 1 March 1966, Reel 61, *SNCC Papers.*

41. Smith interview.

42. Piven and Cloward, *Regulating the Poor*, 256–63.

43. Community Action Programs were established by the Office of Economic Opportunity under the Economic Opportunity Act (1964). The programs concentrated on urban poverty and specified that the poor would determine community needs and develop comprehensive services and programs.

44. Wiley Branton, "UPO Report of Programs and Budgets," City Council Hearings on the United Planning Organization, 25 June 1968, District of Columbia City Council Papers, Gelman Library, George Washington University; "Statement by Wiley A. Branton, Executive Director, UPO," 27 June 1968, Wiley A. Branton Papers, Box 187–11 Folder 33, Moorland-Spingarn Research Center, Howard University.

45. Branton, "UPO Report of Programs and Budgets," City Council Papers, GWU; William Raspberry, "Anacostia: 'City Dump' of Housing," *Washington Post,* 19 June 1968, B1.

46. Smith, *Captive Capital,* 73–75; memo from Kenneth Schlossberg to Edgar May, 17 August 1966, UPO August 1966–October 1966, IR 1964–1967, Office of Economic Opportunity, General Records of the Community Services Administration, Record Group 381, National Archives, College Park, Md.

47. Dorothy Boulding Ferebee, interview by Merze Tate, 28 and 31 December 1979 in *Black Women Oral History Project,* edited by the Schlesinger Library, 444–50 (Cambridge, Mass.: Radcliffe College, 1980); Felix, "African American Women in Social Reform."

48. "Southeast House Celebrates 50 Years of Community Service," *Washington Afro-American,* 3 May 1980, 3.

49. Ophelia S. Egypt, "Ten Year Report on Program of Community Education, February, 1956 to June, 1966," Folder 8, Box 16, Ophelia Egypt Papers, Moorland-Spingarn Research Center, Howard University.

50. Zora Martin-Felton, interview by author, 20 March 1995.

51. Burlage interview; Schlossberg to May, 14 July 1967, IR 1964–1967, OEO Papers.

52. Ten people worked as antipoverty organizers and three as consumer education aides. Betty James, "First Anti-Poverty Workers Graduate at SEH," *Washington Star,* 6 March 1965, Southeast House Article File, MLK Library; Pharnal Longus, "Change in a Public Housing Development: A Case Study, Barry Farms," 1978, unpublished document in author's possession.

53. Nancy Naples found that War on Poverty workers in New York and Philadelphia similarly moved into paid positions that resembled work they already performed in their neighborhoods and communities. Naples, *Grassroots Warriors.*

54. Theresa Jones, interview by author, 24 August 1995; Felix, "African American Women in Social Reform," 56–64.

55. Dorothy Gilliam and Willard Clopton, "Anti-Poverty War Is Giving the Poor the Weapons to Fight Back," *Washington Post,* 20 February 1966, B1; Jesse W. Lewis Jr., "Poor Ask to Run Anti-Poverty Unit," *Washington Post,* 16 February 1966, C1; Branton, "UPO Report of Programs and Budgets," Appendix, City Council Papers, GWU Library; Carol Williams, "Cleaning Up Washington's Forgotten Backyard," *Communities in Action,* 2 (April–May 1967), 3–6; Smith, "From Cracker Barrel to Laundromat."

56. Leroy F. Aarons, "Barry Farms Group Sows Seeds of 'Rebellion,'" *Washington Post,* 27 February 1966, B9.

57. Burlage, "Truths of the Heart," in Curry et al., *Deep in Our Hearts;* Ken Schlossberg to Edgar May, 14 July 1967, Inspection Reports, Box 16, OEO Papers.

58. Longus, "Change in a Public Housing Development."

59. "Getting the Message Across," *Communities in Action* 1 (December 1966): 7. Antipoverty organizers affiliated with SDS similarly discovered women's effectiveness as organizers, according to Frost, *"An Interracial Movement of the Poor,"* 23, 77–79.

60. Longus memo of June 1966, quoted in Schlossberg to May, 14 July 1967, Inspection Reports, Box 16, OEO Papers.

61. Burlage, "Truths of the Heart," in Curry et al., *Deep in Our Hearts,* 122; Longus, "Change in a Public Housing Development," 10–11.

62. Martin-Felton interview; Theresa Jones interview; Burlage interview; Naples, *Grassroots Warriors,* 148.

63. "Cleaning Up Washington's Forgotten Backyard"; "Barry Farm Group Sows Seeds of 'Rebellion'"; "Band of Angels, Rebels with a Cause, Give Housing Chief Tough Afternoon," *Washington Post,* 28 February 1966, B2; Schlossberg to May, 14 July 1967, IR 1964–1967, OEO Papers.

64. Ruth Jenkins, "Divided Day of Work, Study Produces Better Men," *Washington Afro-American,* 26 February 1966, 13.

65. The emphasis on creating jobs for men as a solution to poverty became apparent during a series of conferences held by the Office of Economic Opportunity. High-level government administrators who spoke at the conferences acknowledged the devastating impact of women's poverty, particularly as it affected children. At the same time, speakers asked women to volunteer in support of new employment training programs to train "the total man." U.S. Office of Economic Opportunity, *Women in the War on Poverty* (Washington, D.C.: Government Printing Office, 1967), 9–10; U.S. Office of Economic Opportunity, *Women in the War on Poverty* (Washington, D.C.: Government Printing Office, 1968), 54–55; U.S. Office of Economic Opportunity, *Women in the War on Poverty* (Washington, D.C.: Government Printing Office, 1969), 4.

66. UPO, *Alternatives: A Special Report on the United Planning Organization* (Washington, D.C.: UPO, 1969), 14, 37; "New 'Dramatic Techniques' in UPO Manpower Proposal."

67. Carol Honsa, "SE Forms Anti-Poverty Sewing Circle," *Washington Post,* 3 February 1968, B4.

68. "Beating the System Together: Interview with a Black Feminist," *off our backs* 4 (October 1973): 2; Lowe, *First Twenty Years,* 26; Carol Honsa, "Red-Faced UPO Still Offers Pill," *Washington Post,* 25 July 1967; "Birth Control Issue Leads to UPO Firing," *Washington Star,* 29 July 1967; Carol Honsa, "UPO Official Is Fired for Birth Control Talk," *Washington Post,* 29 July 1967, from Birth Control 1965–1969 Article File, MLK Library; Task Force on Women in Poverty Report, 1967, reprinted in Carabillo, Meuli, and Csida, *Feminist Chronicles,* 171.

69. John Barber, "Project Organizes Youth in District for Self-Help," *Hilltop,* 13 October 1967, 5; Ivan Brandon, "Pride Becomes 'The Man' as Apartment Landlord," *Washington Post,* 25 August 1970, C1, C3; "Civic, Business Leaders Give $1,000 to Help Pride Firm Stave Off Crisis," *Washington Post,* 26 November 1970, A31; Diane Brockett, "Pride Lands New Contract," *Washington Star,* 11 November 1979, E1, E8.

70. Frank Speltz, untitled interview with UPO employees, *Washington Free Press,* 31 May 1968, 12–13; "UPO Employees Dismissed, Resign," *Washington Afro-American,* 27 April 1968, 1. Members of the D.C. chapter of the Black Panther Party accused the federal government of using the antipoverty program to suppress political activism. Reginald "Malik" Edwards, quoted in Terry, *Bloods,* 12.

71. "UPO Employees Dismissed, Resign," *Washington Afro-American,* 27 April 1968, 1; Dorothy Gilliam and Willard Clopton, "UPO's Bank Rolls with Criticism, Looks to Best Year," *Washington Post,* 24 February 1966, B1, B4.

72. Marion Barry and H. Rap Brown both worked for the UPO and UPO-funded Pride, Inc. Brown, *Die Nigger Die!,* 75–79; Speltz, untitled interview with UPO employees; "UPO Employees Dismissed, Resign," *Washington Afro-American,* 27 April 1968, 1; Burlage, "Truths of the Heart," in Curry et al., *Deep in Our Hearts,* 123–24.

73. Smith, *Captive Capital,* 254–56. Historian Michael Katz concluded that the War on Poverty's community action programs "nourished and intensified a growing citizens' movement, reshaped local politics, and launched a new generation of minority leaders, many of them women, into public life." Katz, *Undeserving Poor,* 114.

74. Longus, "Change in a Public Housing Development."

75. Williams, "Cleaning Up Washington's Forgotten Backyard"; "Getting the Message Across." A 1972 survey conducted by one of the city's newspapers named Hobson the "individual who has fought the hardest for positive change in the District." Marion Barry was the runner-up. "Hobson Picked in Poll as Person Who Worked Hardest for Change," *Washington Post,* 27 May 1972, A24. On Hobson, see "Julius Hobson: A Goad for Change," *Washington Post,* 2 July 1972, B1, B3; Elizabeth Shelton, "There's No Room in the Hobsons' Life for Ennui," *Washington Post,* 23 August 1970, E1, E4.

76. Many journalists have attempted to explain Marion Barry's political successes; see Barras, *Last of the Black Emperors*; Agronsky, *Marion Barry*; Jaffe and Sherwood, *Dream City.*

77. Kranz interview; Smith interview.

78. Burlage, "Truths of the Heart," in Curry et al., *Deep in Our Hearts,* 125; Klatch, *Generation Divided,* 172.

79. Felix, "African American Women in Social Reform," 56–64; Theresa Jones interview; 1978 D.C. Mayoral Transition Taskforce, Box 27, Anne B. Turpeau papers, Library of Congress; Lowe, *First Twenty Years.*

Chapter 2: Defining Welfare Rights

1. Etta Horn interview by Mary Kotz, 20 November 1974, Tape 143, Collection 1304A, State Historical Society of Wisconsin; Felix, "African American Women in Social Reform"; Juliette Harris, "Etta Horne on Welfare: 'It's a Disgrace!'" *Washington Examiner,* 5–8 October 1967, in Public Welfare Article File, MLK Library.

2. Horn interview; Harris, "Etta Horne on Welfare: 'It's a Disgrace!'"

3. Senate Committee on Appropriations, *Supplemental Appropriations for Fiscal Year 1971* (Washington, D.C.: Government Printing Office, 1970), 322. Racial differentials are primarily a result of the larger size of black families as compared to white. U.S. Bureau of the Census, *1970 Census of the Population, Subject Report: Low-Income Areas in Large Cities* (Washington, D.C.: Government Printing Office, 1973), 841–46.

4. "Food Money Often Goes to Pay the Landlord," *Washington Afro-American*, 9 April 1966, 1–2; Carol Honsa, "Welfare Mothers Fighting for Dignity," *Washington Post*, 5 February 1967, M4.

5. Nationally, African American women composed the majority of NWRO members, although white recipients accounted for 53 percent of those on welfare. Nadasen, "Expanding the Boundaries of the Women's Movement," 277; West, *National Welfare Rights Movement*, 45–46. On the establishment of the NWRO, see Kotz and Kotz, *Passion for Equality*, 214–18; Piven and Cloward, *Poor People's Movements*, 294–95; Nadasen, *Welfare Warriors*.

6. Affiliation with the national organization required at least twenty-five members, each paying annual dues of one dollar. To qualify for membership, the majority of each chapter's members had to be welfare recipients; others could qualify for affiliation if their incomes fell below poverty level. "1968 Membership Report, November 9, 1968" and "National Welfare Rights Organization—Membership Reports for 1969," Box 2018, National Welfare Rights Organization Papers, Moorland-Spingarn Library, Howard University; Carol Honsa, "District to Ask Federal Welfare Aid," *Washington Post*, 26 June 1970, C8. No membership figures could be found for the period after 1970. The CWA is also referred to as the Citywide Welfare Rights Organization.

7. Horn interview; Statement of Etta Horn, U.S. Congress, Senate, Subcommittee on Financial Institutions of the Committee on Banking and Currency, *Credit in Low-Income Areas* (Washington, D.C.: Government Printing Office, 1970), 111–32; "More WRO Testimony before Senate Committee," *Welfare Fighter* 3 (March 1972): 12.

8. *Welfare Fighter*, November 1971, 11; J. Y. Smith, "Welfare Rights Protestors Fail to 'Evict' System's Chief," *Washington Post*, 28 October 1971, B2; Valk, "'Mother Power.'"

9. "Welfare Clients Say They Need Back-to-School Money," *Washington Afro-American*, 27 August 1966, 1. Michael Lipsky's study of rent strikes in Harlem in the early 1960s found low-income activists effectively used mass protest to generate sympathetic publicity, win middle-class allies, and build a following. Lipsky, *Protest in City Politics*, 188–92; see also Lipsky, "Protest as a Political Resource."

10. Eve Edstrom, "Protesting Welfare Mothers Rebuked," *Washington Post*, 21 September 1967, A2.

11. Long, quoted in White, *Too Heavy a Load*, 235; Long statement during *Hearings on the Nomination of Elliot L. Richardson to Be Secretary of HEW* (Washington, D.C.: Government Printing Office, 1970), 11.

12. Quote from "Byrd Urges Birth Control for Slum-Area Negroes," *Washington Post*, 17 August 1967, B3. As chair of the Senate Appropriations' District Subcommittee, Byrd had encouraged Washington health officials to develop a birth control program targeting welfare recipients for several years. See Cornelia Ball, "Byrd Backs Birth Control," *Washington Daily News*, 15 October 1963; William Grigg, "Birth Control Study Started by District," *Washington Star*, 16 October 1963, all from Birth Control Article File, MLK Library.

13. Moynihan, *Negro Family*; "Woman Power," *Washington Afro-American,* 6 July 1968, 4.

14. A vast literature addresses the issue of women's use of motherhood and maternalist politics to establish their participation in reform and public work. See White, *Too Heavy a Load*; Hine, "Rape and the Inner Lives of Black Women"; Borris, "Power of Motherhood"; Gordon, "Black and White Visions of Welfare"; Wolcott, *Remaking Respectability.*

15. "Mother Power" signs appeared, for example, during the May 1968 Mother's Day march through D.C. that opened the Poor People's Campaign. Elsie Carper, "3,000 March in Opening of Drive by Poor," *Washington Post,* 13 May 1968, A10.

16. Ernest Holsendolph, "A Test of Wills at Welfare," *Washington Evening Star,* 1 July 1967, 1.

17. Nadasen, *Welfare Warriors,* 49, 135.

18. For other examples of the use of the term "slavery" to refer to work requirements or to the welfare system more generally, see Carol Honsa, "Job Training Delayed," *Washington Post,* 24 June 1968, B1; Elsie Carper, "3000 March in Opening of Drive by Poor," *Washington Post,* 13 May 1968, A10; Elsie Carper, "District's Welfare Policies Must Change, Hill Warned," *Washington Post,* 4 May 1968, B2.

19. Carol Honsa, "Welfare Bill Called 'Betrayal of Poor,'" *Washington Post,* 29 August 1967, A4; Eve Edstrom, "Irate Welfare Mothers Hold 'Wait-In,'" *Washington Post,* 20 September 1967, A1, A7.

20. Organizations invited to the meeting included the League of Women Voters, the American Association of University Women, the National Association of Social Workers, the Women's International League for Peace and Freedom, United Church Women, the National Council of Negro Women, the National Council of Catholic Women, the National Council of Jewish Women, the Society of Friends, the Urban League, and the National Council of Christians and Jews. Etta Horn letter, 23 February 1968, Folder 11, Box 24, George A. Wiley Papers, SHSW; Carolyn Lewis, "Welfare Alliance Cries 'Coercion,'" *Washington Post,* 2 March 1968, B10.

21. "Statement for the Department of Public Welfare Hearing on 1963 Budget Needs—May 15, 1961," and Mrs. Jehu Hunter, to Representative Robert N. Giaimo, 12 April 1963, Washingtoniana Division, D.C. Community Archives, Collection 33, Series 1, Sub-series 2, Box 22, Records of the League of Women Voters of the District of Columbia, MLK Library.

22. "Statement Before Subcommittee of the House Committee on the District of Columbia on H.R. 6528, to Provide a Public Child Day Care Program," 13 September 1967, Box 22, LWV Collection.

23. According to Marisa Chappell, the League of Women Voters had a long-standing commitment to welfare reform and the notion of federal responsibility for the economic well-being of families. By the late 1970s, however, the league supported work requirements. Chappell, "Rethinking Women's Politics."

24. National Organization for Women Papers, Folder 48, Box 170, Schlesinger Library.

25. Task Force on Women in Poverty Report (1967) and National Organization for Women Bill of Rights in 1968 in Carabillo, Meuli, and Csida, *Feminist Chronicles*, 171, 210, 214, and 217–20.

26. Honsa, "Welfare Mothers Fighting for Dignity," M4; Lewis, "Welfare Alliance Cries 'Coercion.'"

27. Bell, "'Rights' of the Poor"; William Chapman, "Man-in-House Rule in Child Aid Voided," *Washington Post*, 18 June 1968, A1, A6; Martin Weil, "Welfare Recipients Question the Givers," *Washington Post*, 18 June 1968, A8.

28. *Mildred v. Stewart, et al., v. Walter E. Washington, et al.*, Folder 14, Box 25, City Council Papers, GWU. In light of this case, the Department of Public Welfare enacted a new policy declaring that refusal to permit inspection of property would not adversely affect any applicant or recipient.

29. Young, "Mama's Welfare Blues"; Ratagick, "Two American Welfare Mothers," 76; Tillmon, "Welfare Is a Women's Issue."

30. Government of the District of Columbia, Department of Public Welfare, Public Assistance Division, Appeal Hearing: Summary of Findings, 8 December 1967 and 5 January 1968, Folder 1, Box 3; and Laurens H. Silver, Deputy Director, Neighborhood Legal Services Program, to Polly Shackleton, D.C. City Council, 9 October 1968, Folder 7, Box 25, City Council Papers, GWU; "A Test of Wills at Welfare," *Washington Star*, 1 July 1967; "Welfare Recipients Stage Tense Three-Hour Protest," *Washington Post*, 1 July 1967, B2; "Welfare Snoopers," *Washington Afro-American*, 4 June 1966, 4; "Welfare Dept. to Resume Hearing on Investigations," *Washington Post*, 12 September 1968, C17.

31. Kotz and Kotz, *A Passion for Equality*, 258–59; Davis, *Brutal Need*, 60–69; Melnick, *Between the Lines*, 85–88; "HEW Chases 'Man in House' from Welfare Regulations," *Washington Afro-American*, 29 June 1968, 26.

32. Etta Horn, "Testimony of the Citywide Welfare Alliance of the District of Columbia," 20 May 1969, Box 24, Folder 11, Wiley Papers.

33. Carol Honsa, "Mothers Welcome Welfare Decision," *Washington Post*, 19 June 1968, C24; Chapman, "Man-in-House Rule in Child Aid Voided"; Carol Honsa, "New Approaches Urged in Welfare Appeals," *Washington Post*, 18 August 1968, D8.

34. "Welfare Snoopers," *Washington Afro-American*, 4 June 1966, 4.

35. Resolution of the District of Columbia City Council, 15 July 1969; Polly Shackleton to William Proxmire, 16 July 1969, Box 22, LWV collection.

36. *Supplemental Appropriations for Fiscal Year 1971*, 321–27; Testimony of Winifred G. Thompson, Hearings before the Subcommittee of the Committee on Appropriations, *District of Columbia Appropriations for 1972*, Pt. 2 (Washington, D.C.: Government Printing Office, 1971), 985–89; *District of Columbia Appropriations for 1973*, 113–16.

37. Paul Hodge, "Welfare Families Fear Cuts Coming," *Washington Post*, 7 January 1972, C1, C3; West, *National Welfare Rights Organization*, 330–31; "Women Protest Welfare Harassment," *Washington Evening Star*, 14 March 1973.

38. J. Y. Smith, "Fauntroy Criticizes City Welfare Slash," *Washington Post*, 7 Decem-

ber 1971, C1, C16; Thomas Crosby, "At Welfare, It Was Just a Matter of Genealogy," *Washington Evening Star,* 21 April 1972; *District of Columbia Appropriations for 1973,* 111–15.

39. J. Y. Smith, "Welfare Training Lagging," *Washington Post,* 9 March 1972, B1, B3; Paul W. Valentine, "Welfare Roll Rate Increase Dips Sharply," *Washington Post,* 18 July 1973, C1, C6.

40. Protests continued but with less frequency. In the fall of 1971, for example, a group from the Mount Pleasant Welfare Rights Organization marched to the city welfare office demanding higher payments and funds to help cover the costs of expenses associated with the holidays. Smith, "Welfare Rights Protesters Fail to 'Evict' System's Chief"; "District of Columbia," *NWRO/Welfare Fighter,* November 1971, 11.

41. J. Y. Smith, "Fauntroy Criticizes City Welfare Slash," *Washington Post,* 7 December 1971, C1, C16; "D.C. Has FAP Hearings," *NWRO/Welfare Fighter,* December 1971, 5.

42. Alice Bonner, "Yedell, Ex-Chief Cited for Inaction on Welfare Pleas," *Washington Post,* 12 December 1976, A1, A7.

43. Carol Honsa, "D.C. Mothers Can Get Pay Supplements," *Washington Post,* 9 April 1971, C1, C7; West, *National Welfare Rights Movement,* 334; Piven and Cloward, *Poor People's Movements,* 294–95.

44. Smith, "Fauntroy Criticizes City Welfare Slash"; "D.C. Has FAP Hearing," *Welfare Fighter* 2 (December 1971): 5.

45. J. Y. Smith, "Welfare Activist Moves from Street to Office," *Washington Post,* 17 May 1975, D1–D2. Along with Horn, Nia Bullock, another welfare rights activist, headed a child care center funded by the city's Department of Human Resources. "Ex-DHR Foes, Now on Payroll, Silent," *Washington Post,* 12 December 1976, A7. Mary Lanier, active in the welfare rights group and antipoverty programs in the Arthur Capper projects in southeast D.C., gained employment in a resource development program at Federal City College, helping to set up and run youth and adult education programs in her neighborhood. Marcia Feldman, "Mary Lanier," *D.C. Gazette* 1 (29 June–12 July 1970): 4–5.

46. D.C. Family Welfare Rights Organization Advocacy and Assistance Project, Proposal to Washington Metropolitan Area Health and Welfare Council, July, 1970, and D.C. Family Welfare Rights Organization Advocacy and Assistance Project, Proposal to Model Cities, August, 1970, Box 2160, NWRO Papers.

47. Activists elected to attend the Gary, Indiana, convention included Etta Horn, Elizabeth Perry, and Theresa Jones. David R. Boldt, "22 D.C. Delegates Elected for Black Political Convention," *Washington Post,* 2 March 1972, D7; "Black United Front Claims Popularity," *Washington Afro-American,* 17 February 1968, 1–2; Feldman, "Mary Lanier"; Kotz and Kotz, *Passion for Equality,* 259.

48. For the challenges confronting NWRO after 1970, see Nadasen, *Welfare Warriors,* ch. 7.

49. Kotz and Kotz, *Passion for Equality,* 279–84; Nadasen, "Expanding the Boundaries of the Women's Movement," 274, 288–91.

50. Tillmon, "Welfare Is a Women's Issue."

51. Citywide Welfare Rights Alliance, Inc., "A Proposal to Office of Economic Opportunity," Box 2160, NWRO Papers.

52. "Report on the Washington Area Conference on Battered Women," 16 December 1976, Box 12, Folder "1974–1985 D.C. Commission for Women, Battered Women, 1976–1981," Anne B. Turpeau Papers, Library of Congress; Bobby McMahon et al., testimony Senate Committee on Labor and Human Resources, Subcommittee on Health, *Family Planning and Population Research* (Washington, D.C.: Government Printing Office, 1970), 276–80; "People in the News," *Welfare Fighter* 2 (April–May 1971): 7; Betty Medsger, "2,000 Women Form a Ring at Capitol," *Washington Post,* 23 June 1972, C1–2.

53. "Operation Give a Damn," *Vocal Majority* 2 (March 1971): 5; 27 September 1967 chapter meeting announcement and 20 January 1972 press release, Folder 48, Box 170, NOW Papers.

54. "Kicking the Traces," *Vocal Majority* 2 (March 1971): 14; "Women in Poverty," *Vocal Majority* 4 (January 1973): 9–10; "Welfare Is a Woman's Issue," *Vocal Majority* 2 (June 1971): 2.

55. "Welfare Is a Woman's Issue," *Vocal Majority* 2 (June 1971): 2. For articles on welfare in other early feminist publications, see Glassman, "Women and the Welfare System," and Schulder, "Does the Law Oppress Women?" in Morgan, *Sisterhood Is Powerful*; Leo, "ADC: Marriage to the State," reprinted in Koedt, Levine, and Rapone, *Radical Feminism*; Warrior, "Females and Welfare," in Tanner, *Voices from Women's Liberation,* 277–78.

56. Marilyn Salzman Webb, "Welfare for the Rich," *off our backs,* 10 July 1970, 5; Nancy Young, "Mama's Welfare Blues," *off our backs,* November 1971, 8–9.

57. "A Black Woman Responds to Women's Liberation," *off our backs,* 15 April 1971, 18; "Horning In," *off our backs,* 14 December 1970, 6.

58. Mary Vogel to Gloria Steinem, 15 February 1972, and "Welfare Dinner" flyer, Box 93, Folder 4, Gloria Steinem Papers, Sophia Smith Collection; "A Proposal to Office of Economic Opportunity from Citywide Welfare Alliance, Inc.," NWRO Papers.

59. Ratagick, "Two American Welfare Mothers," 75–77.

60. Ibid, 112, 76.

61. Smith, "What Would You Do?" 12.

Chapter 3: Washington Women's Liberation Movement

1. Marilyn Webb advertisement, *Washington Free Press,* 7 March 1968, 4.

2. On women in SDS and antipoverty programs, see Frost, "*Interracial Movement of the Poor.*"

3. The Rankin Brigade's call is quoted in Swerdlow, *Women Strike for Peace,* 137.

For descriptions of the protest, see Rosen, "Day They Buried 'Traditional Womanhood'"; Echols, "'Woman Power,'" in Small and Hoover, *Give Peace a Chance.*

4. Estimates of the numbers who took part in the alternative activities range from 200 to 500 who abandoned the formal Brigade program to 30 to 50 women who met to develop a radical women's program. Marilyn Salzman Webb, "Towards a Radical Women's Movement," *Washington Free Press,* 29 February 1968, 4; Marilyn Salzman Webb, "Women: We Have a Common Enemy," *New Left Notes,* 10 June 1968, 15; Elaine Fuller, "A Rankin March," *Washington Free Press,* 3 February 1968, 8; Marilyn Salzman Webb, "Rankin Rebuttal," *Washington Free Press,* 20 February 1968, 10; Pam Allen, "beyond a . . . feminist stance," *Guardian,* 27 January 1968, 2; Firestone, "Jeannette Rankin Brigade," in New York Radical Women, *Notes from the First Year,* 18–19.

5. Echols, *Daring to Be Bad,* 72–92.

6. Amatniek, "Funeral Oration," in New York Radical Women, *Notes from the First Year,* 20–21; Firestone, "Jeannette Rankin Brigade," in New York Radical Women, *Notes from the First Year,* 18.

7. Recollections of women's role in the antiwar and New Left movements are included in Fraser, *1968*; Klatch, *Generation Divided*; Evans, *Personal Politics.* SDS's statement on women's liberation appeared in *New Left Notes,* 10 July 1967, 4.

8. Marilyn Salzman Webb, "Women's Liberation," *Washington Free Press,* 29 February 1968, 4. Michael S. Foley argues that the draft resistance movement in Boston offered some satisfying opportunities for women's growth and activism. Nonetheless, the women at the Rankin Brigade described draft resistance as typical of women's position in the larger movement and the broader society. Foley, "'Point of Ultimate Indignity' or a 'Beloved Community?'" in McMillan and Buhle, *New Left Revisited.* For D.C. women's complaints about their opportunities, see also Nicholas von Hoffman, "Feminine Revolution-within-the-Revolution," *Washington Post* (n.d., circa January 1969), Women, 1968–1969 Article File, MLK Library.

9. Information about D.C.'s chapter of SDS comes from Reel 8 and Reel 22, *Students for a Democratic Society Papers, 1958–1970* (Glen Rock, N.J.: Microfilming Corporation of America, 1977); Cathlyn Wilkerson interview by Ronald Grele, 17 February 1985, transcript, Student Movement of the 1960s Collection, Oral History Collection, Columbia University.

10. Charlotte Bunch, interview by author, 15 February 1995; Betty Garman, interview by author, 17 April 1994; Marcia Kopit Sprinkle, interview by author, 15 May 1994 and 27 June 1994.

11. Bunch, *Passionate Politics,* 5–6; Charlotte Bunch et al., "Ourstory Herstory: A Working Paper on the D.C. Women's Liberation Movement, 1968–1971" (unpublished manuscript), Sharon Deevey Papers; Echols, *Daring to Be Bad,* 70; Webb, "*Off Our Backs* and the Feminist Dream," in Wachsberger, *Voices from the Underground,* 124–25.

12. Wilkerson transcript, 77.

13. The Sandy Springs and Lake Villa conferences are discussed in Echols, *Daring to Be Bad,* 105; Bunch, *Passionate Politics,* 5–6; Freeman, *Politics of Women's Liberation,* 106–8; Brownmiller, *In Our Time,* 30–33, 52–54.

14. Webb, "Woman as Secretary, Sexpot, Spender, Sow, Civic Actor, Sickie," *Motive* 29 (March–April 1969): 48–59.

15. Cathy Wilkerson, *Women: The Struggle for Liberation* (Washington, D.C.: Students for a Democratic Society, n.d.), 8–10, Folder 2, Carton 1, Bunch Papers.

16. "Who We Are. Descriptions of Women's Liberation Groups" undated (circa November 1968), Folder 19, Carton 1, Bunch Papers; Barbara Stubbs, "The Angry Young Women," *Washington Star,* 25 May 1969, in Women 1968–69 Article File, MLK Library.

17. Webb, "Woman as Secretary, Sexpot, Spender."

18. Sarachild, "Feminist Consciousness Raising," in Tanner, *Voices from Women's Liberation,* 154–57; Allen, "Free Space," in Koedt, Levine, and Rapone, *Radical Feminism*; Freeman, *Politics of Women's Liberation,* 104–5.

19. Linda Carcionne, "A Proposal," 13 August 1968, Folder 19, Carton 1, Bunch Papers; Sharon Deevey, interview by author, 25 September 1993.

20. Bunch, "Ourstory Herstory," 2; Stubbs, "Angry Young Women."

21. Fraser, "Insiders and Outsiders," in Tinker, *Women in Washington.*

22. For descriptions of the development of *off our backs,* see Webb, "*Off Our Backs* and the Feminist Dream," and Douglas and Moira, "*Off Our Backs:* The First Decade," in Wachsberger, *Voices from the Underground,* 107–30; "Critique of Women's Liberation and Proposal for a Magazine," October 1970, *off our backs* Papers, Washington, D.C.; "Marlene Wicks and Marilyn Webb: Co-Founders of *Off Our Backs,*" *off our backs* (January 1980): 4, 32.

23. 1970–71 log book, *off our backs* Papers.

24. Echols, *Daring to Be Bad,* 97–98.

25. Kovacs, "'Witch' at the Justice Department," 4.

26. Heidi Steffens, "Bananas and Rifles—Sugar and Death: A Saga of the United Fruit Company," Folder 58, Carton 2, Bunch Papers.

27. Steffens, "W.I.T.C.H.," 10, 19.

28. Stubbs, "Angry Young Women."

29. Coral Conspiracy, "To Liberate Children"; Marcia and Norma, "Children's House."

30. "Action Planned for November 14th Moratorium—Washington Women's Liberation," Addendum Carton 1, Folder 33, Bunch Papers.

31. Carcione, "State of the Struggle"; "$5500 or fight!" *off our backs,* 4 May 1970, 10.

32. Bunch, "Ourstory, Herstory." Smaller groups generally organized to focus on particular issues or to unite women who lived in specific parts of the city. One very active group was the Coral Conspiracy, comprising residents of Takoma Park; others

represented southeast D.C., northwest D.C., and some Virginia suburbs. "Washington Women's Liberation Groups," unpublished manuscript prepared for November 1968 conference, Carton 1, Folder 19, Bunch Papers.

33. Mary Wiegers, "Beneath Those Charred Bras, Revolution Smolders," *Washington Post,* 8 March 1970, G1, G3; "Women's Work among the Radicals," *Washington Post,* 9 March 1970, B1–B2; "Lib Sees Women's Limited Roles: 'Sow to Sexpot to Sickie'"; "Women's Lib: 'Only Active Radicals in Town,'" *Washington Post,* 11 March 1970, B1, B3.

34. Deevey interview; Bunch interview; Sprinkle interview.

35. Bunch, "Ourstory, Herstory," 5–7.

36. Frances Chapman, "Sage Advice," *off our backs* 2 (May–June 1972): 17; Frances Chapman, "Women's Fest," *off our backs* 3 (April 1973): 8.

37. "Bev Fisher," *off our backs* 2 (November 1972): 2–3.

38. Fraser, "Insiders and Outsiders," in Tinker, *Women in Washington.*

39. Jenness, *Feminism and Socialism*; Randy Furst, "YSA Charts Program for 1970," *Guardian* 22 (January 1970): 5.

40. Elizabeth Shelton, "'Federally Employed Women' Is Formed to Push Equal Rights," *Washington Post,* 24 September 1968, C3.

41. "To Be—or Not to Be—Belligerent," *F.E.W.'s News and Views* 2 (April 1970): 2.

42. Claudia Levy, "Rally Here to Push Senate Rights Vote," *Washington Post,* 20 August 1970, B2; "She-Power Is on the March," *Washington Daily News,* 26 August 1970, 2; Karl E. Meyer, "Women's Lib Asks Boycott of 4 Products," *Washington Post,* 26 August 1970, A1, A10.

43. The position taken by the DCWLM on the ERA resembled that held by most women labor organizers and sympathizers until the early 1970s. U.S. Senate, Congress, Committee on the Judiciary, *"Equal Rights" Amendment: Hearings before the Subcommittee on Constitutional Amendments* (Washington, D.C.: Government Printing Office, 1970), 78–81; Deevey interview.

44. Bunch, *Passionate Politics,* 8.

45. YSA representatives who helped plan the event claimed that more than 3,000 women attended the march. Alice Woznack, "Power in Unity," *off our backs,* 25 October 1970, 15.

46. Claudia Levy and Alex Ward, "Women Rally to Publicize Grievances," *Washington Post,* 27 August 1970, A1, A7; Claudia Levy, "City Names Wednesday for Women," *Washington Post,* 21 August 1970, C4.

47. "Speakers from Many Women's Organizations Urged Support of Equal Rights for Women," *F.E.W.'s News and Views* 2 (September 1970): 2–3.

48. Levy and Ward, "Women Rally to Publicize Grievances"; "It's NOW for a FEW Bold Ladies," *Washington Daily News,* 27 August 1970, 5.

49. "Speakers from Many Women's Organizations," 2.

50. Lillian Wiggins, "I'll Fight Not with Men, but with the System," *Washington Afro-American,* 29 August 1970, 1, 18; Jackie Washington, "Appeal to Black Women: 'Lib'

Strike Boycott Urged," *Washington Star,* 23 August 1970, Women Article File, MLK Library; "Howard Unit Won't Join Women's Lib," *Washington Post,* 23 August 1970, D3. For accounts of opposition, see Myra MacPherson, "Battle of the Sexes Becomes a Word War," *Washington Post,* 27 August 1970, C1, C4; "Black View," *Washington Daily News,* 27 August 1970, 5, 7; "Men's View Biggest Lady's Day of All," *Washington Daily News,* 27 August 1970, 5.

51. OOB Collective, "Strength in Change," *off our backs,* 25 October 1970, 15; Bunch, "Ourstory, Herstory," 9; Anne, Lynn, Pam, and Sharon, "If Not N.O.W., Who?," *off our backs,* 30 September 1970, 2.

52. Bunch, *Passionate Politics,* 8; "It's NOW for a FEW Bold Ladies." The speech delivered by Joanne Carmodey (or Comedy), the black lesbian speaker at the Women's Strike Day, is available in Folder 54, Carton 2, Bunch Papers.

53. Anne et al., "If Not N.O.W., Who?"; Women's Jail Collective, "Jailbreak," *off our backs,* 30 September 1970, 3. Analysis of criminality as a product of women's oppression appeared earlier in *off our backs,* suggesting that the march to the Women's Detention Center may have been poorly organized, but was based on views already developed by activists. See Marilyn Salzman Webb, "Empty the Women's Jails," *off our backs,* 31 July 1970, 1.

54. Bunch, "Ourstory, Herstory," 9; Levy and Ward, "Women Rally to Publicize Grievances"; "Women's Liberation Movement" file, Federal Bureau of Investigation.

55. Women's Jail Collective, "Jailbreak."

56. Bunch, "Ourstory, Herstory," 9; Biren interview.

57. Anne et al., "If Not N.O.W., Who?"; OOB Collective, "Strength in Change."

58. "News from Women's Centers in New York," *Rat,* 17 November–6 December, 1970, 13; Anne et al., "If Not N.O.W., Who?"

59. "Toward a Mass Feminist Movement," resolution passed at the 1971 national convention of the Socialist Workers Party, reprinted in Jenness, *Feminism and Socialism,* 148.

60. *G.W. Women's Liberation Newsletter,* January 1971, Folder 4, Box 8, Women's Liberation Collection, Sophia Smith Collection; "Operation Give a Damn," *Vocal Majority* 1 (March 1971): 5.

61. "Clancy Lowers the Boom—What Next?" *off our backs,* 25 March 1971, 16; "Operation Give a Damn."

62. *off our backs* (Summer 1971): 31; Karlyn Barker, "Divisions Slow Women's Lib Drive," *Washington Post,* 14 November 1971, D1, D6.

Chapter 4: Organizing for Reproductive Control

1. New scholarship on black women's organizations and nationalist groups such as the Young Lords Party has challenged the view that all women of color opposed abortion and contraception on the grounds that these forms of population control represented federally orchestrated forms of genocide. Nelson, *Women of Color and*

the Reproductive Rights Movement; Polatnick, "Diversity in Women's Liberation Ideology"; Silliman et al., *Undivided Rights.*

2. Mary Wiegers, "Women's Lib: 'Only Active Radicals in Town,'" *Washington Post,* 11 March 1970, B3.

3. Wolfson, "Clenched Fist, Open Heart," in DuPlessis and Snitow, *Feminist Memoir Project.*

4. *Roe* was followed in 1973 by *Doe v. Dalton,* a Supreme Court ruling striking down restrictive laws specifying eligibility requirements. For background on the struggle for abortion rights, see Reagan, *When Abortion Was a Crime*; Garrow, *Liberty and Sexuality*; Fried, *From Abortion to Reproductive Freedom.*

5. Jennifer A. Nelson also argues that women of color were critical to transforming feminists' approach to abortion, although she dates their influence to the late 1970s. Nelson, *Women of Color and the Reproductive Rights Movement.*

6. In 1972, the Court extended the right to contraception to unmarried men and women in its *Eisenstadt v. Baird* decision. On the popularity of the birth control pill, see William D. Mosher, *Trends in Contraceptive Practice: United States, 1965–76,* DHHS Publication No. (PHS) 82–1986 (Hyattsville, Md.: National Center for Health Statistics, 1982), 11.

7. "Family Planning," Folder 3, Box 10, Ophelia Egypt Papers, Moorland-Spingarn Research Center.

8. Cornelia Ball, "Byrd Backs Birth Control," *Washington Daily News,* 15 October 1963; William Grigg, "Birth Control Study Started by District," *Washington Star,* 16 October 1963, both in Birth Control 1965–1969 Article File, MLK Library.

9. 1964 Year-End Report, PPFA Records, Sophia Smith Collection.

10. "Byrd Urges Birth Control for Slum-Area Negroes," *Washington Post,* 17 August 1967, Birth Control Article File, MLK Library.

11. The history of U.S.-sponsored family planning initiatives is covered by Critchlow, "Birth Control, Population Control, and Family Planning"; Reed, *Birth Control Movement and American Society.*

12. National Center for Health Statistics, *Utilization of Family Planning Services by Currently Married Women 15–44 Years of Age,* DHEW Publication No. (PHS) 78–1977 (Hyattsville, Md.: U.S. Department of Health, Education, and Welfare Public Health Service, 1977), 20–21.

13. See assorted articles from Birth Control Article File, MLK Library.

14. Calvin Zon, "In Memory of Sisters Murdered By Abortion," *Washington Star,* 8 May 1972, Abortion, 1972–1978 Article File, MLK Library; Nelson, *Women of Color and the Reproductive Rights Movement,* 64–70; Lawrence, "Indian Health Service and the Sterilization of Native American Women."

15. Marilyn Salzman Webb, "Nixon on Birth Control: A Hard Pill to Swallow," *Guardian,* 23 August 1969, 10.

16. "Who Says Too Many?" *off our backs,* Health Supplement, Summer 1971, 24–25; Judith Coburn, "Off the Pill?" *Ramparts,* June 1970, 46–49.

17. These arguments are covered in Nelson, *Women of Color and the Reproductive Rights Movement*; Davis, *Women, Race, and Class*; Ross, "African American Women and Abortion," in Solinger, *Abortion Wars.*

18. *Muhammad Speaks* and *Black Panther* quoted in Nelson, *Women of Color and the Reproductive Rights Movement,* 85.

19. Evette Pearson, "White America Today," *Black Panther,* 4 January 1969, reprinted in Foner, *Black Panthers Speak,* 26; Judi Douglas, "Birth Control," *Black Panther,* 7 February 1970, 7.

20. Nelson, *Women of Color and the Reproductive Rights Movement,* 85–86.

21. Sally Quinn, "Abortions in the City," *Washington Post,* 25 March 1970, B3. Another report on this conference appears in Box 1, Hearing Files, 1967–1974, Records of the City Council, National Archives.

22. Bobby McMahan testimony, Committee on Labor and Human Resources, U.S. Senate, *Family Planning and Population Research* (Washington, D.C.: Government Printing Office, 1970), 276–80.

23. Judge Gesell, who made the ruling, may have been influenced by his wife, who sat on the board of the city's Planned Parenthood Association chapter in 1964–65. Only spotty records of the PPA chapter are available, making it difficult to determine whether she still served on the association's board when her husband ruled in the Vuitch case. Minutes, Board of Trustees, PPAF Papers, Sophia Smith Collection; Lader, *Abortion II,* 1–17; *United States of America v. Milan Vuitch,* 305 F. Supp. 1032 (1969).

24. The CWA established a Health Group, although it is unclear what activities the group undertook. Press release issued by D.C. Citywide Alliance, 5 November 1968, Box 2083, NWRO Papers.

25. Wolfson, "Clenched Fist," 270–71; "Washington Women's Liberation Project Groups," Fall 1969, Folder 21, Carton 1, Bunch Papers; Webb, "Hard Rain's Gonna Fall."

26. Meeting the conditions for therapeutic abortion did not guarantee that women would receive the procedure, as in the case of two women reportedly turned away by D.C. General in August 1969, despite having obtained the proper certification. Myra MacPherson, "Abortion Protest Stymied," *Washington Post,* 9 September 1969, B1–B2.

27. "Abortions at D.C. General Hospital," *off our backs,* 27 February 1970, 4. Historian Leslie Reagan similarly has argued that the enforcement of abortion laws in the 1950s and 1960s led to the emergence of a system wherein white women with private health insurance were most likely to receive therapeutic abortions in private hospitals, while poor, African American, and Latina women were more likely to seek criminal abortions. Reagan, *When Abortion Was a Crime,* 193.

28. The 1967 figures used by abortion proponents ranged from 500 to more than 800 women who received treatment at D.C. General for complications from illegal abortions. In contrast, official figures compiled by the D.C. Department of Public

Health show a total of forty-two deaths from abortions between 1960 and 1967 and a sharp increase in the number of therapeutic abortions performed at four Washington hospitals between 1959 and 1969. "Statement by Washington Women's Liberation to the Mayor's Task Force on Public Health Goals" and "Committee on Abortions Meeting," Folder 42, Carton 2, Addenda, Bunch Papers. Other reports present different numbers but reveal the same trend of extremely low numbers of therapeutic abortions completed at D.C. General relative to the higher numbers of women who sought treatment there after illegal abortions. Statement by Alyce C. Gullattee in *Report of the City Council's Health and Welfare Committee on Abortions in the District of Columbia, October 1970* (Washington, D.C.: Government of the District of Columbia City Council, 1970); Donald Hirzel, "Court Turns Down Plea for Abortion," *Washington Evening Star,* 7 March 1970, Abortion Article File, MLK Library.

29. Irma Moore, "Hearings Set on State of D.C. General," *Washington Post,* 11 September 1969, A26; Stuart Auerbach, "Hospital Employees Join Doctors' Protest," *Washington Post,* 17 September 1969, C3; Carl Bernstein, "Hospital Needs Told at Probe," *Washington Post,* 18 September 1969, B2.

30. "Committee on Abortions Meeting," minutes, 23 September 1969, Folder 42, Carton 2, Bunch Papers.

31. Richard E. Prince, "Panel Backs Abortions at D.C. General," *Washington Post,* 4 December 1969, Abortion Article File, MLK Library; Sidney Lippman, "Mayor's Unit Asks Abortions at D.C. General," *Washington Daily News,* 2 December 1969, 5.

32. "School Clothing for Welfare Children," *NWRO/Welfare Fighter,* September 1969, 7; Malcolm Kovacs, "'Witch' at the Justice Department," *Quicksilver Times,* 1–11 October 1969, 4.

33. Washington, D.C., Women's Liberation, "'It's Alright Ma (I'm Only Bleeding),'" Folder 41, Carton 2, Bunch Papers.

34. Coburn, "Off the Pill?" 49.

35. Alice Wolfson, "Women and Health," Folder 42, Carton 2, Bunch Papers.

36. "'It's Alright Ma'"; Webb, "Hard Rain's Gonna Fall," 4; Coburn, "Off the Pill?" Women in Chicago went a step further and created their own abortion service. Kaplan, *Story of Jane.*

37. "Washington Women's Liberation Statement on Birth Control Pills," Appendix X, U.S. Congress, Senate, Committee on Small Business, Subcommittee on Monopoly, *Competitive Problems in the Drug Industry,* 2nd Session, Pt. 17 (Washington, D.C.: Government Printing Office, 1970); Malcolm Kovacs, "The Pill Hearings," *D.C. Gazette,* 23 March 1970, 6–7; Committee on Labor and Human Resources, Senate, *Family Planning and Population Research* (Washington, D.C.: Government Printing Office, 1970), 277.

38. Bunch, "Ourstory, Herstory: A Working Paper on the D.C. Women's Liberation Movement, 1968–1971," Sharon Deevey Papers, Columbus Ohio.

39. "Horning In," *off our backs,* 14 December 1970, 6.

40. "'It's Alright Ma.'"

41. Peter Osnos, "D.C. General Is Sued Again over Abortion," *Washington Post,* 30 April 1970, A1–A2; Mary Ann Kuhn, "Mother at 14 Decries Hospital," *Washington Daily News,* 30 April 1970, 26; Peter Osnos, "Woman Testifies in Private for Abortion at D.C. General," *Washington Post,* 10 March 1970, A1, A8; Peter Osnos, "Abortion Pleas Is Rejected, Appeal Set," *Washington Post,* 12 March 1970, A1, A14; Peter Osnos, "Mental Health Abortion Ordered at D.C. General," *Washington Post,* 13 March 1970, A1, A11.

42. District of Columbia Health and Welfare Council, "Position Paper on Abortion," 27 July 1970, Subject Files, Box 10, City Council Papers, GWU; "Health Crisis Breaks in D.C.: Systemic Conditions Are Showing Up," Folder 42, Carton 2, Bunch Papers. For information on the collective action suit, see "Contempt for Women," *off our backs,* 19 March 1970, 4; and front-page *Washington Post* articles, March 10–13, 1970.

43. Stuart Auerbach, "Women Disrupt Hearing on the Pill," *Washington Post,* 24 January 1970, B1, B3; Regina Sigal, "Politics of the Pill," *off our backs,* 27 February 1970, 3.

44. Judith Coburn, "Off the Pill?" *Village Voice,* 5 February 1970, 14–15; Wolfson, "Clenched Fist, Open Heart," in DuPlessis and Snitow, *Feminist Memoir Project,* 271.

45. Wolfson and Wolfson, "Food and Drug Administration and the Pill"; Alice Wolfson, "More on the Pill," *off our backs,* 19 March 1970, 6.

46. Nancy Beezley, "How Safe the Pill?" *Quicksilver Times,* 3–13 April 1970, 8.

47.Women's liberation and welfare activists' testimony eventually became part of the official record of the Senate hearings. Washington Women's Liberation Statement on Birth Control Pills, *Competitive Problems in the Drug Industry,* 7283–85; Alex Ward, "Women Hold Own Hearing on Pill," *Washington Post,* 8 March 1970, L7; "Women Hold Their Own," *off our backs,* 19 March 1970, 3.

48. Accounts of these hearings appear in Alex Ward, "Repeal of Abortion Laws Urged," *Washington Post,* 27 June 1970, B1; *Report of the City Council's Health and Welfare Committee on Abortions in the District of Columbia;* Hearing Files, 1967–1974, Box 1, Records of the City Council, RG351, National Archives; D.C. Health and Welfare Council, "Position Paper on Abortion," 27 July 1970, Abortion Subject File, Box 10, City Council Files, GWU.

49. "Records of 22 October 1971 Hearing Regarding the Proposed Licensing of Abortion Clinics," Box 1, Records of the City Council, Hearing Files, 1967–1974, National Archives. In 1972, the City Council instituted a twenty-four-hour waiting period, but proabortion groups sued to stop the implementation. WONAAC to Dr. Henry Robinson, Chair, Health and Welfare Committee of the D.C. City Council, 14 July 1972, Abortion Subject Files, Box 10, City Council Papers, GWU; Ron Taylor, "D.C. City Council Backs New Abortion Rules," *Washington Post,* 12 July 1972, C1; "D.C. Is Upheld on Enforcement of Abortion Law," *Washington Post,* 21 October 1972, A3.

50. *U.S. v. Vuitch,* 402 U.S. 62 (1971).

51. "Rules for Abortion," *Washington Post,* 21 March 1972, A18; "Abortion Law Repeal Gathers Speed," *NOW Acts* 3 (Winter 1970): 16; "Clinics: An Answer to Hospital Overcrowding?" *NOW Acts* 4 (Spring 1971): 9–10; *Vocal Majority* 2 (June 1971): 24; "Abortion Clinic to Open at Washington Hospital," *Washington Daily News,* 15 January 1971; "Abortion Clinic to Open Downtown," *Washington Daily News,* 25 March 1971; Ned Scharff, "I Was Just So Grateful," *Washington Star,* 17 October 1971, Abortion Article File, MLK Library; *News Notes: Planned Parenthood of Metropolitan Washington, D.C.* 21 (Fall 1971), Folder 10, Box 16, Egypt Papers.

52. "MAA: The Metropolitan Abortion Alliance," *Vocal Majority* 2 (March 1971): 7; "D.C. Women Campaign for Free Abortions," *Washington Daily News,* 16 April 1971, 4.

53. "D.C. Women Campaign for Free Abortions," *Washington Daily News,* 16 April 1971, 4; Jean Powell, "Women Don't Agree," *Washington Evening Star,* 28 July 1971, Abortion 1971 Article File, MLK Library; MAA Position Paper, Women's Ephemera Collection, Abortion—Metropolitan Abortion Alliance Folder, Northwestern University.

54. "If Men Could Get Pregnant, Abortion Would Be a Sacrament," *off our backs,* 24 June 1971, 20; Joy Billington, "NOW to Challenge All," *Washington Star,* 27 April 1971, Abortion Article File, MLK Library.

55. "Another Reaction," *off our backs,* 24 June 1971, 20; Jeannie Reynolds, "Metropolitan Abortion Alliance Rally," *Vocal Majority* 2 (June 1971): 23.

56. Jeannie Reynolds, "Abortion Committee Proposed," *Vocal Majority* 2 (July 1971): 7.

57. Gail Martens, "Another Reaction," *off our backs,* 24 June 1971, 20.

58. Elizabeth Barnes, "Panel Foresees Mass Women's Movement," *The Militant,* 16 January 1970, 8; Jaquith, "Issues before the Abortion Movement," in Jenness, *Feminism and Socialism.*

59. Toba Singer, "Suit Contests D.C. Abortion Statutes," *The Militant,* 4 October 1972, 16; "Abortion Law Change Hit," *Washington Star,* 16 July 1972; Calvin Zon, "In Memory of Sisters Murdered by Abortion," *Washington Star,* 8 May 1972, Abortion, 1972–1978 Article File, MLK Library.

60. *WONAAC* Newsletter, 21 October 1971, 4; "Women for Abortion Action," *D.C. Gazette,* 15 December 1971; "Women March on Washington," *Space City!* 16 December 1971, 11; Caroline Lund, "Nov. 20 Spurs Int'l. Abortion Struggle," *The Militant,* 3 December 1971, 4–5; John Mathews and Jacqueline Trescott, "Abortion—2 Points of View," *Washington Evening Star,* 21 November 1971, A3; "November 20th—Some Reporting, Some Diatribe, Some Analysis," *off our backs,* 12 December 1971, 16; Scrapbook, Reel 2, WONAAC Papers.

61. "Black Women," *WONAAC Newsletter,* 21 October 1971, 13.

62. Mary Treadwell, "Black Women," *WONAAC Newsletter,* 21 October 1971, 7. A variation of this article appeared as "Is Abortion Black Genocide?" in *Family Plan-*

ning Perspectives 4 (January 1972): 4–5 and in Treadwell's testimony before Congress, Committee of the Judiciary, Subcommittee on Constitutional Amendments, *Abortion,* Pt. 4 (Washington, D.C.: Government Printing Office, 1975), 683–85.

63. Committee on the Judiciary, *Abortion,* 684–85.

64. Varda One, "Women's Liberation Where Are You Going?" *Everywoman,* February 1971, 16–18; Caroline Lund, "Red-Baiting and Women's Liberation," *The Militant,* 13 November 1970, 9; Caroline Lund, "Issues in Female Liberation Split," *The Militant,* 5 February 1971, 14, 22.

65. Jean Powell, "Women Don't Agree," *Washington Star,* 28 July 1971, Abortion Article File, MLK Library; "Bringing Abortion Home," *off our backs,* October 1971, 10; "A House Divided," *off our backs,* October 1971, 11; "November 20th—Some Reporting, Some Diatribe, Some Analysis."

66. "November 20—Some Reporting, Some Diatribe, Some Analysis"; Karlyn Barker, "Divisions Slow Women's Lib Drive," *Washington Post,* 14 November 1971, D1, D6.

67. Carol Edelson, "Supreme Court Abortion Ruling," *off our backs,* 31 March 1971, 4; Clark and Wolfson, "Class, Race, and Reproductive Rights."

68. The Buckley Amendment proposed to expand the definition of "person" in the Constitution to apply to all human beings, including their unborn offspring. The Helms Amendment proposed to prohibit abortion from the time of conception, without exception.

69. The amendment that passed in 1976 allowed Medicaid payments for abortion in cases to protect a mother's life. Lawsuits challenging the amendment were immediately filed by health care providers and abortion rights groups.

70. According to a 1975 survey of Washington, D.C., residents conducted by the Bureau of Social Science Research, 77 percent agreed that decisions about abortions should be left to a woman and her doctor. Support among white respondents (78 percent) was somewhat higher than support among nonwhite respondents (69 percent). Jay Mathews, "Abortion, Homosexual Rights Backed," *Washington Post,* 8 August 1975, C1, C3; D.C. Women's Health and Abortion Information Project, "Abortion: A Woman's Right to Choose," Women's Ephemera Collection, Abortion—Washington Area Women's Center Folder, Northwestern University.

71. Mary Bailey, "Senate Abortion Hearings: Do They Really Hear," *off our backs,* 31 May 1974, 6; "Memorial," *off our backs* 7 (December 1977): 9; Folder 48, Box 1970, NOW Papers, Schlesinger Library; "Since the Supreme Court Decision on Abortion," *Vocal Majority* 4 (June 1973): 5, 7.

72. Elizabeth Becker, "Abortion Recipients Attack Proposed Ban on Medicaid Help," *Washington Post,* 20 October 1974, B7; Lillian Wiggins, "Bartlett Amendment Discriminatory to the Poor," *Washington Afro-American,* 5 October 1974, 4.

73. Committee on the Judiciary, *Abortion,* Pt. 4, 683–94, 698–706.

74. Mary Treadwell Barry, "The Poor's Right to Abortion," letter to the editor, *Washington Star,* 18 June 1977, A6.

Chapter 5: Women and Black Liberation

1. R. C. Newell, "Black Feminists or Liberators?" *Washington Afro-American,* 12 October 1974, 13.

2. Renee Ferguson, "Women's Liberation Has Different Meaning for Blacks," *Washington Post,* 3 October 1970, A18; Jay Mathews, "Abortion, Homosexual Rights Backed," *Washington Post,* 8 August 1975, C1, C3.

3. A poll conducted by Louis Harris and Associates of more than 4,000 women and men found that 67 percent of black women expressed sympathy for the efforts of women's liberation, compared to 35 percent of white women; 22 percent of black women reported being unsupportive, compared to 53 percent of white women. Figures for black and white men revealed a similar pattern, with 50 percent of black men indicating their support compared to 41 percent of white men, and 31 percent of black men unsympathetic to feminism compared to 41 percent of white men. J. V. Reistrup, "Women Still Cool to Lib but Want Better Status," *Washington Post,* 24 March 1972, A1, A10; Reid, *"Together" Black Women,* 32–55.

4. "A Black Woman Responds to Women's Liberation," *off our backs,* 15 April 1971, 18.

5. Recent reconsiderations of the history of Black Power include Tyson, *Radio Free Dixie*; Joseph, "Black Liberation without Apology"; Lang, "Between Civil Rights and Black Power."

6. For overviews about the Black Panther Party, see Jones, *Black Panther Party Reconsidered*; Joseph, *Waiting 'til the Midnight Hour.*

7. For definitions of Black Power, see Van Deburg, *New Day in Babylon*; Kopkind, "Future of 'Black Power'"; McCartney, *Black Power Ideologies*; Franklin, "Political Economy of Black Power."

8. Van Deburg, *New Day in Babylon,* 112–91; White, "Africa on My Mind."

9. Moynihan, *Negro Family.*

10. Minutes of Strategy and Tactics Committee Meeting, 8 August 1965, ACT, Minutes of Meetings, Series 2, Box 2, Hobson Papers.

11. Reginald H. Booker, interview by Robert Wright, 24 July 1970, interview RJB 585, transcript, Moorland-Spingarn Research Center; Cleaver, *Soul on Ice,* 162.

12. Angela Terrell, "Priority: Liberating Black Communities," *Washington Post,* 1 April 1973, G10.

13. Patton, "Black People and the Victorian Ethos," in Cade, *Black Woman,* 147; Tony Gittens, "Black Anti-War Movement to Work Independently," *Hilltop,* 9 February 1968, 10.

14. Hampton and Fayer, *Voices of Freedom,* 425–48; interviews with Gittens, Giddings, and Manns Israel, conducted by Blackside, Inc., for *Eyes on the Prize II,* Hampton Collection, Washington University, St. Louis.

15. Jean M. White, "'Revival of Blackness' Is Applauded at Howard," *Washington Post,* 27 October 1966, A4.

16. Brown, "Black University," in Weaver and Weaver, *University and Revolution,* 146.

17. Hampton and Fayer, *Voices of Freedom,* 427–36.

18. U.S. Senate, Committee on Government Operations, Subcommittee on Investigations, *Riots, Civil and Criminal Disorders,* Pt. 22 (Washington, D.C.: Government Printing Office, 1969), 4769–73.

19. Don Robinson and Leon Dash, "Thousands Quit Classes in Boycott at Howard University," *Washington Post,* 11 May 1967, A1, A12; Jack White and Ivan Brandon, "120 Walk Out on Nabrit at Howard Talk," *Washington Post,* 19 September 1967, A1, A7; Gregory and Manns Israel interviews, Hampton Collection.

20. Gittens, quoted in Hare, "Behind the Black College Student Revolt," 59; Hare, "Battle for Black Studies."

21. Brown, *Die Nigger Die!*

22. "Black Power Committee Holds Press Conference," *Hilltop,* 7 April 1967, 1.

23. *Riots, Civil and Criminal Disorders,* 4771–72.

24. *Riots, Civil and Criminal Disorders,* 4772; Robert Jeffers, "Students Take Nabrit Flag, List of Demands," *Hilltop,* 23 February 1968, 1; Loretta Ross interview by Joyce Follet, Voices of Feminism Oral History Project, Sophia Smith Collection.

25. de Graf, "Howard," in Foster and Long, *Protest!*

26. Gittens interview.

27. Jacqueline Trescott and Paul Hendrickson, "What Happened to the Howard Class of '68?" *Washington Post,* 15 May 1968, B3.

28. Lowe and McDowell, "Participant-Nonparticipant Differences"; Sanders Bebura and Brenda Adams, "Howard University Students Take Over," *Washington Free Press,* 27 March 1968, 5; Ivan C. Brandon, "Tight Organization Ran Howard Sit-In," *Washington Post,* 24 March 1968, A17. For the students' demands and the administration's response, see Board of Trustees of Howard University, "Policy Statement on the Black University," in Wallerstein and Starr, *University Crisis Reader,* Vol. 1, *Liberal University Under Attack*; Howard University Students, "February 1968, *The Spear and Shield,*" in Wallerstein and Starr, *University Crisis Reader,* Vol. 2, *Confrontation and Counterattack.*

29. Susan Jacoby, "Changed Howard: Students Speak Up," *Washington Post,* 24 September 1968, A1, A10; Trescott and Hendrickson, "What Happened to the Howard Class of 68?"; de Graf, "Howard," in Foster and Long, *Protest!* 339–41; Martin Well and Ivan C. Brandon, "Howard Ends Studies," *Washington Post,* 16 May 1970, A1, A8.

30. Stanfiel, "Profile of the 1972 Freshman Class."

31. See interviews with Marilyn Robinson and Anita James Sanders in Trescott and Hendrikson, "What Happened to the Howard Class of '68?"

32. Diana Onley Campbell, interview by author, 5 August 1993; Wallace, "Black Feminist's Search for Sisterhood," in Hull, Scott, and Smith, *All the Women Are White, All the Blacks Are Men,* 8–9; and Wallace, "To Hell and Back," in DuPlessis and Sni-

tow, *Feminist Memoir Project.* Wallace also describes her experience at Howard in "Anger in Isolation: A Black Feminist's Search for Sisterhood," *Village Voice,* 28 July 1975, 6–7; Ross interview by Follet.

33. "Black View," *Washington Daily News,* 27 August 1970, 5, 7; flyer for "Conference to Unite Women," 16–18 October 1970, sponsored by George Washington Women's Liberation, in Box 1, Student Protest Collection, GWU Library.

34. Lonnie Kashif, "Color, Class Status Big Factors in Women's Liberation," *Muhammad Speaks,* 4 September 1970, 22.

35. "Howard Unit Won't Join Women's Lib," *Washington Post,* 23 August 1970, D3; Lillian Wiggins, "I'll Fight Not with Men, but with the System," *Washington Afro-American,* 29 August 1970, 1, 18; Jackie Washington, "Lib Strike Boycott Urged," *Washington Star,* 23 August 1970, in Women Article File, MLK Library.

36. Renee Ferguson, "Women's Liberation Has Different Meaning for Blacks," *Washington Post,* 3 October 1970, A18.

37. On BPP chapters, see Williams, "No Haven"; Jeffries, "Black Radicalism and Political Repression."

38. Hayes and Kiene, "'All Power to the People,'" in Jones, *Black Panther Party Reconsidered.*

39. Washington, D.C., Chapter, "Press Release," *The Black Panther,* 18 July 1970, 9; "The Panther Raid," *D.C. Gazette,* 13 July–26 July 1970, 12; "Third World," *off our backs,* 30 September 1970, 10; "3 Panthers Seized in Scuffle," *Washington Post,* 11 May 1970, B3; "Prologue to July 4 Black Panther Raid," *Quicksilver Times* 2 (28 July–August 6, 1970): 6; "D.C. Panthers Busted," *Quicksilver Times* 2 (14 July–24 July 1970): 7. The report of the congressional study on internal security refers to the arrest of several D.C. Panthers and indicates federal surveillance and, no doubt, interference with the group's activities. Committee on Internal Security of the House of Representatives, *The Black Panther Party: Its Origin and Development as Reflected in Its Official Weekly Newspaper, The Black Panther Black Community News Service* (Washington, D.C.: U.S. Government Printing Office, 1970). Panther members later won at least two suits against local police as a result of these raids. "Panthers Win Police Raid Suit," *Washington Afro-American,* 25 May 1974, 1.

40. Jacqueline Bolder, "Panthers Shelve Militant Image," *Washington Star,* 9 July 1973, Black Panthers Clipping File, MLK Library; Mitch Ratner, "The Panthers Settle In," *D.C. Gazette* 1 (29 June–12 July 1970): 2, 8; Terry Becker, "Panthers," *Quicksilver Times* 2 (3 April–13 April 1970): 3; Sherry Brown, interview by author.

41. "Towards a Revolutionary Morality," *Black Panther,* 15 March 1970, 14; Becker, "Panthers."

42. Interview with Reginald "Malik" Edwards, in Terry, *Bloods,* 11–12.

43. Maurice, "We Serve the People," *Black Panther,* 17 October 1970, 4; untitled announcement, *Black Panther,* 3 April 1971, 3.

44. "Black Panther Party," *Washington Afro-American,* 1 August 1970, 1–2; "Towards a Revolutionary Morality," *Black Panther,* 15 March 1970, 14.

45. Nkenge Toure, interview by author; Paul W. Valentine, "20,000 Join Protest of Welfare Plan," *Washington Post,* 26 March 1972, A1, A3.

46. Bolder, "Panthers Shelve Militant Image"; John Saar, "Health Clinic Is Opened by Panthers," *Washington Post,* 21 May 1973, C1–C2; Stephen E. Colter, "No Doctor, Clinic to Close," *Washington Afro-American,* 24 August 1974, 1.

47. Former members' discussions of women's roles in the party include Abu-Jamal, *We Want Freedom*; Jennings, "African Womanism in the Black Panther Party"; Brown, *Taste of Power*; Cleaver, "Women, Power, and Revolution," in Cleaver and Katsiaficas, *Liberation, Imagination, and the Black Panther Party*; and chapters in Jones, *Black Panther Party Reconsidered.* See also Matthews, "'No One Ever Asks,'" in Collier-Thomas and Franklin, *Sisters in the Struggle.*

48. Eldridge Cleaver, "Message to Sister Erica Huggins," *Black Panther,* 5 July 1969, 9; Untitled Memo, 1970, Box 2136, NWRO Papers; Claudia Levy and Alex Ward, "Women Rally to Publicize Grievances," *Washington Post,* 27 August 1970, A1; Myra MacPherson, "Battle of the Sexes Becomes a Word War," *Washington Post,* 27 August 1970, C1. For other statements about the party's position on women, see "Revolution and Women," *Black Panther,* 16 March 1970, 3; Bobby Seale, "Women and the Black Panther Party," *Quicksilver Times* 2 (3 March–13 March 1970): 9; Eve, "Women's Liberation," *Black Panther,* 11 July 1970, 18–19.

49. Brown interview; Toure interview.

50. Nkenge Toure profile in Baker and Kline, *Conversation Begins,* 353.

51. Osa Massen, "My Experiences as a Community Worker in the BPP," www.itsabouttimebpp.com/Chapter_History (16 March 2005); Israel, interview by author.

52. Gerald Wood, "The BPP Calls for a RPCC," *Black Panther,* 21 August 1970, 6. For an analysis of the convention, see Katsiaficas, "Organization and Movement," in Cleaver and Katsiaficas, *Liberation, Imagination, and the Black Panther Party.*

53. Newton's statement largely disregarded lesbians, implying that the gay liberation movement comprised only men. See "The Women's Liberation and Gay Liberation Movements: August 15, 1970," in Newton, *To Die for the People,* 152–55.

54. "Panther Women Discuss Their Oppression," *Quicksilver Times,* 31 October–9 November 1970, 8.

55. Some reports claim as many as 10,000–15,000 people attended the convention. See Katsiaficas, "Organization and Movement," in Cleaver and Katsiaficas, *Liberation, Imagination, and the Black Panther Party,* 146; Abu-Jamal, *We Want Freedom,* 75–76.

56. "The People and the People Alone Were the Motive Power," *Black Panther,* 12 September 1970, 3; "Workshops," *Quicksilver Times,* 24 November–4 December 1970, 9–11; "Lesbian Demands: Panther Constitution Convention," *Come Out* 1, no. 7 (1970): 16. The documents drafted by delegates at the convention are included in Cleaver and Katsiaficas, *Liberation, Imagination, and the Black Panther Party,* 289–300.

57. For coverage of the September Revolutionary People's Constitutional Convention, see "Newton, at Panther Parley, Urges Socialist System," *New York Times,* 6

September 1970, 40; Paul Delaney, "Panthers Weigh New Constitution," *New York Times,* 7 September 1970, 13; "Philly Convention," *Rat* 3 (11–25 September 1970): 17; "We Shall Be Free," *Quicksilver Times* 2 (15–25 September 1970): 3, 15; "The Days Belonged to the Panthers," *off our backs,* 30 September 1970, 4–5; Lois Hart, "Black Panthers Call a Revolutionary People's Constitutional Convention: A White Lesbian Responds," *Come Out* 1 (September–October 1970): 15; "YAWF Women's Statement," *Philadelphia Free Press* 4, nos. 14–16 (1970): 7–8; "Philly Convention," *Rat* 3 (September 1970): 17.

58. Paul Delaney, "Panthers to Reconvene in Capital to Ratify Their Constitution," *New York Times,* 8 September 1970, 57; Abu-Jamal, *We Want Freedom,* 77–78.

59. "Interview with Elaine Brown," *Black Panther,* 3 October 1970, 7.

60. "Dear Sisters," *off our backs,* 14 December 1970, 3; Bread and Roses, "Women and the Panther Convention," *Rat,* 17 November–6 December 1970, 24.

61. "Black Panthers Want Howard U. to Cancel Fee," *Washington Post,* 22 November 1970, A5; Ivan C. Brandon, "Panthers, Howard U. Still at Odds," *Washington Post,* 25 November 1970, C2; Ivan C. Brandon, "Panthers Seek Site for Talk," *Washington Post,* 27 November 1970, C1, C10; Hilliard and Cole, *This Side of Glory,* 314.

62. "Notes from Women's Liberation Project Group to Discuss Relating to the Revolutionary People's Constitutional Convention and the Black Panther Party," September 1970, Folder 29, Carton 1, Bunch Papers.

63. Notes on Workshops, October 1970, Folder 29, Carton 1, Bunch Papers.

64. "Huey Speaks," *Quicksilver Times,* 8–18 December 1970, 7.

65. "Revolutionary People's Constitutional Convention"; "Three Women Talk on the Revolutionary People's Constitutional Convention," *Ain't I a Woman,* 29 January 1971, 10–11; Bunch, "Ourstory, Herstory," Deevey Papers.

66. Stewart interview; "People's Law and Order," *Quicksilver Times,* 25 September–4 October 1970, 15.

67. *Hilltop* editorial reprinted as "Cultural Nationalism," *Quicksilver Times* 2 (8–18 December 1970): 7.

68. "Plain Facts," *Quicksilver Times,* 8–18 December 1970, 6; Austin Scott, "Huey Newton Asks End to Boundaries," *Washington Post,* 29 November 1970, D1, D6; Ivan C. Brandon and Jim Mann, "Panthers End D.C. Convention," *Washington Post,* 30 November 1970, C1, C3.

69. Bolder, "Panthers Shelve Militant Image."

70. Judy Bachrach, "Battling the Devils of Sexism and Racism," *Washington Post,* 23 August 1974, B2.

71. Wilson Morris, "600 Black Women Confer," *Washington Post,* 16 November 1975, B16; Mary Ellen Perry, "Blacks Have Varied Views of Liberation," *Washington Star,* 2 April 1976, E1, E3.

72. Jacqueline Trescott, "Dorothy Height, Feminist," *Washington Post,* 14 November 1975, C3.

73. Jo Benoit to Margaret Sloan, 7 August 1974 and 22 September 1974, Box 1, Folders 7 and 8, National Black Feminist Organization Papers, University of Illinois Chicago; White, *Too Heavy a Load*; Roth, *Separate Roads to Feminism*; Springer, *Living for the Revolution.*

74. "Beating the System Together: Interview with a Black Feminist," *off our backs,* October 1973, 2–3.

75. "Uniting and Conquering," *off our backs,* December–January 1974, 1; Fran Pollner, "Black Feminists up Front," *off our backs,* December–January 1974, 2–3.

Chapter 6: Lesbian Feminism and Separatism

1. Sue Fox, "The Furies," *Washington Blade,* 16 June 1995, 63, 65, 67.

2. Rita Mae Brown to the Furies (n.d., circa 1972), Sharon Deevey Papers.

3. The pressures for conformity and political correctness that emerged within the Furies resembled those experienced by many other lesbian feminist and New Left groups. Shugar, *Separatism and Women's Community*; Klatch, *Generation Divided.*

4. Beemyn, "Queer Capital," in Beemyn, *Creating a Place for Ourselves*; Johnson, "'Homosexual Citizens'"; Lilli Vincenz, interviewed by Mark Meinke, 21 April 2001, Rainbow History Project, Washington, D.C. An extremely useful chronology of significant political events in the District's gay and lesbian past can be found at the Web site maintained by the Rainbow History project, www.rainbowhistory.org.

5. Allen Young, a member of SDS and employee of the Liberation News Service in Washington, D.C., described his silence about his homosexuality in "Out of the Closet: A Gay Manifesto," *Ramparts* 10 (November 1971): 52–59. For other accounts of gay men and women's experiences in 1960s movements, see D'Emilio, *Lost Prophet*; Lekus, "Queer and Present Dangers"; Deming, *Prisons That Could Not Hold*; Nestle, *Restricted Country.*

6. Along with the *Gay Blade,* the *D.C. Gazette,* the *Washingtonian, Quicksilver Times,* and *off our backs* intermittently covered activities organized by or deemed relevant to the city's gay population.

7. Thomas Shales, "Gay Liberation in D.C.," *D.C. Gazette,* 24 May 1971, 4, 17; *Gay Blade* 3 (November 1971): 1; *Gay Blade* 3 (December 1971): 1; Carlene Cheatam, interview by Mark Meinke, 23 February 2001, Rainbow History Project; Valerie Papaya Mann interview, Rainbow History Project.

8. Joan Carmodey speech in Carton 2, Folder 54, Bunch Papers; DCWLM Bulletin, 17 September 1970, Carton 1, Folder 26, Bunch Papers.

9. Background information comes from Sharon Deevey, interview by author, 25 September 1993; Sharon Deevey, "Such a Nice Girl," *The Furies* 1 (January 1972): 2; Fox, "The Furies": Joan Biren, interview by author, 30 December 1992; Charlotte Bunch, interview by author, 15 February 1995.

10. Bunch interview; Biren interview; Deevey interview; Helaine Harris, interview with author, 16 August 1993; Fox, "The Furies"; Tasha Peterson, "Class Will Tell," *off*

our backs, 15 April 1971. See also autobiographical articles by Coletta Reid, Helaine Harris, and Nancy Myron in *Motive* 32 (January 1972).

11. Jacobs, *Way the Wind Blew*; Varon, *Bringing the War Home,* 56–58; Joan Biren, personal communication, 9 September 2004; Fox, "The Furies."

12. Stein, *City of Sisterly and Brotherly Loves.*

13. Hayden, *Reunion,* 420–21; Lekus, "Queer and Present Dangers," ch. 6; U.S. Senate, Committee on the Judiciary, Subcommittee to Investigate the Administration of the Internal Security Act and Other Internal Security Laws, *The Weather Underground* (Washington, D.C.: Government Printing Office, 1975), 10.

14. DCWLM, "What Is a Collective?" Folder 1970–1971, Box 1, Joan E. Biren Papers, Lesbian Herstory Archives.

15. Echols, *Daring to Be Bad,* 220–22; Women's Commune, "Mind Bogglers," *off our backs,* 31 July 1970, 13; interview with Susan Gregory, *off our backs* 3 (September 1973): 18–19.

16. Radicalesbians, "Woman-Identified Woman," *Women: A Journal of Liberation* 1 (Summer 1970): 39.

17. Rita Mae Brown, "Hanoi to Hoboken," *off our backs,* 25 March 1971, 4–5.

18. Deevey, "Such a Nice Girl"; Deevey interview; Echols, *Daring to Be Bad,* 224–25; Ginny Berson, "Slumming It in the Middle Class," *The Furies* 1 (March–April 1972): 12–13; Myron, "Lace Curtains and a Plastic Jesus"; Reid, "Coming Out in the Women's Movement," in Myron and Bunch, *Lesbianism and the Women's Movement,* 95; Those Women (Statement of the Furies at Day Care Center), May 1971, Carton 2, Folder 54, Bunch Papers.

19. Women who did not join the Furies generally do not recall a problem with homophobia among D.C. feminists. Wolfson, "Clenched Fist, Open Heart," in DuPlessis and Snitow, *Feminist Memoir Project*; "A Month of Tuesdays," *off our backs,* Summer 1971, 30; "Good-By Ruby Tuesday," *off our backs,* 6 May 1971, 18; Frances Chapman, "Sage Advice," *off our backs* 2 (May–June 1972): 17. A description of the women's movement retreat, which handles the issues raised by lesbians in a positive way, is Helene Gardell, "Politics and Sex," *off our backs,* 24 June 1971, 22.

20. Rita Mae Brown, "Roxanne Dunbar: How a Female Heterosexual Serves the Interests of Male Supremacy," *The Furies* 1 (January 1972): 5–6; Brown, "Hanoi to Hoboken"; Charlotte Bunch, "Out Now," *The Furies* 1 (June–July 1972): 12–13; Ginny Berson, "The Furies," *The Furies* 1 (January 1972): 1.

21. Charlotte Bunch, "Lesbians in Revolt," *The Furies* 1 (January 1972): 8–9. See also "Statement of the Furies at Day Care Center."

22. Rita Mae Brown, "The Shape of Things to Come," *Women: A Journal of Liberation* (January 1972), reprinted in *Plain Brown Rapper* (Oakland: Diana Press, 1976), 110.

23. Berson, "The Furies."

24. Ibid.; Deevey interview; Bunch interview; Biren interview; Deevey, "Such a Nice Girl."

25. For critical responses to the Furies issued by other Washington, D.C., activists, see Wolfson, "Clenched Fist, Open Heart," in DuPlessis and Snitow, *Feminist Memoir Project*; Fox, "The Furies," 67; "Bev Fisher," *off our backs*, November 1972, 2–3; Fran Chapman, "Commentary," *off our backs,* January 1972, 7; Betty Garman, Memo to Those Women, 1 July 1971, Deevey Papers; Fran Pollner, "One Day in the Life of the Women's Movement," *off our backs* 2 (May–June 1972): 16.

26. "Brief Summary of Resolutions Passed at the Recent National NOW Convention in L.A.," *Vocal Majority* 2 (October 1971): 10; Eva Freund, interview by Mark Meinke, 3 November 2002, Rainbow History Project.

27. Berson, "The Furies," in Wachsberger, *Voices from the Underground,* 316.

28. Charlotte Bunch, "Notes for the Cell Meeting, January, 1972," Box 1, Biren Papers.

29. *Gay Blade* 3 (November 1971): 1; *Gay Blade* 3 (February 1972): 1; *Gay Blade* 3 (March 1972): 1; *Gay Blade* 4 (December 1972): 1; *Gay Blade* 4 (June 1973): 1.

30. Rita Mae Brown, "Leadership vs. Stardom," *The Furies* 1 (February 1972): 20; Ginny Berson, "Beyond Male Power," *The Furies* 1 (May 1972): 13–14. Rita Mae Brown later repeated her argument about the need for a national organization in Rita Mae Brown, "Take State Power!" *The Tide* 3 (June 1974): 3, 23.

31. Coletta Reid, "Details," *The Furies* 1 (June–July 1972): 7.

32. Brown, "The Shape of Things to Come"; "Teach Each Other, Teach Ourselves," pamphlet, 1971, Addenda, Carton 2, Folder 49, Bunch Papers.

33. Biren interview. The Furies quickly discontinued their skills workshops, but Bunch's notes from a January 1972 meeting indicate that the group still considered skills centers an important activity. Bunch, "Notes for the Cell Meeting, January 1972," Biren Papers.

34. Charlotte Bunch to parents, 14 October 1971, Carton 1, Folder 23, Bunch Papers; *The Gay Blade* 3 (March 1972): 1–2.

35. Berson, "The Furies."

36. "What's Going On?" *The Furies* 1 (January 1972): 15.

37. Linda Carcione et al., "The State of the Struggle," Folder 21, Box 1, Bunch Papers.

38. Brown, "Leadership vs. Stardom."

39. Sharon Deevey and Nancy Myron took printing classes at a technical school in Washington, D.C. According to Deevey, she took classes for political reasons and because she did not have firm ideas for her career. Deevey interview.

40. "What's Going On?" *The Furies* 1 (January 1972): 15.

41. Bunch and Reid, "Revolution Begins at Home."

42. Berson, "Only by Association."

43. Fox, "The Furies," 67.

44. Harris interview. The formula designed by the group for sharing income is described in Reid, "Details"; Berson, "The Furies," in Wachsberger, *Voices from the Underground,* 314; Fox, "The Furies."

45. Bunch and Reid, "Revolution Begins at Home." Rita Mae Brown, one of the working-class women in the group, recalled that the middle-class women were "good about sharing, a lot better than I would have been if the shoe were on the other foot." Brown, *Rita Will,* 269–70; Biren interview.

46. Bunch et al., "Ourstory, Herstory: A Working Paper on the D.C. Women's Liberation Movement, 1968–1971," Deevey Papers. The March 1971 issue of *Vocal Majority* notes the nine consciousness-raising groups affiliated with the local NOW chapter.

47. Berson, "The Furies," in Wachsberger, *Voices from the Underground*; Deevey and Reid, "Emotionalism—Downward Spiral," 11.

48. U.S. Department of Justice, "The Furies, 1967–1975," Federal Bureau of Investigation File; Fox, "After the Revolution"; Journal Entry, Deevey Papers; Brown, *Rita Will,* 271.

49. Biren's photographs appear in the group's newspaper, but no articles in *The Furies* attribute authorship to Biren. She left the group by the time the paper started, but, like Sharon Deevey, Biren assisted with its publication even after she was kicked out of the collective. Fox, "After the Revolution"; Biren interview.

50. Deevey interview; Harris interview; Biren interview; Fox, "The Furies."

51. Biren interview.

52. Fox, "After the Revolution," 43, 45; Harris interview; Biren interview; Brown, *Plain Brown Rapper,* 17–19.

53. The North Carolina lesbian feminist group, Feminary, acknowledged the Furies' role in shaping their own ideas about lesbianism and collective living. Knowlton, "Rita Mae Brown." A recent study of the women's movement in Dayton, Ohio, also credits *The Furies* newspaper with influencing the Dayton Women's Liberation group's thinking about lesbianism as a political issue. Ezekiel, *Feminism in the Heartland,* 50–51. Bunch stressed the influence of the Furies, and of lesbian separatism more generally, in forcing women's organizations to recognize the legitimacy of lesbian civil rights in "Learning from Lesbian Separatism."

54. Kollias, "Spiral of Change."

55. For descriptions of individuals' goals and accomplishments after they left the collective, see Reid, "Taking Care of Business"; "The Muses of Olivia: Our Own Economy, Our Own Song," *off our backs* 4 (August–September 1974): 2–3; Bunch, *Passionate Politics*; Brown, *Plain Brown Rapper.* Biren's photographs appear in numerous publications, including two collections she published of her own work, *Eye to Eye: Portraits of Lesbians* (Washington, D.C.: Glad Hag Books, 1979) and *Making a Way: Lesbians Out Front* (Washington, D.C.: Glad Hag Books, 1987).

56. Taylor and Rupp, "Women's Culture and Lesbian Feminist Activism."

57. Fran Chapman, "Sage Advice," *off our backs* 2 (May–June 1972): 17; "Bev Fisher," *off our backs* 2 (November 1972): 2–3.

58. "Bev Fisher"; "The Washington Feminists" flyer (1971), Box 5, Folder "Women's Liberation Movements and Studies," Liberal/Left Collection, GWU; "Women's Center," *Washington Area Women's Center Newsletter,* April 1972.

59. Rhudy, "Opinion," 11; Freund, "Once Upon a Time," 17; Announcement of Sexuality and Lesbianism Action Group, *Vocal Majority* 4 (April 1973): 19; Freund interview.

60. Charlotte Bunch, "Lesbian Feminist Politics," *off our backs* 3 (April 1973): 17.

61. Michelle Parkerson, interview by Mark Meinke, 7 March 2001, Rainbow History Project; Mann interview. The sentiments expressed by Parkerson and Mann echo those articulated by Boston's Combahee River Collective in their 1978 "Black Feminist Statement."

62. *Gay Blade* 3 (September 1972): 1.

63. Sidney Brinkley, "Black Gay History in the Making," *Washington Blade*, 7 February 1997, 12, 23; Jim Marks, "Of Gems and Nurturing Women," *Gay Blade*, 16 March 1984, 1, 13; Brett Beemyn, "'It Was Like the Sun Rose': The Coffeehouse and the Development of a Black LGB Community in Washington, D.C.," 24 September 2000, paper presented at the Eighth Annual Lavender Languages and Linguistics Conference, American University, Washington, D.C.; Parkerson interview; Mann interview; Cheatam interview.

Chapter 7: Coalition Building against Sexual Violence

1. Interview with Nkenge Toure from Baker and Kline, *Conversation Begins*, 349–57; Nkenge Toure interview by author, 24 February 2005. Information about the health clinic is from Stephen E. Colter, "No Doctor, Clinic to Close," *Washington Afro-American*, 24 August 1974, Clinics 1972–1978 Article File, MLK Library.

2. "Interview: Black Women and Rape," *Aegis* 31 (Winter/Spring 1981): 31–38; Wendy Stevens, "Learning to Survive," *off our backs* 8 (March 1978): 8.

3. Davis, "Joanne Little"; McGuire, "'It Was Like All of Us Had Been Raped,'" 907.

4. The Department of Justice acknowledged these racial disparities in its annual *Uniform Crime Reports for the United States.*

5. In 1972, the number of rapes in the D.C. metropolitan area was exceeded by that recorded in sixteen other locales in the United States with populations over 250,000 people. Federal Bureau of Investigation, *Uniform Crime Reports for the United States* (Washington, D.C.: Government Printing Office, 1973).

6. "Protestors Lay Killing in SE to Police Neglect," *Washington Post*, 28 August 1966, A3.

7. Brownmiller, *In Our Time*, 199–203; Bevacqua, *Rape on the Public Agenda*, 54–57.

8. Connell and Wilson, *Rape*, xv–xvi.

9. *Washington Area Women's Center Newsletter*, January 1972.

10. Freeman and MacMillan, "Feminist Workplace"; Scott, "How to Stop the Rapists?"; Schechter, *Women and Male Violence*, 35; "Found Women Activists," *Ms.* 1 (January 1973): 67.

11. Washington Area Women's Center Brochure, July 1973, Reel 16, Herstory 2,

Herstory: Women's History Collection (Berkeley, Calif.: Women's History Research Center, 1974); Bevacqua, *Rape on the Public Agenda,* 33, 39, 52.

12. Connell and Wilson, *Rape,* 176–80; Schechter, *Women and Male Violence,* 39.

13. Schmidt, "Rape Crisis Centers"; Matthews, *Confronting Rape,* 10; Carol Eron, "The Rape Crisis Center," *Washington Post,* 15 July 1973, Potomac Section, 10–11, 22–23, 27.

14. Eron, "Rape Crisis Center."

15. Rape Crisis Center Collective, "Our Sisters Speak," *Women: A Journal of Liberation* 3 (Winter 1972): 68–69.

16. Eron, "Rape Crisis Center."

17. "Women Talk Sex from Lesbianism to Rape," *Washington Star,* 12 May 1974, Women 1972–1975 Article File, MLK Library.

18. WPEC members included Big Sisters of Washington, Black Women Organized for Action, NOW, the National Committee for Household Employment, the Women's Equity Action League, the Washington Area Women's Center, and the Women's Legal Defense Fund. Subject Files, Box 16, City Council Papers, GWU.

19. Cities across the United States recorded similar increases in the numbers of reported rapes. According to the FBI's Uniform Crime Reports, the number of reported rapes nationally grew by 70 percent from 1967 to 1972, the highest increase of any type of violent crime. National League of Cities, *Rape* (Washington, D.C.: National League of Cities, 1974); Kirk Scharfenberg, "Changes in Rape Laws Urged by Council Study," *Washington Post,* 10 July 1973, A1, A11.

20. Under the D.C. codes, rape convictions were possible only if the complainant's "consent was induced by physical force or by threats which put her in reasonable fear of death or grave bodily harm." Corroborative evidence of resistance, such as bruises or physical scars, was required to back up the victim's claims that physical force had been used. National League of Cities, *Rape,* 5.

21. Jim Mann, "Mother Files Suit in GW Coed's Rape," *Washington Post,* 7 March 1972, C1; Lawrence Meyer, "Confession Unveiled after Rape Acquittal," *Washington Post,* 1 December 1972, A1, A16; J. Y. Smith, "The Rape Victim's Dilemma: How to React?" *Washington Post,* 2 December 1972, E1, E3; Karlyn Barker, "She Felt Like a Defendant," *Washington Post,* 2 December 1972, E1, E3; Wood, "Victim in a Forcible Rape Case," in Connell and Wilson, *Rape,* 149–50.

22. "Testimony of the Washington, D.C. Rape Crisis Center to the Public Safety Committee Task Force on Rape, City Council, Washington, D.C.," 18 September 1973, Hearing Files 1967–1974, City Council Papers, National Archives; Sharon Thompson, "Demystifying Rape," *off our backs* 3 (October 1973): 15; DeLoach, "Rape Task Force Report."

23. Some of these recommendations reappeared in the position paper issued by the Women's Political Education Coalition a year later, indicating that the task force's 1973 suggestions had either not been implemented or not been enforced. For example, the WPEC again demanded the elimination of the corroboration requirement in

rape cases and asked that courts forbid the use of a victim's prior sexual experience as evidence in rape cases.

24. In the Washington Area Women's Center newsletter, the RCC indicated that they would have preferred stronger recommendations by the task force, but they backed the proposed changes and the WPEC. *Washington Area Women's Center Newsletter,* September 1973, 5–6.

25. D.C. Commission on the Status of Women, *Seventh Annual Report* (May 1974), Herstory 3, Reel 1, Herstory Microfilm Collection; Lowe, *First Twenty Years,* 32.

26. Testimony of Mary Treadwell Barry to City Council Hearings on Rape, September 18, 1973, Rape Hearing Files 1967–1974, Box 29, City Council Papers, National Archives.

27. Ibid.

28. Barakso, *Governing NOW,* 24.

29. In 1978, the FAAR newsletter merged with *Aegis,* published by the National Communication Network (NCN), a project created by grassroots shelter workers at the Wisconsin Conference on Battered Women. Later, the Boston Alliance Against Sexual Coercion joined FAAR and the NCN to publish *Aegis* as a joint project. Schechter, *Women and Male Violence,* 38; *Aegis,* March–April 1979, 1.

30. *In Our Own Write,* August 1977, 3; Valle Jones, interview by author, 13 March 1994; "D.C. Task Force on Abused Women," n.d., Valle Jones Papers; Alice Bonner, "Shelter for Battered Wives Opens," *Washington Post,* 10 August 1976, C1, C5.

31. Loretta Ross testimony before House Committee on Appropriations, *Departments of Labor, Health and Human Services, Education, and Related Agencies Appropriations for 1982,* Pt. 8 (Washington, D.C.: Government Printing Office, 1981), 1143–45; Schmidt, "Rape Crisis Centers."

32. Schechter, *Women and Male Violence,* 41–42; Matthews, "Surmounting a Legacy"; Ezekiel, *Feminism in the Heartland,* 129–30, 140. Lois Ahrens noted a similar transformation in the battered women's shelter in Austin, Texas. Ahrens, "Battered Women's Refuges."

33. Valle Jones interview; Sally Quinn, "The Rape Crisis Center: An 'Alternative' to the Police," *Washington Post,* 15 June 1975, E17.

34. Bevacqua, *Rape on the Public Agenda,* 39; Scott, "How to Stop the Rapists," 353.

35. Hall, "Mind That Burns in Each Body," in Snitow, Stansell, and Thompson, *Powers of Desire,* 345; MacMillan and Lenaerts, "Interview: Black Women and Rape," 36.

36. Toure interview; Bevacqua, *Rape on the Public Agenda,* 78–79; "Interview: Black Women and Rape," *Aegis* (1976), reprinted (Winter/Spring 1981), 31–37.

37. Hare, "Revolution without a Revolution"; Davis, "Rape, Racism, and the Capitalist Setting."

38. Angela Terrell, "Priority: Liberating Black Communities," *Washington Post,* 1 April 1973, G10; Delaplaine, "*Mujeres y la Comunidad Latina*"; Loretta Ross, interview

by Joyce Follet, transcript of video recording, 3 November 2004, Voices of Feminism Oral History Project, Sophia Smith Collection.

39. Ross interview by Follet.

40. "Interview: Black Women and Rape." Yulanda Ward, a Howard University student, was another critical figure in these movements. In the late 1970s, Ward, like Toure and Ross, was active in the Citywide Housing Coalition and the National Black United Front and sat on the board of the RCC. She was murdered in 1980, a crime that some of her colleagues attributed to her political activities. See "In Memorium," *Quest* 5, no. 3 (1981): 8–9; Thomas Morgan, "Robbers Kill D.C. Housing Unit Leader," *Washington Post,* 3 November 1980, C1, C7; Yulanda Ward obituary, *Washington Post,* 6 November 1980, C4.

41. Pronounced (and frequently spelled) "Joanne."

42. McNeil, "'Joanne Is You and Joanne Is Me,'" in Collier-Thomas and Franklin, *Sisters in Struggle.*

43. Julie Alibrando, "Interview with Kathie Gottesman of the San Francisco Bay Area Dessie Woods' Support Coalition," *Aegis,* March–April 1979, 11; Blitman and Green, "On Trial," *Ms.* 3 (May 1975): 49–54, 84–88; Davis, "Joanne Little"; Karenga, "Joanne Little Case"; Bevacqua, *Rape on the Public Agenda,* 127–29.

44. Springer, *Living for the Revolution,* 49–50; Nelson, *Women of Color and the Reproductive Rights Movement,* 62–63.

45. "On Violence," *off our backs* 5 (February 1975): 8, 21; Reagon and Sweet Honey in the Rock, *We Who Believe in Freedom,* 29–31.

46. Diana Onley Campbell, interview by author, 5 August 1993.

47. Valle Jones interview.

48. Campbell, a black lesbian, worked at My Sister's Place until the mid-1980s, followed by an appointment with the National Coalition Against Domestic Violence.

49. Campbell interview.

50. Testimony of Maria Orrego, D.C. Commission for Women, *Hispanic Women Speak Out, a Public Hearing,* 31 August 1982, Women's Pamphlets File, MLK Library; Delaplaine, "*Mujeres y la Comunidad Latina.*"

51. Sally Quinn, "'Prisoners Against Rape': Trying to Unlock Myths and Images," *Washington Post,* 16 June 1975, B1, B3; "The Rape Crisis Center: An 'Alternative' to the Police"; Charles R. Babcock, "Men's Unit Trying to Curb Rape," *Washington Post,* 30 May 1976, D4; Vernon Thompson, "Group Voices Concerns about Rise in SE Rapes," *Washington Post,* 14 August 1976, B2; Ross interview by Follet.

52. Interview with Nkenge Toure and Patrice Toure, *FAAR News,* September–October 1977, 5.

53. Loretta Ross, interview by author, 14 February 2005.

54. Ross, interview by Follet; Loretta J. Ross, "Working with Minority Men Committing Violence against Women," *Report from the First National Conference on Third World Women and Violence* (1981), Box 2, Loretta Ross Papers, Sophia Smith Collection.

55. Friedman, "Rape, Racism, and Reality." Reprinted, in a shortened form, in *Aegis* (Winter/Spring 1981): 25–28.

56. The D.C. Area Feminist Alliance formed in 1977 as a coalition of local women's organizations. The alliance was intended to diminish feminists' sense of isolation from each other and create a mechanism for sharing ideas, problems, and resources and collectively responding to local matters that affected women. See "D.C. Feminist Coalition," *off our backs* 7 (April 1977): 7; "D.C. Feminist Alliance," *off our backs* 7 (June 1977): 8; "IWY," *off our backs* 7 (July–August 1977): 12.

57. Marcy Rein and Carol Anne Douglas, "Women Unite: Reclaim the Night," *off our backs* 8 (June 1978): 8–9; "March and Rally Details and List of Endorsers," 21 April 1978; and "Anti-Rape Week" flyer, Alexa Freeman Papers.

58. "Press Conference Statement," 21 April 1978. Endorsers included local chapters of NOW, churches, women's publications, feminist research centers, abortion rights groups, and economic organizations. "March and Rally Details," Freeman Papers.

59. The march principles were published in *Women: A Journal of Liberation* 6 (1979): 30–31.

60. Deb Friedman, "KGWP—Another View," *FAAR News*, January–February 1978, 9–10; Rein and Douglas, "Women Unite: Reclaim the Night," 8.

61. Rein and Douglas, "Women Unite: Reclaim the Night," 8; Chris Lundberg to D.C. Area Feminist Alliance, 13 February 1978, Valle Jones Papers.

62. Rein and Douglas, "Women Unite: Reclaim the Night"; Alexa Freeman, interview by author, 23 August 1995.

Conclusion

1. Carol Anne Douglas, "DCAFA Background," *off our backs*, June 1978, 9.

2. *Alliance News: Newsletter of the D.C. Area Feminist Alliance* 1 (February 1978), Jones Papers.

3. "Combating Racism in the Women's Movement," Conference Program, May 1980, Jones Papers.

4. Loretta Ross, interview by Follet, transcript of video recording, pp. 127–28.

5. Toure, "Report on the First National Third World Women's Conference"; Schechter, *Women and Male Violence*, 277; Loretta J. Ross, "Third World Women and Violence," August 1980, Box 2, Ross Papers.

6. Williams, "Violence against Women"; Ross interview by Follet, transcript of video recording, pp. 128–30.

7. Toure, "Report on the First National Third World Women's Conference," 72.

Selected Bibliography

Manuscript Collections

Duke University, Durham, N.C.
  Rare Books, Manuscripts, and Special Collections Library
    Atlanta Lesbian Feminist Alliance Collection
    Milo Guthrie Papers
George Washington University, Washington, D.C.
  Department of Special Collections, Gelman Library
    District of Columbia City Council Papers
    Liberal/Left Archival Materials/Studies Collection
    Student Protest Collection
Howard University, Washington, D.C.
  Moorland-Spingarn Research Center
    Wiley A. Branton Papers
    Ophelia Settle Egypt Papers
    National Welfare Rights Organization Papers
Lesbian Herstory Archives, New York
    Joan E. Biren Papers
Library of Congress, Washington, D.C.
  Manuscripts Division
    Anne B. Turpeau Papers
Martin Luther King Jr., Memorial Library, Washington, D.C.
  Washingtoniana Division, D.C. Community Archives
    Julius W. Hobson Papers
    League of Women Voters Collection
    Articles Files

National Archives, Washington, D.C.
District of Columbia City Council Papers, Record Group 351
National Archives, College Park, Md.
Office of Economic Opportunity, General Records of the Community Services Administration, Record Group 381
Northwestern University, Evanston, Ill.
Charles Deering McCormick Library of Special Collections
Women's Ephemera Files
Radcliffe Institute, Harvard University, Cambridge, Mass.
Arthur and Elizabeth Schlesinger Library on the History of Women in America
Charlotte Bunch Papers
NOW Papers
Smith College, Northampton, Mass.
Sophia Smith Collection
Planned Parenthood Federation of America Records II
Loretta Ross Papers
Gloria Steinem Papers
Women's Liberation Collection
State Historical Society of Wisconsin, Madison, Wis.
George A. Wiley Papers, 1949–1975
Women's National Abortion Action Coalition Papers
University of Illinois at Chicago, Chicago, Ill.
Special Collections Department, University Library
National Black Feminist Organization Papers
University of Missouri–St. Louis, St. Louis, Mo.
Western Historical Manuscripts Collection
Women's Studies Periodicals Collection

Privately Held Collections

Dorothy Burlage Papers, Cambridge, Mass.
Sharon Deevey Papers, Columbus, Ohio
Alexa Freeman Papers, Washington, D.C.
Valle Jones Papers, Durham, N.C.
off our backs Papers, Washington, D.C.

Microfilm Collections

Congress on Racial Equality Papers, 1941–1968. Sanford, N.C.: Microfilming Corporation of America, 1982.

Herstory: Women's History Collection. Berkeley, Calif.: Women's History Research Center, 1974.

Papers of Mary Church Terrell, 1951–1962. Washington, D.C.: Library of Congress, 1977.

Students for a Democratic Society Papers, 1958–1970. Glen Rock, N.J.: Microfilming Corporation of America, 1977.

Student Nonviolent Coordinating Committee Papers, 1959–1972. Sanford, N.C.: Microfilming Corporation of America, 1980.

Underground Newspaper Microfilm Collection, 1963–1976. Wooster, Ohio: Micro Photo Division of Bell and Howell, 1976.

Oral Interviews

Allen, Norma. Interview by author, 22 June 1994, Washington, D.C. Tape recording.

Biren, Joan E. Interview by author, 30 December 1992, Takoma Park, Md. Tape recording.

———. Interview by Lucia Valeska, 1978. Transcript. In author's possession.

———. Interview by Judith Schwarz, 7 June 1979, Takoma Park, MD. Transcript. In author's possession.

Booker, Reginald. Interview by Robert Wright, 24 July 1970. Interview RJB 585, transcript. Civil Rights Documentation Project, Moorland-Spingarn Research Center, Howard University.

Brown, Sherry. Telephone interview by author, 13 February 2005.

Bunch, Charlotte. Interview by author, 15 February 1995, New York. Tape recording.

Burlage, Dorothy. Interview by author, 21 February 1995, Cambridge, Mass. Tape recording.

Butler, Josephine. Interview by author, 21 June 1994, Washington, D.C. Tape recording.

Campbell, Diana Onley. Interview by author, 5 August 1993, Washington, D.C. Tape recording.

Cheatam, Carlene. Interview by Mark Meinke, 23 February 2001, Washington, D.C. Rainbow History Project, Washington, D.C. Transcript.

Colom, Audrey. Interview by Mary Kotz, 7 January 1975. Tape recording. Interview 216, Collection 1304A, State Historical Society of Wisconsin.

Deevey, Sharon. Interview by author, 25 September 1993, Columbus, Ohio. Tape recording.

Douglas, Carol Anne. Interview by author, 11 May 1994, Washington, D.C. Tape recording.

Edgcombe, Gabrielle. Interview by author, 17 March 1994, Washington, D.C. Tape recording.

Ferebee, Dorothy Boulding. Interview by Merze Tate, 28 and 31 December 1979. In *Black Women Oral History Project,* ed. Schlesinger Library, 433–81. Cambridge, Mass.: Radcliffe College, 1980.

Freeman, Alexa. Interview by author, 23 August 1995, Washington, D.C. Tape recording.

Freund, Eva. Interview by Mark Meinke, 3 November 2002, Washington, D.C. Rainbow History Project, Washington, D.C. Transcript.

Garman, Betty. Interview by author, 17 April 1994, Baltimore, Md. Tape recording.

Giddings, Paula. Interview by Blackside, Inc., for *Eyes on the Prize II,* n.d. Transcript. Washington University in St. Louis Libraries, Film and Media Archive, Henry Hampton Collection.

Gittens, Anthony. Interview by Blackside, Inc., for *Eyes on the Prize II,* 16 October 1988. Transcript. Washington University in St. Louis Libraries, Film and Media Archive, Henry Hampton Collection.

Gregory, Robin. Interview by Blackside, Inc., for *Eyes on the Prize II,* 12 October 1988. Transcript. Washington University in St. Louis Libraries, Film and Media Archive, Henry Hampton Collection.

Harris, Helaine. Interview by author, 16 August 1993, Hyattsville, Md. Tape recording.

Hobson, Julius. Interview by Katherine Shannon, 3 July 1967 and 17 May 1968. Interview RJB 4 and RJB 322, transcript. Civil Rights Documentation Project, Moorland-Spingarn Research Center, Howard University.

Horn, Etta. Interview by Mary Kotz, 20 November 1974. Tape recording. Tape 143, Collection 1304A, State Historical Society of Wisconsin.

———. Interview by Blackside, Inc., for *Eyes on the Prize II,* 4 December 1988. Tape recording. Washington University in St. Louis Libraries, Film and Media Archive, Henry Hampton Collection.

Israel, Adrienne Manns. Interview by author, 1 March 1993, Greensboro, N.C. Transcript.

———. Interview by Blackside, Inc., for *Eyes on the Prize II,* 16 October 1988. Transcript. Washington University in St. Louis Libraries, Film and Media Archive, Henry Hampton Collection.

Jones, Theresa. Interview by author, 24 August 1995, Washington, D.C. Tape recording.

Jones, Valle. Interview by author, 13 March 1994, Durham, N.C. Tape recording.

Kranz, Sharlene. Interview by author, 23 August 2004, Washington, D.C. Tape recording.

Mann, Valerie Papaya. Interview by Mark Meinke, 5 March 2001, Washington, D.C. Rainbow History Project, Washington, D.C. Transcript.

Manns, Adrienne. Interview by H. O. Lewis, 9 August 1968. Interview RJB 267, transcript. Civil Rights Documentation Project, Moorland-Spingarn Research Center, Howard University.

Martin-Felton, Zora. Interview by author, 30 March 1995, Washington, D.C. Transcript.

Neal, Gaston. Interview by James Mosby, 1 July 1968. Interview RJB 232, transcript. Civil Rights Documentation Project, Moorland-Spingarn Research Center, Howard University.

Parkerson, Michelle. Interview by Mark Meinke, 7 March 2001, Washington, D.C. Rainbow History Project, Washington, D.C. Transcript.

Richardson, Judy. Interview by author, 22 February 1995, Cambridge, Mass. Tape recording.

Ross, Loretta. Telephone interview by author, 14 February 2005.

———. Interview by Joyce Follet. Transcript of video recording, November and December 2004, February 2005. Voices of Feminism Oral History Project, Sophia Smith Collection, Smith College.

Smith, Tina. Interview by author, 17 May 1994, Washington, D.C. Tape recording.

Sprinkle, Marcia. Interview by author, 15 May 1994 and 27 June 1994, Washington, D.C. Tape recording.

Stewart, Pearl. Interview by Allen Coleman, 27 October 1970. Interview RJB 670, transcript. Civil Rights Documentation Project, Moorland-Spingarn Research Center, Howard University.

Toure, Nkenge. Telephone interview by author, 24 February 2005.

Vincenz, Lilli. Interview by Mark Meinke, 21 April 2001, Washington, D.C. Rainbow History Project, Washington, D.C. Transcript.

Weaver, Juanita. Interview by author, 18 June 1994, Takoma Park, Md. Tape recording.

Wilkerson, Cathlyn. Interview by Ronald Grele, 17 February 1985, Brooklyn, N.Y. Transcript. Student Movements of the 1960s Oral History Project, Oral History Research Office, Columbia University.

Newspapers, Magazines, and Journals

Aegis (originally known as the *Feminist Alliance Against Rape Newsletter*), 1974–81

Black News, 1970

Black Panther, 1969–74

Black Scholar, 1970–81

Communities in Action, 1966–67

D.C. Gazette, 1970–78

Daily Rag, 1973–74

Ebony, 1965–74

F.E.W.'s News and Views, 1969–74

Furies, 1972–73

Guardian, 1968–71

Hilltop (Howard University), 1967–68

In Our Own Write (also known as *Washington Area Women's Center Newsletter* and *Raising Cain*), 1971–84

Militant, 1970–72

Motive, 1969–72

Muhammad Speaks, 1960–64, 1971

New Left Notes, 1967–68

New York Times, 1967–70

off our backs, 1970–80

Quest, 1974–81
Quicksilver Times, 1969–71
Ramparts, 1970–71
Spectre, 1971–72
The Tide, 1974
Unity and Struggle, 1973–76
Vocal Majority (National Capital Area Chapter of NOW), 1970–73 (previously *The Activist*, 1968)
Washington Afro-American, 1964–80
Washington Blade (also known as *Gay Blade*), 1969–95
Washington Daily News, 1970–71
Washington Free Press, 1967–69
Washington Post, 1964–80
Washington Star (also known as *The Evening Star*), 1965–77
Washingtonian, 1973
Women: A Journal of Liberation, 1970–83
Women's National Abortion Action Coalition (WONAAC) Newsletter, 1970–72

Government Documents

D.C. Commission on Status of Women. *Seventh Annual Report*. Washington, D.C.: Commission on Status of Women, 1974.

Department of Health, Education, and Welfare, National Center for Health Statistics. *Vital Statistics of the United States, 1970*. Vol. 2, *Mortality*. Rockville, Md.: Public Health Service, 1974.

Department of Health and Human Services, National Center for Health Statistics. *Vital Statistics of the United States, 1980*. Vol. 2, *Mortality*. Washington, D.C.: Government Printing Office, 1984.

District of Columbia, Department of Public Welfare. *Annual Report*. Washington, D.C.: Department of Public Welfare, 1966.

Federal Bureau of Investigation Files and Records (Freedom of Information Act and Other Releases)
D.C. Chapter, Congress on Racial Equality
D.C. Committee to Free Angela Davis
The Furies
off our backs
Washington Women's Liberation

Moynihan, Daniel Patrick. *The Negro Family: The Case for National Action*. Washington, D.C.: U.S. Government Printing Office, 1965.

National Center for Health Statistics. *Utilization of Family Planning Services by Currently Married Women, 15–44 Years of Age*. DHEW Pub. No. (PHS) 78–1977. Hyattsville, Md.: U.S. Department of Health, Education, and Welfare, Public Health Service, 1977.

Report of the City Council's Health and Welfare Committee on Abortions in the District of Columbia, October 1970. Washington, D.C.: Government of the District of Columbia, 1970.

United Planning Organization. *Alternatives: A Special Report on the UPO.* Washington, D.C.: UPO, 1969.

U.S. Department of Commerce, Bureau of the Census. *Historical Statistics of the United States, Colonial Times to 1970.* Washington, D.C.: Government Printing Office, 1975.

———. *Sixteenth Census of the United States: 1940.* Detailed Population Characteristics. Vol. 3, *The Labor Force, District of Columbia.* Washington, D.C.: Government Printing Office, 1941.

———. *A Report of the Seventeenth Decennial Census of the United States. Census of Population: 1950.* Vol. 2, *Characteristics of the Population.* Pt. 9, *District of Columbia.* Washington, D.C.: Government Printing Office, 1952.

———. *The Eighteenth Decennial Census of the United States. Census of Population: 1960.* Vol. 1, *Characteristics of the Population.* Pt. 10, *District of Columbia.* Washington, D.C.: Government Printing Office, 1961.

———. *1970 Census of Population.* Vol. 1, *Characteristics of the Population.* Pt. 10, *District of Columbia.* Washington, D.C.: Government Printing Office, 1973.

———. *1970 Census of the Population. Subject Report: Low-Income Areas in Large Cities.* Washington, D.C.: Government Printing Office, 1973.

———. *1980 Census of Population.* Vol. 1, *Characteristics of the Population.* Ch. B, *General Population Characteristics.* Pt. 10, *District of Columbia.* Washington, D.C.: Government Printing Office, 1982.

———. *1980 Census of Population.* Vol. 1, *Characteristics of the Population.* Ch. C, *General Social and Economic Characteristics.* Pt. 1, *United States Summary.* Washington, D.C.: Government Printing Office, 1983.

———. *1980 Census of Population.* Vol. 1, *Characteristics of the Population.* Ch. C, *General Social and Economic Characteristics.* Pt. 10, *District of Columbia.* Washington, D.C.: Government Printing Office, 1983.

———. *Statistical Abstract of the United States, 1970,* 91st ed. Washington, D.C.: Government Printing Office, 1970.

———. *Statistical Abstract of the United States, 1980,* 101st ed. Washington, D.C.: Government Printing Office, 1980.

U.S. Department of Commerce, Bureau of Economic Analysis. *Local Area Personal Income, 1973–1978.* Vol. 1, *Summary.* Washington, D.C.: Government Printing Office, 1980.

U.S. Congress, House Committee on Appropriations. *Departments of Labor, Health and Human Services, Education, and Related Agencies Appropriations for 1982: Hearings before a Subcommittee of the Committee on Appropriations, U.S. Senate, Ninety-seventh Congress, First session.* Washington, D.C.: Government Printing Office, 1981.

U.S. Congress, House Committee on Education and Labor, Subcommittee on Select Education. *Domestic Violence. H.R. 7927 and H.R. 8948.* 2nd session. Washington, D.C.: Government Printing Office, 1978.

———. *Domestic Violence: Prevention and Services.* 1st session. Washington, D.C.: Government Printing Office, 1979.

U.S. Congress, House Committee on Internal Security. *The Black Panther Party: Its Origin and Development as Reflected in Its Official Weekly Newspaper "The Black Panther Community News Service."* Washington, D.C.: Government Printing Office, 1970.

U.S. Congress, Senate Committee on Banking, Housing, and Urban Affairs, Subcommittee on Financial Institutions. *Credit in Low-Income Areas.* Washington, D.C.: Government Printing Office, 1970.

U.S. Congress, Senate Committee on Government Operations, Subcommittee on Investigations. *Riots, Civil and Criminal Disorders.* 1st session, Pts. 19 and 22. Washington, D.C.: Government Printing Office, 1969.

U.S. Congress, Senate Committee on Labor and Human Resources, Subcommittee on Health. *Family Planning and Population Research.* Washington, D.C.: Government Printing Office, 1970.

U.S. Congress, Senate Committee on Labor and Human Resources, Special Subcommittee on Human Resources. *Family Planning Services and Population Research Amendments of 1973.* Washington, D.C.: Government Printing Office, 1973.

U.S. Congress, Senate Committee on Labor and Public Welfare, Subcommittee on Children and Youth. *Child and Family Services Act, 1975.* Washington, D.C.: Government Printing Office, 1975.

U.S. Congress, Senate Committee on Small Business, Subcommittee on Monopoly. *Competitive Problems in the Drug Industry: Hearings Before the Subcommittee on Monopoly of the Select Committee on Small Business.* 2nd session on Present Status of Competition in the Pharmaceutical Industry, Pt. 17. Washington, D.C.: Government Printing Office, 1970.

U.S. Congress, Senate Committee on the District of Columbia. *Crime in the National Capital: District of Columbia Omnibus Crime Bill.* 2nd session, Pt. 9. Washington, D.C.: Government Printing Office, 1970.

———. *Crime in the National Capital: Narcotics-Crime Crisis in the Washington Area.* 2nd session, Pt. 12. Washington, D.C.: Government Printing Office, 1971.

U.S. Congress, Senate Committee on the Judiciary. *"Equal Rights" Amendment: Hearings Before the Subcommittee on Constitutional Amendments of the Committee on the Judiciary.* Washington, D.C.: Government Printing Office, 1970.

———. *The Weather Underground: Report of the Subcommittee to Investigate the Administration of the Internal Security Act and Other Internal Security Laws.* Washington, D.C.: Government Printing Office, 1975.

U.S. Office of Economic Opportunity. *Women in the War on Poverty: Conference Proceedings.* Washington, D.C.: Government Printing Office, 1967.

———. *Women in the War on Poverty: Conference Proceedings.* Washington, D.C.: Government Printing Office, 1968.

———. *Women in the War on Poverty: Conference Proceedings.* Washington, D.C.: Government Printing Office, 1969.

Books and Articles

Abu-Jamal, Mumia. *We Want Freedom: A Life in the Black Panther Party.* Cambridge, Mass.: South End Press, 2004.

Agronsky, Jonathan I. Z. *Marion Barry: The Politics of Race.* Latham, N.Y.: British American Publishing, 1991.

Ahrens, Lois. "Battered Women's Refuges: Feminist Cooperatives vs. Social Service Institutions." *Radical America* 14 (May/June 1980): 41–47.

Allen, Pamela. "Free Space," in *Notes from the Third Year,* reprinted in *Radical Feminism,* edited by Anne Koedt, Ellen Levine, and Anita Rapone, 271–79. New York: Quadrangle Books, 1973.

Amatniek, Kathie. "Funeral Oration for the Burial of Traditional Womanhood." In *Notes from the First Year,* edited by New York Radical Women, n.p. New York: New York Radical Women, 1968.

Bailis, Lawrence Neil. *Bread or Justice: Grassroots Organizing in the Welfare Rights Movement.* Lexington, Mass.: D.C. Heath, 1974.

Baker, Christina Looper, and Christina Baker Kline. *The Conversation Begins: Mothers and Daughters Talk About Living Feminism.* New York: Bantam Books, 1996.

Banks, Manley Elliott, et al. "Transformative Leadership in the Post–Civil Rights Era: The 'War on Poverty' and the Emergence of African American Political Leadership." *Western Journal of Black Studies* 20 (Winter 1996): 173–87.

Barakso, Maryann. *Governing NOW: Grassroots Activism in the National Organization for Women.* Ithaca, N.Y.: Cornell University Press, 2005.

Barbour, Floyd B., ed. *The Black Power Revolt.* Boston, Mass.: Porter Sargent, 1968.

———, ed. *The Black Seventies.* Boston, Mass.: Porter Sargent, 1970.

Barras, Jonetta Rose. *The Last of the Black Emperors: The Hollow Comeback of Marion Barry in the New Age of Black Leaders.* Baltimore: Bancroft Press, 1998.

Baxandall, Rosalyn. "Re-Envisioning the Women's Liberation Movement's Narrative: Early Second Wave African American Feminists." *Feminist Studies* 27 (Spring 2001): 225–45.

Beemyn, Brett. "A Queer Capital: Race, Class, Gender, and the Changing Social Landscape of Washington's Gay Communities, 1940–1955." In *Creating a Place for Ourselves: Lesbian, Gay, and Bisexual Community Histories,* edited by Brett Beemyn, 183–210. New York: Routledge, 1997.

———, ed., *Creating a Place for Ourselves: Lesbian, Gay, and Bisexual Community Histories.* New York: Routledge, 1997.

Bell, Winifred. "The 'Rights' of the Poor: Welfare Witch-Hunts in the District of Columbia." *Social Work* 13 (January 1968): 60–67.

Berson, Ginny Z. "The Furies: Goddesses of Vengeance." In *Voices from the Underground: Insider Histories of the Vietnam Era Underground Press,* Vol. 1, edited by Ken Wachsberger, 313–24. Tempe, Ariz.: Mica's Press, 1993.

———. "Only by Association." *The Furies* 1 (June–July 1972): 5–6.

Bevacqua, Marie. *Rape on the Public Agenda: Feminism and the Politics of Sexual Assault.* Boston: Northeastern University Press, 2000.

Blitman, Nan, and Robin Green. "On Trial." *Ms.* 3 (May 1975): 49–54, 84–88.

Board of Trustees of Howard University. "A Policy Statement on the Black University." In *The University Crisis Reader,* Vol. 1, *The Liberal University Under Attack,* edited by Immanuel Wallerstein and Paul Starr, 361–63. New York: Random House, 1971.

Booker, Simeon. "Washington's Civil Rights Maverick." *Ebony* 20 (May 1965): 140–45.

Borris, Eileen. "The Power of Motherhood: Black and White Activist Women Redefine the 'Political.'" *Yale Journal of Law and Feminism* 2, no. 25 (1989): 25–49.

Breines, Wini. "What's Love Got to Do With It? White Women, Black Women, and Feminism in the Movement Years." *Signs* 27 (Summer 2002): 1095–133.

Brent, William Lee. *Long Time Gone.* New York: Random House, 1996.

Brown, Elaine. *A Taste of Power: A Black Woman's Story.* New York: Anchor Books, 1992.

Brown, Ewart. "The Black University." In *University and Revolution,* edited by Gary R. Weaver and James H. Weaver, 141–51. Englewood Cliffs, N.J.: Prentice-Hall, 1969.

Brown, H. Rap. *Die, Nigger Die!* New York: Dial Press, 1969.

Brown, Rita Mae. *A Plain Brown Rapper.* Oakland, Calif.: Diana Press, 1976.

———. *Rita Will: Memoir of a Literary Rabble-Rouser.* New York: Bantam Books, 1997.

Brownmiller, Susan. *Against Our Will: Men, Women, and Rape.* New York: Simon and Schuster, 1975.

———. *In Our Time: Memoir of a Revolution.* New York: Dial Press, 1999.

Bunch, Charlotte. "Learning from Lesbian Separatism." *Ms.* 5 (November 1976): 60–61, 99–102.

———. *Passionate Politics: Feminist Theory in Action, 1968–1986.* New York: St. Martin's Press, 1987.

———, and Nancy Myron, eds. *Class and Feminism: A Collection of Essays from the Furies.* Baltimore: Diana Press, 1974.

——— and Coletta Reid. "Revolution Begins at Home." *The Furies* 1 (May 1972): 2–4.

Burlage, Dorothy Dawson. "Truths of the Heart." In *Deep in Our Hearts: Nine White Women in the Freedom Movement,* edited by Constance Curry et al., 85–130. Athens: University of Georgia Press, 2000.

Cade Bambara, Toni, ed. *The Black Woman.* New York: Mentor Books, 1970.

Caplan, Marvin. *Farther Along: A Civil Rights Memoir.* Baton Rouge: Louisiana State University Press, 1999.

Carabillo, Toni, Judith Meuli, and June Bundy Csida. *Feminist Chronicles, 1953–1993.* Los Angeles: Women's Graphics, 1993.

Carmichael, Stokely, with Ekwueme Michael Thelwell. *Ready for Revolution: The Life and Struggles of Stokely Carmichael (Kwame Ture).* New York: Scribner, 2003.

Carone, Simone M. "Birth Control and the Black Community in the 1960s: Genocide or Power Politics?" *Journal of Social History* 31 (Spring 1998): 545–69.

Carson, Clayborne. *Malcolm X: The FBI File.* New York: Carroll and Graf, 1991.

———. *In Struggle: SNCC and the Black Awakening of the 1960s.* Cambridge, Mass.: Harvard University Press, 1981.

Cary, Francine Curro, ed. *Urban Odyssey: A Multicultural History of Washington, D.C.* Washington, D.C.: Smithsonian Institution Press, 1996.

Chappell, Marisa. "Rethinking Women's Politics in the 1970s: The League of Women Voters and the National Organization for Women Confront Poverty." *Journal of Women's History* 13 (Winter 2002): 155–79.

Churchill, Ward, and Jim Vander Wall. *The COINTELPRO Papers: Documents from the FBI's Secret Wars against Dissent in the United States.* Boston: South End Press, 2002.

Clark, Adele, and Alice Wolfson. "Class, Race, and Reproductive Rights." *Socialist Review* 78 (November–December 1984): 110–20.

Cleaver, Eldridge. *Soul on Ice.* New York: Dell, 1968.

Cleaver, Kathleen. "Women, Power, and Revolution." In *Liberation, Imagination, and the Black Panther Party,* edited by Kathleen Cleaver and George Katsiaficas, 123–27. New York: Routledge, 2001.

———, and George Katsiaficas, eds. *Liberation, Imagination, and the Black Panther Party.* New York: Routledge, 2001.

Cobb, Charlie. "Black Power: A Defiant Young Stokely Carmichael Gave Rise to a Warning." *Emerge* 8 (June 1997): 38–47.

Coburn, Judith. "Off the Pill?" *Village Voice,* 5 February 1970, 14–15.

———. "Off the Pill?" *Ramparts* 8, no. 12 (June 1970): 46–49.

Collier-Thomas, Bettye, and V. P. Franklin, eds. *Sisters in the Struggle: African American Women in the Civil Rights–Black Power Movement.* New York: New York University Press, 2001.

Collins, Patricia Hill. *Black Feminist Thought: Knowledge, Consciousness, and the Politics of Empowerment.* New York: Routledge, 1990.

Connell, Noreen, and Cassandra Wilson, eds. *Rape: The First Sourcebook for Women.* New York: New American Library, 1974.

Cooke, Joanne, Charlotte Bunch-Weeks, and Robin Morgan, eds. *The New Women: An Anthology of Women's Liberation.* Greenwich, Conn.: Fawcett, 1970.

Crawford, Vicki L., Jacqueline Anne Rouse, and Barbara Woods, eds. *Women in the Civil Rights Movement: Trailblazers and Torchbearers, 1941–1965.* Brooklyn, N.Y.: Carlson, 1990.

Critchlow, Donald T. "Birth Control, Population Control, and Family Planning: An Overview." *Journal of Policy History* 7 (1995): 1–21.

Curry, Constance, et al. *Deep in Our Hearts: Nine White Women in the Freedom Movement.* Athens: University of Georgia Press, 2000.

Davis, Angela Y. *Angela Davis: An Autobiography.* New York: Random House, 1974; reprint, New York: International, 1988.

———. "Joanne Little: The Dialectics of Rape." *Ms.* 3 (June 1975): 74–77, 106–8.

———. "Rape, Racism, and the Capitalist Setting." *Black Scholar* 9 (April 1978): 24–30.

———. *Women, Race and Class.* New York: Vintage Books, 1983.

Davis, Flora. *Moving the Mountain: The Women's Movement in America since 1960.* New York: Simon and Schuster, 1991.

Davis, Martha F. *Brutal Need: Lawyers and the Welfare Rights Movement, 1960–1973.* New Haven, Conn.: Yale University Press, 1993.

———. "Welfare Rights and Women's Rights in the 1960s." *Journal of Policy History* 8, no. 1 (1996): 144–65.

de Graf, Lawrence B. "Howard: The Evolution of a Black Student Revolt." In *Protest! Student Activism in America,* edited by Julian Foster and Durward Long, 319–44. New York: William Morrow, 1970.

Deevey, Sharon, and Coletta Reid. "Emotionalism—Downward Spiral." *The Furies* 1 (February 1972): 11.

Delaplaine, Jo. "*Mujeres y la Comunidad Latina:* Women and the Latin Community." *Quest* 4 (Fall 1978): 11–13.

DeLoach, Tim. "The Rape Task Force Report: A Second and Closer Look." *The Gay Blade* 4 (September 1973): 6–7.

D'Emilio, John. *Lost Prophet: The Life and Times of Bayard Rustin.* New York: Free Press, 2003.

———. *Sexual Politics, Sexual Communities: The Making of a Homosexual Minority in the U.S., 1940–1970.* Chicago: University of Chicago Press, 1983.

Deming, Barbara. *Prisons That Could Not Hold.* Athens: University of Georgia Press, 1995.

Douglas, Carol Anne, and Fran Moira. "*Off Our Backs:* The First Decade, 1970–1980." In *Voices from the Underground: Insider Histories of the Vietnam Era Underground Press,* Vol. 1, edited by Ken Wachsberger, 107–23. Tempe, Ariz.: Mica's Press, 1993.

Dudziak, Mary L. *Cold War Civil Rights: Race and the Image of American Democracy.* Princeton, N.J.: Princeton University Press, 2000.

Due, Tananarive, and Patricia Due Stevens. *Freedom in the Family: A Mother-Daughter Memoir of the Fight for Civil Rights.* New York: One World/Ballantine, 2003.

Ebony Magazine. *The Black Revolution: An Ebony Special Issue.* Chicago: Johnson, 1970.

Echols, Alice. *Daring to Be Bad: Radical Feminism in America, 1967–1975.* Minneapolis: University of Minnesota Press, 1989.

———. "'We Gotta Get Out of This Place': Notes toward a Remapping of the Sixties." *Socialist Review* 92 (April–June 1992): 9–33.

———. "'Woman Power': Exploring the Relationship between the Antiwar Movement and the Women's Liberation Movement." In *Give Peace a Chance,* edited by Melvin Small and William D. Hoover, 170–81. Syracuse, N.Y.: Syracuse University Press, 1992.

Elliot, Jeffrey M. *Black Voices in American Politics.* San Diego: Harcourt, Brace Jovanovich, 1986.

Enke, Anne. "Smuggling Sex through the Gates: Race, Sexuality, and the Politics of Space in Second Wave Feminism." *American Quarterly* 55, no. 4 (2003): 635–67.

Epstein, Barbara. *Political Protest and Cultural Revolution: Nonviolent Direct Action in the 1970s and 1980s.* Berkeley: University of California Press, 1991.

Evans, Sara. *Personal Politics: The Roots of the Women's Liberation Movement in the Civil Rights Movement and the New Left.* New York: Knopf/Vintage Books, 1979.

———. *Tidal Wave: How Women Changed America at Century's End.* New York: Free Press, 2003.

Ezekiel, Judith. *Feminism in the Heartland.* Columbus: Ohio State University Press, 2002.

Ferree, Myra Marx, and Patricia Yancey Martin, eds. *Feminist Organizations: Harvest of the New Women's Movement.* Philadelphia: Temple University Press, 1995.

Firestone, Shulamith. "The Jeannette Rankin Brigade: Woman Power?" In *Notes from the First Year,* edited by New York Radical Women, n.p. New York: New York Radical Women, 1968.

———, and Anne Koedt, eds. *Notes from the Third Year: Women's Liberation.* New York: New York Radical Feminists, 1971.

Foley, Michael S. "The 'Point of Ultimate Indignity' or a 'Beloved Community'? The Draft Resistance Movement and New Left Gender Dynamics." In *The New Left Revisited,* edited by John McMillan and Paul Buhle, 178–198. Philadelphia: Temple University Press, 2003.

Foner, Philip S., ed. *The Black Panthers Speak.* Philadelphia: J. B. Lippincott, 1970.

Franklin, Raymond S. "The Political Economy of Black Power." *Social Problems* 16 (Winter 1969): 286–301.

Fraser, Arvonne S. "Insiders and Outsiders: Women in the Political Arena." In *Women in Washington: Advocates for Public Policy,* edited by Irene Tinker, 120–39. Beverly Hills, Calif.: Sage, 1983.

Fraser, Ronald. *1968: A Student Generation in Revolt.* New York: Pantheon Books, 1988.

Freedman, Estelle. *No Turning Back: The History of Feminism and the Future of Women.* New York: Ballantine Books, 2002.

Freeman, Jo. "The Origins of the Women's Liberation Movement." *American Journal of Sociology* 78 (January 1973): 30–49.

———. *The Politics of Women's Liberation: A Case Study of an Emerging Social Movement and Its Relation to the Policy Process.* New York: David McKay, 1975.

Freeman, Lexi, and Jackie MacMillan. "The Feminist Workplace: Interview with Nancy McDonald." *Quest* 3 (Winter 1976–77): 65–80.

Freeman, Susan K. "From the Lesbian Nation to the Cincinnati Lesbian Community: Moving toward a Politics of Location." *Journal of the History of Sexuality* 9 (January–April 2000): 137–74.

Fried, Marlene Gerber, ed. *From Abortion to Reproductive Freedom: Transforming a Movement.* Boston: South End Press, 1990.

Friedman, Deb. "Rape, Racism, and Reality." *Aegis* 31 (July–August 1978): 17–26.

Frost, Jennifer. *"An Interracial Movement of the Poor": Community Organizing and the New Left in the 1960s.* New York: New York University Press, 2001.

Freund, Eva. "Once Upon a Time." *Vocal Majority* 4 (April 1973): 17.

Garcia, Alma M. "The Development of Chicana Feminist Discourse, 1970–1980." *Gender and Society* 3 (June 1989): 217–38.

Gardiner, Judith Kegan, ed. *Provoking Agents: Gender and Agency in Theory and Practice.* Urbana: University of Illinois Press, 1995.

Garrow, David. *Liberty and Sexuality: The Right to Privacy and the Making of Roe v. Wade.* New York: MacMillan, 1994.

Gilbert, Ben W. *Ten Blocks from the White House.* London: Pall Mall Press, 1968.

Gilmore, Stephanie. "The Dynamics of Second-Wave Feminist Activism in Memphis, 1971–1982: Rethinking the Liberal/Radical Divide." *NWSA Journal* 15 (Spring 2003): 94–117.

Glassman, Carol. "Women and the Welfare System." In *Sisterhood Is Powerful,* edited by Robin Morgan, 102–14. New York: Vintage Books, 1970.

Gluck, Sherna Berger. "Whose Feminism, Whose History? Reflections on Excavating the History of (the) U.S. Women's Movement(s)." In *Community Activism and Feminist Politics: Organizing across Race, Class, and Gender,* edited by Nancy A. Naples, 31–56. New York: Routledge, 1998.

Gordon, Linda. "Black and White Visions of Welfare: Women's Welfare Activism, 1890–1945." *Journal of American History* 78 (September 1991): 559–90.

———. *Woman's Body, Woman's Right: Birth Control in America,* rev. ed. New York: Penguin Books, 1990.

Greenberg, Cheryl Lynn, ed. *A Circle of Trust: Remembering SNCC.* New Brunswick, N.J.: Rutgers University Press, 1998.

Guy-Sheftall, Beverly, ed. *Words of Fire: An Anthology of African American Feminist Thought.* New York: New Press, 1995.

Halberstam, David. *The Children.* New York: Random House, 1998.

Hall, Jacquelyn Dowd. "The Mind That Burns in Each Body: Women, Rape and Racial Violence." In *Powers of Desire: The Politics of Sexuality,* edited by Ann Snitow, Christine Stansell, and Sharon Thompson, 328–49. New York: Monthly Review Press, 1983.

Hampton, Henry, and Steve Fayer, eds. *Voices of Freedom: An Oral History of the*

Civil Rights Movement from the 1950s through the 1980s. New York: Bantam Books, 1990.

Hare, Nathan. "The Battle for Black Studies." *Black Scholar* 3 (May 1972): 36–39.

———. "Behind the Black College Student Revolt." *Ebony* 22 (August 1967): 58–61.

———. "Revolution without a Revolution: The Psychology of Sex and Race." *Black Scholar* 9 (April 1978): 4–5.

Harrington, Michael. *The Other America: Poverty in the United States.* New York: Macmillan, 1963.

Hartmann, Susan M. *The Other Feminists: Activists in the Liberal Establishment.* New Haven, Conn.: Yale University Press, 1998.

Hayden, Tom. *Reunion: A Memoir.* New York: Random House, 1988.

Hayes, Floyd W., III, and Francis A. Kiene III. "'All Power to the People': The Political Thought of Huey P. Newton and the Black Panther Party." In *The Black Panther Party Reconsidered,* edited by Charles E. Jones, 157–76. Baltimore: Black Classic Press, 1998.

Hertz, Susan Handley. *The Welfare Mothers Movement: A Decade of Change for Poor Women?* Washington, D.C.: University Press of America, 1981.

Hilliard, David, and Lewis Cole. *This Side of Glory: The Autobiography of David Hilliard and the Story of the Black Panther Party.* Boston: Little, Brown, 1993.

Hine, Darlene Clark. "Rape and the Inner Lives of Black Women in the Middle West: Preliminary Thoughts on the Culture of Dissemblance." *Signs* 14, no. 4 (1989): 912–20.

hooks, bell. *Ain't I a Woman: Black Women and Feminism.* Boston: South End Press, 1981.

Howard University Students. "February 1968, *The Spear and Shield.*" In *The University Crisis Reader,* Vol. 2, *Confrontation and Counterattack,* edited by Immanuel Wallerstein and Paul Starr, 485–86. New York: Random House, 1971.

Hull, Gloria T., Patricia Bell Scott, and Barbara Smith. *All the Women Are White, All the Blacks Are Men, but Some of Us Are Brave: Black Women's Studies.* New York: Feminist Press, 1982.

Jacobs, Ron. *The Way the Wind Blew: A History of the Weather Underground.* London: Verso, 1997.

Jaffe, Harry S., and Tom Sherwood. *Dream City: Race, Power, and the Decline of Washington, D.C.* New York: Simon and Schuster, 1994.

Jaquith, Cindy. "Issues before the Abortion Movement." In *Feminism and Socialism,* edited by Linda Jenness, 58–62. New York: Pathfinder Press, 1972.

Jeffries, Judson L. "Black Radicalism and Political Repression in Baltimore: The Case of the Black Panther Party." *Ethnic and Racial Studies* 25 (January 2002): 64–98.

Jenness, Linda, ed. *Feminism and Socialism.* New York: Pathfinder Press, 1972.

Jennings, Regina. "African Womanism in the Black Panther Party: A Personal Story." *Western Journal of Black Studies* 25, no. 3 (2001): 146–52.

———. "A Panther Remembers." *Essence* 21 (February 1991): 122.

Johnson, Allen Griswold. "On the Prevalence of Rape in the United States." *Signs* 6 (Autumn 1980): 136–46.

Johnson, David K. "'Homosexual Citizens': Washington's Gay Community Confronts the Civil Service." *Washington History* 6 (Fall/Winter 1994–1995): 44–63.

Jones, Charles E., ed. *The Black Panther Party Reconsidered.* Baltimore: Black Classic Press, 1998.

Joseph, Peniel E. "Black Liberation without Apology: Reconceptualizing the Black Power Movement." *The Black Scholar* 31 (Fall/Winter 2001): 2–19.

———. *Waiting 'til the Midnight Hour: A Narrative History of Black Power in America.* New York: Henry Holt, 2006.

Kaplan, Laura. *The Story of Jane: The Legendary Underground Feminist Abortion Service.* New York: Pantheon Books, 1995.

Karenga, Maulana Ron. "Joanne Little Case: In Defense of Sis. Joanne: For Ourselves and History." *Black Scholar* 7 (July–August 1975): 37–42.

Katsiaficas, George. "Organization and Movement: The Case of the Black Panther Party and the Revolutionary People's Constitutional Convention of 1970." In *Liberation, Imagination, and the Black Panther Party,* edited by Kathleen Cleaver and George Katsiaficas, 141–55. New York: Routledge, 2001.

Katz, Michael B. *The Undeserving Poor: From the War on Poverty to the War on Welfare.* New York: Pantheon Books, 1990.

Kesselman, Amy. "Women's Liberation and the Left in New Haven, Connecticut, 1968–1972." *Radical History Review* 81 (Fall 2001): 15–33.

King, Katie. *Theory in Its Feminist Travels: Conversations in U.S. Women's Movements.* Bloomington: Indiana University Press, 1994.

King, Mary. *Freedom Song: A Personal Story of the 1960s Civil Rights Movement.* New York: William Morrow, 1987.

Klatch, Rebecca E. *A Generation Divided: The New Left, the New Right, and the 1960s.* Berkeley: University of California Press, 1999.

Kluger, Richard. *Simple Justice: The History of Brown v. Board of Education and Black Americans' Struggle for Equality.* New York: Vintage Books, 1975.

Knowlton, Elizabeth. "Rita Mae Brown," *Feminary* 10 (1979): 74.

Koedt, Anne, Ellen Levine, and Anita Rapone, eds. *Radical Feminism.* New York: Quadrangle Books, 1973.

Kollias, Karen. "Spiral of Change: An Introduction to Quest." *Quest* 1 (Summer 1974): 6.

Kopkind, Andrew. "The Future of 'Black Power': A Movement in Search of a Program." *New Republic,* 7 January 1967, 16–18.

———. "Washington: The Lost Colony." *New Republic,* 23 April 1966, 13–17.

———. "Washington: The Lost Colony—II." *New Republic,* 30 April 1966, 19–22.

Kotz, Nick, and Mary Lynn Kotz. *A Passion for Equality: George A. Wiley and the Movement.* New York: W. W. Norton, 1977.

Kovacs, Malcolm. "'Witch' at the Justice Department," *Quicksilver Times* 1, no. 11 (October 1969): 4.

Lader, Lawrence. *Abortion II: Making the Revolution.* Boston: Beacon Press, 1973.

Lang, Clarence. "Between Civil Rights and Black Power in the Gateway City: The Action Committee to Improve Opportunities for Negroes (Action), 1964–75." *Journal of Social History* 37, no. 3 (2004): 725–54.

Lawrence, Jane. "The Indian Health Service and the Sterilization of Native American Women." *American Indian Quarterly* 24, no. 3 (2000): 400–19.

Lederer, Laura, ed. *Take Back the Night: Women on Pornography.* New York: William Morrow, 1980.

Leo, Andre. "ADC: Marriage to the State." In *Notes from the Third Year* (1971) reprinted in *Radical Feminism,* edited by Anne Koedt, Ellen Levine, and Anita Rapone, 222–27. New York: Quadrangle Books, 1973.

Levitan, Sar A., ed. *The Great Society's Poor Law: A New Approach to Poverty.* Baltimore: Johns Hopkins Press, 1969.

Lipsky, Michael. "Protest as a Political Resource." *American Political Science Review* 62 (December 1968): 1144–58.

———. *Protest in City Politics.* Chicago: Rand McNally, 1970.

Lowe, Carol Hill, ed. *The First Twenty Years: Women's Rights to Women Leaders: The District of Columbia Commission for Women Highlights and Legislative History, 1967–1987.* Washington, D.C.: District of Columbia Commission for Women, 1987.

Lowe, Gilbert A., Jr., and Sophia F. McDowell. "Participant-Nonparticipant Differences in the Howard University Student Protest." *Journal of Negro Education* 40 (Winter 1971): 81–90.

Marotta, Toby. *The Politics of Homosexuality.* Boston: Houghton Mifflin, 1981.

Matthews, Nancy A. *Confronting Rape: The Feminist Anti-Rape Movement and the State.* London: Routledge, 1994.

———. "Surmounting a Legacy: The Expansion of Racial Diversity in a Local Anti-Rape Movement." *Gender and Society* 3 (December 1989): 518–32.

Matthews, Tracye A. "'No One Ever Asks What a Man's Role in the Revolution Is': Gender Politics and Leadership in the Black Panther Party, 1966–1971." In *Sisters in the Struggle: African American Women in the Civil Rights–Black Power Movement,* edited by Bettye Collier-Thomas and V. P. Franklin, 230–56. New York: New York University Press, 2001.

McCartney, John T. *Black Power Ideologies: An Essay in African-American Political Thought.* Philadelphia: Temple University Press, 1992.

McGuire, Danielle L. "'It Was Like All of Us Had Been Raped': Sexual Violence, Community Mobilization, and the African American Freedom Struggle." *Journal of American History* 91 (December 2004): 906–31.

McMillan, John, and Paul Buhle, eds. *The New Left Revisited.* Philadelphia: Temple University Press, 2003.

McNeil, Genna Rae. "'Joanne Is You and Joanne Is Me': A Consideration of African

American Women and the 'Free Joan Little' Movement, 1974–1975." In *Sisters in Struggle: African American Women in the Civil Rights—Black Power Movement,* edited by Bettye Collier-Thomas and V. P. Franklin, 259–79. New York: New York University Press, 2001.

Meier, August, and Elliott Rudwick. *CORE: A Study in the Civil Rights Movement.* Urbana: University of Illinois Press, 1975.

Melnick, R. Shep. *Between the Lines: Interpreting Welfare Rights.* Washington, D.C.: Brookings Institution, 1994.

Meyer, David S., and Nancy Whittier. "Social Movement Spillover." *Social Problems* 14 (May 1994): 277–98.

Morgan, Robin, ed. *Sisterhood Is Powerful.* New York: Vintage Books, 1970.

Moynihan, Daniel Patrick. *The Negro Family: The Case for National Action.* Washington, D.C.: Office of Planning and Research, U.S. Department of Labor, 1965.

Murray, Pauli. *The Autobiography of a Black Activist, Feminist, Lawyer, Priest, and Poet.* Knoxville: University of Tennessee Press, 1987.

Myron, Nancy. "Lace Curtains and a Plastic Jesus." *Motive* 32 (January 1972): 36.

———, and Charlotte Bunch, eds. *Lesbianism and the Women's Movement.* Baltimore: Diana Press, 1975.

Nadasen, Premilla. "Expanding the Boundaries of the Women's Movement: Black Feminism and the Struggle for Welfare Rights." *Feminist Studies* 28 (Summer 2002): 271–301.

———. *Welfare Warriors: The Welfare Rights Movement in the United States.* New York: Routledge, 2005.

Naples, Nancy A., ed. *Community Activism and Feminist Politics: Organizing across Race, Class, and Gender.* New York: Routledge, 1998.

———. *Grassroots Warriors: Activist Mothering, Community Work, and the War on Poverty.* New York: Routledge, 1998.

National Committee on Segregation in the Nation's Capital. *Segregation in Washington.* Chicago: National Committee on Segregation in the Nation's Capital, 1948.

National League of Cities. *Rape.* Washington, D.C.: National League of Cities, 1974.

National Welfare Rights Organization. *Six Myths about Welfare.* Washington, D.C.: National Welfare Rights Organization, 1971.

Nelson, Jennifer A. "'Abortions under Community Control': Feminism, Nationalism, and the Politics of Reproduction among New York City's Young Lords." *Journal of Women's History* 13 (Spring 2001): 157–80.

———. *Women of Color and the Reproductive Rights Movement.* New York: New York University Press, 2003.

Nestle, Joan. *A Restricted Country.* Ann Arbor, Mich.: Firebrand Books, 1987.

Newton, Huey P. *To Die for the People.* New York: Random House, 1972.

New York Radical Women, ed. *Notes from the First Year.* New York: New York Radical Women, 1968.

Patton, Gwen. "Black People and the Victorian Ethos." In *The Black Woman,* edited by Toni Cade Bambara, 143–48. New York: Mentor Books, 1970.

Payne, Charles. *I've Got the Light of Freedom: The Organizing Tradition and the Mississippi Freedom Struggle.* Berkeley: University of California Press, 1995.

Phelan, Shane. *Identity Politics: Lesbian Feminism and the Limits of Community.* Philadelphia: Temple University Press, 1989.

Piven, Frances Fox, and Richard Cloward. *Poor People's Movements: Why They Succeed, How They Fail.* New York: Pantheon Books, 1977.

———. *Regulating the Poor: The Functions of Federal Welfare.* New York: Pantheon Books, 1971.

Pogrebin, Letty Cottin. "The FBI Was Watching You." *Ms.* 5 (June 1977): 37–44, 69–76.

Polatnick, M. Rivka. "Diversity in Women's Liberation Ideology: How a Black and a White Group of the 1960s Viewed Motherhood." *Signs* 21 (Spring 1996): 679–706.

Radicalesbians. "Woman-Identified Woman." *Women: A Journal of Liberation* 1 (Summer 1970): 39.

Rainwater, Lee, and William L. Yancey. *The Moynihan Report and the Politics of Controversy.* Cambridge, Mass.: MIT Press, 1967.

Ransby, Barbara. *Ella Baker and the Black Freedom Movement: A Radical Democratic Vision.* Chapel Hill: University of North Carolina Press, 2003.

Ratagick, Marie. "Two American Welfare Mothers." *Ms.* 1 (June 1973): 74–77, 112.

Reagan, Leslie J. *When Abortion Was a Crime: Women, Medicine, and Law in the United States, 1867–1973.* Berkeley: University of California Press, 1997.

Reagon, Bernice Johnson. "Coalition Politics: Turning the Century." In *Home Girls: A Black Feminist Anthology,* edited by Barbara Smith, 356–69. New York: Kitchen Table Press, 1983.

———, and Sweet Honey in the Rock. *We Who Believe in Freedom: Sweet Honey in the Rock . . . Still on the Journey.* New York: Anchor Books, 1993.

Reed, James. *The Birth Control Movement and American Society: From Private Vice to Public Virtue.* Princeton, N.J.: Princeton University Press, 1984.

Reid, Coletta. "Coming Out in the Women's Movement." In *Lesbianism and the Women's Movement,* edited by Nancy Myron and Charlotte Bunch, 91–103. Baltimore: Diana Press, 1975.

———. "Taking Care of Business." *Quest* 1 (Fall 1974): 6–23.

Reid, Inez Smith. *"Together" Black Women.* New York: Emerson Hall, 1972.

"Revolutionary People's Constitutional Convention." *Women: A Journal of Liberation* 2 (Winter 1970): 63–65.

Rhudy, Frances Thompson. "Opinion: Thoughts on Lesbianism." *Vocal Majority* 4 (April 1973): 11.

Rigsby, Gregory U. "Afro-American Studies at Howard University: One Year Later." *Journal of Negro Education* 39 (Summer 1970): 209–13.

Rodriguez, Noelie Maria. "Transcending Bureaucracy: Feminist Politics at a Shelter for Battered Women." *Gender and Society* 2 (June 1988): 214–27.

Rosen, Ruth. "The Day They Buried 'Traditional Womanhood': Women and the Politics of Peace Protest." *Vietnam Generation* 1 (1989): 208–34.

———. "The Female Generation Gap: Daughters of the Fifties and the Origins of Contemporary American Feminism." In *U.S. History as Women's History,* edited by Linda Kerber et al., 313–34. Chapel Hill: University of North Carolina Press, 1995.

———. *The World Split Open: How the Modern Women's Movement Changed America.* New York: Viking Press, 2000.

Ross, Loretta J. "African American Women and Abortion." In *Abortion Wars: A Half Century of Struggle, 1950–2000,* edited by Rickie Solinger, 161–207. Berkeley: University of California Press, 1998.

Roth, Benita. *Separate Roads to Feminism: Black, Chicana, and White Feminist Movements in America's Second Wave.* Cambridge: Cambridge University Press, 2004.

Rucker, Madalynn C., and JoNina M. Abron. "'Comrade Sisters': Two Women of the Black Panther Party." In *Unrelated Kin: Race and Gender in Women's Personal Narratives,* edited by Gwendolyn Etter-Lewis and Michele Foster, 139–67. New York: Routledge, 1996.

Sacks, Karen Brodkin. "Gender and Grassroots Leadership." In *Women and the Politics of Empowerment,* edited by Ann Bookman and Sandra Morgen, 77–94. Philadelphia: Temple University Press, 1988.

Sales, William W., Jr. *From Civil Rights to Black Liberation.* Boston: South End Press, 1994.

Sarachild, Kathie. "Feminist Consciousness Raising and 'Organizing.'" In *Voices from Women's Liberation,* edited by Leslie B. Tanner, 153–57. New York: Signet Books, 1970.

Schechter, Susan. *Women and Male Violence: The Visions and Struggles of the Battered Women's Movement.* Boston: South End Press, 1982.

Schmidt, Peggy. "Rape Crisis Centers." *Ms.* 2 (September 1973): 15.

Schulder, Diane B. "Does the Law Oppress Women?" In *Sisterhood Is Powerful,* edited by Robin Morgan, 39–57. New York: Vintage Books, 1970.

Schultz, Debra L. *Going South: Jewish Women in the Civil Rights Movement.* New York: New York University Press, 2001.

Scott, Ellen Kaye. "How to Stop the Rapists? A Question of Strategy in Two Rape Crisis Centers." *Social Problems* 40 (August 1993): 343–61.

Sellers, Cleveland, with Robert Terrell. *The River of No Return: The Autobiography of a Black Militant and the Life and Death of SNCC.* New York: William Morrow, 1973.

Shakur, Assata. *Assata: An Autobiography.* Westport, Conn.: Lawrence Hill, 1987.

Shugar, Dana R. *Separatism and Women's Community.* Lincoln: University of Nebraska Press, 1995.

Silliman, Jael, et al., *Undivided Rights: Women of Color Organize for Reproductive Justice.* Boston: South End Press, 2004.

Small, Melvin, and William D. Hoover, eds. *Give Peace a Chance: Exploring the Antiwar Movement.* Syracuse, N.Y.: Syracuse University Press, 1992.

Smith, Barbara, ed. *Home Girls: A Black Feminist Anthology.* New York: Kitchen Table, Women of Color Press, 1983.

Smith, Deborah. "What Would You Do?" *Welfare Fighter* 2 (April–May 1971): 12.

Smith, Jean. "I Learned to Feel Black." In *The Black Power Revolt,* edited by Floyd B. Barbour, 207–18. Boston: Porter Sargent, 1968.

Smith, Patricia. "From Cracker Barrel to Laundromat." *Communities in Action* 1 (December 1966): 20.

Smith, Sam. *Captive Capital: Colonial Life in Modern Washington.* Bloomington: Indiana University Press, 1974.

Snitow, Ann, Christine Stansell, and Sharon Thompson, eds. *Powers of Desire: The Politics of Sexuality.* New York: Monthly Review Press, 1983.

Solinger, Rickie, ed. *Abortion Wars: A Half Century of Struggle, 1950–2000.* Berkeley: University of California Press, 1998.

Spitzer, Neil. "Secret City." *Wilson Quarterly* 13 (January 1989): 102–15.

Springer, Kimberly. *Living for the Revolution: Black Feminist Organizations, 1968–1980.* Durham, N.C.: Duke University Press, 2005.

———, ed. *Still Lifting, Still Climbing: Contemporary African American Women's Activism.* New York: New York University Press, 1999.

Stanfiel, James D. "A Profile of the 1972 Freshman Class at Howard." *Journal of Negro Education* 45 (Winter 1976): 61–69.

Steffens, Heidi. "W.I.T.C.H.," *Quicksilver Times,* 1, no. 11 (October 1969): 10, 19.

Stein, Mark. *City of Sisterly and Brotherly Loves: Lesbian and Gay Philadelphia, 1945–1972.* Chicago: University of Chicago Press, 2000.

Stoper, Emily. *The Student Nonviolent Coordinating Committee: The Growth of Radicalism in a Civil Rights Organization.* Brooklyn, N.Y.: Carlson, 1989.

"Survey Recommends End to Segregation in Washington." *Events and Trends in Race Relations: A Monthly Summary* 9 (January 1947): 180–82.

Swerdlow, Amy. *Women Strike for Peace: Traditional Motherhood and Radical Politics in the 1960s.* Chicago: University of Chicago Press, 1993.

Tanner, Leslie, ed. *Voices from Women's Liberation.* New York: Signet Books, 1970.

Taylor, Ula. "The Historical Evolution of Black Feminist Theory and Praxis." *Journal of Black Studies* 29 (November 1998): 234–53.

Taylor, Verta, and Leila J. Rupp. "Women's Culture and Lesbian Feminist Activism: A Reconsideration of Cultural Feminism." *Signs* 19 (Autumn 1993): 32–61.

Terry, Wallace. *Bloods: An Oral History of the Vietnam War by Black Veterans.* New York: Ballantine, 1984.

Theoharis, Jeanne, and Komozi Woodard. *Freedom North: Black Freedom Struggles outside the South, 1940–1980.* New York: Palgrave, 2003.

Thompson, Becky. "Multiracial Feminism: Recasting the Chronology of Second Wave Feminism." *Feminist Studies* 28 (Summer 2002): 337–60.

Tillmon, Johnnie. "Welfare Is a Women's Issue." *Ms.* 1 (Spring 1972): 111.

Tinker, Irene, ed. *Women in Washington: Advocates for Public Policy.* Beverly Hills, Calif.: Sage, 1983.

Toure, I. Nkenge. "Report on the First National Third World Women's Conference on Violence." *Aegis* (Summer/Autumn 1980): 70–72.

Tyson, Timothy B. *Radio Free Dixie: Robert F. Williams and the Roots of Black Power.* Chapel Hill: University of North Carolina Press, 1999.

Umansky, Lauri. "The Sisters Reply: Black Nationalist Pronatalism, Black Feminism, and the Quest for a Multiracial Women's Movement, 1965–1974." *Critical Matrix* 8 (1994): 19–50.

Valk, Anne M. "Living a Feminist Lifestyle: The Intersection of Theory and Action in a Lesbian Feminist Collective." *Feminist Studies* 28 (Summer 2002): 303–32.

———. "'Mother Power': The Movement for Welfare Rights in Washington, D.C., 1966–1972." *Journal of Women's History* 11 (Winter 2000): 34–58.

Van Deburg, William L. *New Day in Babylon: The Black Power Movement and American Culture, 1965–1975.* Chicago: University of Chicago Press, 1992.

Varon, Jeremy. *Bringing the War Home: The Weather Underground, the Red Army Faction, and Revolutionary Violence in the Sixties and Seventies.* Berkeley: University of California Press, 2004.

Wachsberger, Ken, ed. *Voices from the Underground.* Vol. 1, *Insider Histories of the Vietnam Era Underground Press.* Tempe, Ariz.: Mica Press, 1993.

Wallace, Michele. "A Black Feminist's Search for Sisterhood." In *All the Women Are White, All the Blacks Are Men, but Some of Us Are Brave: Black Women's Studies,* edited by Gloria Hull, Patricia Bell Scott, and Barbara Smith, 5–12. New York: Feminist Press, 1982.

———. "To Hell and Back: On the Road with Black Feminism." in *The Feminist Memoir Project: Voices from Women's Liberation,* edited by Rachel Blau DuPlessis and Ann Snitow, 426–42. New York: Three Rivers Press, 1998.

Wallerstein, Immanuel, and Paul Starr, eds. *The University Crisis Reader.* New York: Random House, 1971.

Warrior, Betsy. "Females and Welfare." In *No More Fun and Games* (November 1969), reprinted in *Voices from Women's Liberation,* edited by Leslie B. Tanner, 277–79. New York: New American Library, 1970.

Washington, Cynthia. "We Started from Different Ends of the Spectrum." *Southern Exposure* 4 (Winter 1977): 14–15.

Webb, Marilyn Salzman. "A Hard Rain's Gonna Fall." *WIN Magazine* 6 (January 1970): 4–6.

———. "*Off Our Backs* and the Feminist Dream." In *Voices from the Underground: Insider Histories of the Vietnam Era Underground Press,* Vol. 1, edited by Ken Wachsberger, 124–30. Tempe, Ariz.: Mica Press, 1993.

———. "Woman as Secretary, Sexpot, Spender, Sow, Civic Actor, Sickie." *Motive* 29 (March–April 1969): 48–59.

"Welfare Rights as an Organizational Weapon: An Interview with George Wiley." *Social Policy* 1 (July–August 1970): 61–62.

West, Guida. *The National Welfare Rights Movement: The Social Protest of Poor Women.* New York: Praeger, 1981.

———. "Twin Track Coalitions in the Black Power Movement." In *Interracial Bonds,* edited by Rhoda Goldstein Blumberg and Wendell James Roye, 71–87. Bayside, N.Y.: General Hall, 1979.

White, Deborah Gray. *Too Heavy a Load: African American Women in Defense of Themselves, 1894–1994*. New York: W. W. Norton, 1999.

White, E. Frances. "Africa on My Mind: Gender, Counter Discourse, and African-American Nationalism." *Journal of Women's History* 2 (Spring 1990): 73–97.

Whittier, Nancy. *Feminist Generations: The Persistence of the Radical Women's Movement.* Philadelphia: Temple University Press, 1995.

Wiggins, Lillian. "Treadwell Has Paid Her Debt to Society." *Washington Informer,* 8 July 1987, 10.

Williams, Lynora. "Violence Against Women." *Black Scholar* 12 (January–February 1981): 24.

Williams, Rhonda Y. "'We're Tired of Being Treated Like Dogs': Poor Women and Power Politics in Black Baltimore." *The Black Scholar* 31 (Fall/Winter 2001): 31–41.

Williams, Yohuru. "No Haven: From Civil Rights to Black Power in New Haven, Connecticut." *The Black Scholar* 31 (Fall/Winter 2001): 54–66.

Wolcott, Victoria. *Remaking Respectability: African American Women in Interwar Detroit.* Chapel Hill: University of North Carolina Press, 2001.

Wolfson, Alice J. "Clenched Fist, Open Heart." In *The Feminist Memoir Project: Voices from Women's Liberation,* edited by Rachel Blau DuPlessis and Ann Snitow, 268–83. New York: Three Rivers Press, 1998.

———, and Philip E. Wolfson. "The Food and Drug Administration and the Pill." *Social Policy* 1 (September–October 1970): 52–53.

Wood, Pamela Lakes. "The Victim in a Forcible Rape Case." In *Rape: The First Sourcebook for Women,* edited by Noreen Connell and Cassandra Wilson, 149–50. New York: New American Library, 1974.

Woodard, Komozi. *A Nation within a Nation: Amiri Baraka (LeRoi Jones) and Black Power Politics.* Chapel Hill: University of North Carolina Press, 1999.

Young, Nancy. "Mama's Welfare Blues." *off our backs* 2 (November 1971): 8.

Zinn, Howard. *SNCC: The New Abolitionists.* Boston: Beacon Press, 1964.

Theses, Dissertations, and Unpublished Papers

Beemyn, Brett. "'It Was Like the Sun Rose': The Coffeehouse and the Development of a Black LGB Community in Washington, D.C." Paper presented at the Eighth Annual Lavender Languages and Linguistics Conference, 24 September 2000, American University, Washington, D.C.

Burlage, Dorothy. "Community Organization and Social Change in Anacostia: 1966–1968." Unpublished manuscript.

Felix, Stephanie Y. "African American Women in Social Reform, Welfare, and Activism: Southeast Settlement House, Washington, D.C., 1950–1970." M.A. thesis, University of Wisconsin–Madison, 1992.

Gilmore, Stephanie. "Rethinking the Liberal/Radical Divide: The National Organization for Women in Columbus, Memphis, and San Francisco, 1966–1982." Ph.D. diss., Ohio State University, 2005.

Lekus, Ian. "Queer and Present Dangers: Homosexuality and American Antiwar Activism During the Vietnam Era." Ph.D. diss., Duke University, 2004.

Longus, Pharnal. "Change in a Public Housing Development: A Case Study, Barry Farms." Unpublished manuscript, 1978.

Ruby, Jenny. "Case Study: *off our backs.*" Unpublished manuscript.

Valk, Anne M. "Separatism and Sisterhood: Race, Sex and Women's Activism in Washington, D.C., 1963–1980." Ph.D. diss., Duke University, 1996.

Index

ANNE M. VALK is the associate director for programs at the John Nicholas Brown Center at Brown University.

WOMEN IN AMERICAN HISTORY

Women Doctors in Gilded-Age Washington: Race, Gender, and Professionalization *Gloria Moldow*

Friends and Sisters: Letters between Lucy Stone and Antoinette Brown Blackwell, 1846–93 *Edited by Carol Lasser and Marlene Deahl Merrill*

Reform, Labor, and Feminism: Margaret Dreier Robins and the Women's Trade Union League *Elizabeth Anne Payne*

Private Matters: American Attitudes toward Childbearing and Infant Nurture in the Urban North, 1800–1860 *Sylvia D. Hoffert*

Civil Wars: Women and the Crisis of Southern Nationalism *George C. Rable*

I Came a Stranger: The Story of a Hull-House Girl *Hilda Satt Polacheck; edited by Dena J. Polacheck Epstein*

Labor's Flaming Youth: Telephone Operators and Worker Militancy, 1878–1923 *Stephen H. Norwood*

Winter Friends: Women Growing Old in the New Republic, 1785–1835 *Terri L. Premo*

Better Than Second Best: Love and Work in the Life of Helen Magill *Glenn C. Altschuler*

Dishing It Out: Waitresses and Their Unions in the Twentieth Century *Dorothy Sue Cobble*

Natural Allies: Women's Associations in American History *Anne Firor Scott*

Beyond the Typewriter: Gender, Class, and the Origins of Modern American Office Work, 1900–1930 *Sharon Hartman Strom*

The Challenge of Feminist Biography: Writing the Lives of Modern American Women *Edited by Sara Alpern, Joyce Antler, Elisabeth Israels Perry, and Ingrid Winther Scobie*

Working Women of Collar City: Gender, Class, and Community in Troy, New York, 1864–86 *Carole Turbin*

Radicals of the Worst Sort: Laboring Women in Lawrence, Massachusetts, 1860–1912 *Ardis Cameron*

Visible Women: New Essays on American Activism *Edited by Nancy A. Hewitt and Suzanne Lebsock*

Mother-Work: Women, Child Welfare, and the State, 1890–1930 *Molly Ladd-Taylor*

Babe: The Life and Legend of Babe Didrikson Zaharias *Susan E. Cayleff*

Writing Out My Heart: Selections from the Journal of Frances E. Willard, 1855–96 *Edited by Carolyn De Swarte Gifford*

U.S. Women in Struggle: A *Feminist Studies* Anthology *Edited by Claire Goldberg Moses and Heidi Hartmann*

In a Generous Spirit: A First-Person Biography of Myra Page *Christina Looper Baker*

Mining Cultures: Men, Women, and Leisure in Butte, 1914–41 *Mary Murphy*

Gendered Strife and Confusion: The Political Culture of Reconstruction *Laura F. Edwards*

The Female Economy: The Millinery and Dressmaking Trades, 1860–1930 *Wendy Gamber*

Mistresses and Slaves: Plantation Women in South Carolina, 1830–80 *Marli F. Weiner*

A Hard Fight for We: Women's Transition from Slavery to Freedom in South Carolina *Leslie A. Schwalm*

The Common Ground of Womanhood: Class, Gender, and Working Girls' Clubs, 1884–1928 *Priscilla Murolo*

Purifying America: Women, Cultural Reform, and Pro-Censorship Activism, 1873–1933 *Alison M. Parker*

Marching Together: Women of the Brotherhood of Sleeping Car Porters *Melinda Chateauvert*

Creating the New Woman: The Rise of Southern Women's Progressive Culture in Texas, 1893–1918 *Judith N. McArthur*

The Business of Charity: The Woman's Exchange Movement, 1832–1900 *Kathleen Waters Sander*

The Power and Passion of M. Carey Thomas *Helen Lefkowitz Horowitz*

For Freedom's Sake: The Life of Fannie Lou Hamer *Chana Kai Lee*

Becoming Citizens: The Emergence and Development of the California Women's Movement, 1880–1911 *Gayle Gullett*

Selected Letters of Lucretia Coffin Mott *Edited by Beverly Wilson Palmer with the assistance of Holly Byers Ochoa and Carol Faulkner*

Women and the Republican Party, 1854–1924 *Melanie Susan Gustafson*

Southern Discomfort: Women's Activism in Tampa, Florida, 1880s–1920s *Nancy A. Hewitt*

The Making of "Mammy Pleasant": A Black Entrepreneur in Nineteenth-Century San Francisco *Lynn M. Hudson*

Sex Radicals and the Quest for Women's Equality *Joanne E. Passet*

"We, Too, Are Americans": African American Women in Detroit and Richmond, 1940–54 *Megan Taylor Shockley*

The Road to Seneca Falls: Elizabeth Cady Stanton and the First Woman's Rights Convention *Judith Wellman*

Reinventing Marriage: The Love and Work of Alice Freeman Palmer and George Herbert Palmer *Lori Kenschaft*

Southern Single Blessedness: Unmarried Women in the Urban South, 1800–1865 *Christine Jacobson Carter*

Widows and Orphans First: The Family Economy and Social Welfare Policy, 1865–1939 *S. J. Kleinberg*

Habits of Compassion: Irish Catholic Nuns and the Origins of the Welfare System, 1830–1920 *Maureen Fitzgerald*

The Women's Joint Congressional Committee and the Politics of Maternalism, 1920–1930 *Jan Doolittle Wilson*

"Swing the Sickle for the Harvest Is Ripe": Gender and Slavery in Antebellum Georgia *Daina Ramey Berry*

Christian Sisterhood, Race Relations, and the YWCA, 1906–46 *Nancy Marie Robertson*

Reading, Writing, and Segregation: A Century of Black Women Teachers in Nashville *Sonya Ramsey*

Radical Sisters: Second-Wave Feminism and Black Liberation in Washington, D.C. *Anne M. Valk*

The University of Illinois Press
is a founding member of the
Association of American University Presses.

University of Illinois Press
1325 South Oak Street
Champaign, IL 61820-6903
www.press.uillinois.edu